FRENCH AND SPANISH QUEER FILM

Audiences, Communities and Cultural Exchange

Chris Perriam and Darren Waldron

EDINBURGH
University Press

Edinburgh University Press is one of the leading university presses in the UK. We publish academic books and journals in our selected subject areas across the humanities and social sciences, combining cutting-edge scholarship with high editorial and production values to produce academic works of lasting importance. For more information visit our website: www.edinburghuniversitypress.com

Edinburgh University Press Ltd
The Tun – Holyrood Road
12 (2f) Jackson's Entry
Edinburgh EH8 8PJ

First published in hardback by Edinburgh University Press 2016

Typeset in 10/12.5 pt Sabon by
Servis Filmsetting Ltd, Stockport, Cheshire,
and printed and bound in Great Britain by
CPI Group (UK) Ltd, Croydon CR0 4YY

A CIP record for this book is available from the British Library

ISBN 978 0 7486 9919 3 (hardback)
ISBN 978 1 4744 2599 5 (paperback)
ISBN 978 0 7486 9920 9 (webready PDF)
ISBN 978 1 4744 1398 5 (epub)

CONTENTS

FIGURES

ACKNOWLEDGEMENTS

The research leading to the publication of this book and much of the time to write it were funded by the Arts and Humanities Research Council ('Queer Cinema from Spain and France: The Translation of Desire and the Formation of Transnational Queer Identities'. Grant reference AH/IO26618/1); in particular this funding secured the engagement of a full-time Research Associate, Ros Murray (now of Kings College, London), whose work on the ground at festivals and focus groups in France and Spain and whose intellectual energy and organisational flair leave the authors forever in her debt. Much of Chapter 4, in particular, was originally drafted by Ros and every chapter bears her mark. We are grateful to Bloomsbury Press for allowing us to include material in the Introduction and Chapter 3 from an essay published elsewhere. The authors wish also to thank Jessie Gibbs, for taking up where Ros left off, for transcribing some of the Spanish focus group and questionnaire responses, and for chasing up contacts, promises, missing fragments of data, and films; Mary Farrelly for transcribing English, Catalan and Spanish questionnaire responses and Kaya Davies Hayon for transcribing English and French questionnaire responses and the Lyon focus group discussion; Scott Frame for transcribing the Barcelona focus group discussion; Miquel Pomar for the text of the Catalan publicity materials; Ochi Reyes for designing a project logo for the publicity materials (and for the team T-shirts); Michael Blyth, Juanma Carrillo, Joako Ezpeleta, Laura Faghol, Antoine Leonetti, Gerjo Pérez Meliá for making time to meet with us on various occasions in interview and structured conversation; to the organisers and volunteers of all the festivals and events we were able to visit, and which are mentioned in the book; to the LGBT Foundation, Manchester, for helping to give the project a local afterlife; and, above all, to all those 440 individuals who made time to respond to our questionnaires and follow-up emails or join our focus groups.

INTRODUCTION

The opening shot of Michèle Massé's 2014 documentary about ageing among four lesbians, *Las ventanas abiertas* (*Open Windows*), shows two instantly recognisable cityscape images, one above the other. The familiar smooth grey tiles and windows of Parisian mansard roofs fill the top half of the screen; in the bottom half, a panorama of Madrid's Palacio Real and the Almudena Cathedral, lit by the setting sun. Two cities, which serve internationally as metonyms for the countries of which they are capitals, countries that have played pivotal roles in the historical evolution of Western Europe, are brought together in a film that examines the experiences of four older lesbians, two in France and two in Spain.

At the heart of Massé's film, albeit unintentionally according to the film-maker, is the issue that preoccupies us in this book: the existence – or not – of a cinematically mediated cross-cultural flow and exchange of tastes, opinions, experiences, desires and values between France and Spain. For Massé, cultural exchange between the two countries in her film is located principally in the fact that older lesbians in both are facing similar challenges (equality, combating homophobia and so on) and working towards the same goals, but she argues that approaches to those challenges differ (in an email exchange with Darren Waldron). A striking example is attitudes to the construction of nursing homes for LGBT people; where the Spanish lesbians worry that queer residents will be forced to return to the closet, the French lesbians are concerned about the potential of segregation in the provision of accommodation specifically for LGBT pensioners. And yet, diversity of attitudes is, of course, explained as much by individual life experiences as by cultural differences. The two Spanish lesbians are prominent activists, one of whom, Boti García, is now single and the other, Empar Pineda, is married. She, and the two French lesbians (Jocelyne Pasqualini and Micheline Boussaingault), in a relationship together, talk of the continuing importance of romantic attachments and sexual pleasure as we age, while Boti has abandoned seduction for fear of rejection because of her age.

In this book, we are interested in examining and analysing such divergences and similarities. However, perhaps of greater importance to us is whether and how commonalities and diversity in perception, approach and stance are claimed in the encounter between the audience and the film. Informing and underpinning this book is one overriding question: how translatable are the tastes, values, desires and fantasies mobilised in films produced in one national, cultural and linguistic space for audiences who reside in another? France and Spain are used as spaces within which the films we include are produced, with their own social, cultural and political contexts that then feed into those films, manifesting themselves in thematic preoccupations and representations. France, Spain and also Britain are explored as spaces within which those films are watched and in which the potential cross-cultural encounter we are interested in exploring – should it exist – might surface and, indeed, flourish. Britain is included because, as specialists of French and Spanish LGBTQ cinemas working in the UK, we were interested in investigating what French and Spanish LGBTQ films might 'mean' for LGBTQ viewers located elsewhere, some of whom were French or Spanish but seeing these films from outside their own country, while others might be attracted to these films for their other points of view, either because or irrespective of their specific national origin or the language of their dialogue.

The book, then, seeks to advance the current state of film audience research and of our knowledge of sexuality in transnational contexts by analysing how these LGBTQ films are negotiated transversally in these ways by different viewing groups in different locations and venues. It is the main publication outcome of an AHRC grant entitled 'Queer Cinema from Spain and France: The Translation of Desire and the Formation of Transnational Queer Identities' (AHRC AH/IO26618/1). In it we study films (in various media and platforms) and audience responses across four languages (Spanish, French, Catalan, English) and engage with participants from across a range of digital and physical audience locations, with a particular focus on LGBTQ film festivals. We examine films that often chronicle the local (in portraying national and subnational identities) or the intimate, but which also draw on, and inform, wider imaginaries and foreign models of non-heterosexual experience.

Given the irreversibly globalised and increasingly networked world in which we live, in which cross-border tastes and social, political and cultural allegiances and practices have been facilitated by consumerism, demographic change and technological advancement, such an investigation into the transnational exchange of films – with audience research at its heart – that probe LGBTQ concerns seemed to us both timely and pressing. It is still the case that actual, social audiences remain underrepresented in published research on LGBTQ cinemas in Europe and beyond. By probing the circulation of French and Spanish LGBTQ cinemas in France, Spain and Britain, and audience responses to them, we seek to address this gap in the field. Border crossings, which have become a key concern for film studies in recent years, thus take shape here in a focus on the trans-Pyrenean and cross-channel exchange of recent LGBTQ films. In these ways, we seek to build on recent work on

French, Spanish and European LGBTQ cinemas and more widely on festivals and audiences.

FRENCH AND SPANISH LGBTQ CINEMAS: DEFINING OUR CORPUS

France and Spain provide ideal case studies through which the kind of transnational interchange and flow of images of desire and identity in which we are interested can be investigated. They boast some of the most high-profile filmmakers associated with LGBTQ issues, including Pedro Almodóvar, François Ozon, Céline Sciamma, Sébastien Lifshitz, Gaël Morel and Ventura Pons, and are among the most prolific producers of LGBTQ films in Europe. Moreover, in their treatment of LGBTQ themes they are frequently characterised as offering productive alternatives to representations circulated by dominant Hollywood cinema and mainstream television culture. For example, while, as elsewhere, ageing among lesbians, gay men and bisexuals has become a concern in global LGBTQ film culture, its impact for physical intimacy has featured prominently in French and Spanish filmic explorations of this theme, as illustrated in *Las ventanas abiertas*, as well as Jon Garaño and Jose Mari Goenaga's 2010 melodrama *80 Egunean* (*En 80 días*; *80 jours*; *For 80 Days*) and Sébastien Lifshitz's acclaimed documentary *Les Invisibles* (*Los invisibles*; *The Invisibles*) (2012), all three explored in Chapter 3, which also includes an analysis of responses to the documentary *Born Naked* (Andrea Esteban 2012).

A similarly frank and uninhibited approach can be found in a series of activist documentaries from both countries that have examined the specificities of transgender and transsexual lived experience, and boldly challenged preconceptions among both the general population and LGB groups. These include Cynthia Arra and Mélissa Arra's political documentary about trans and intersex activism *L'Ordre des mots* (*El orden de las palabras*; *Binding Word* – unofficial titles) (2007), Valérie Mitteaux's *Fille ou garçon, mon sexe n'est pas mon genre* (*Boy or Girl, My Sex Is Not My Gender*) (2011) and Montse Pujantell's *Guerriller@s* (*W@rriors*) (2010). These films, along with Lifshitz's sequel to *Les Invisibles*, *Bambi* (2013), reclaim the means of self-representation (or self-narration in the case of *Bambi*) for trans-identifying people and, combined with Céline Sciamma's acclaimed naturalistic melodrama about gender non-conformity in children, *Tomboy* (2011), bring authentic and less consensual perspectives to bear on the trans theme, which has provided a staple of queer politics, theories and cinema in recent years. In their emphasis on self-determination, they differ from more mainstream exploitations of trans issues, as can be seen in Almodóvar's horror-thriller fusion *La piel que habito* (*The Skin I Live In*) (2011) and Ozon's comedy-melodrama *Une nouvelle amie* (*Una nueva amiga*; *The New Girlfriend*) (2014). Responses to all these are studied in Chapters 4 and 5.

Other fictional films have offered fresh and at times unsettling perspectives on the familiar theme of lesbian and gay desires and relationships. These include Abdellatif Kechiche's polemical story about love and seduction among two young women, *La Vie d'Adèle* (*La vida de Adèle*; *Blue is the Warmest Colour*) (2013), Xavier Villaverde's bisexual rom-com *El sexo de los ángeles* (*Le Sexe des anges*; *The Sex of the Angels*) (2012) and three thrillers: Alain Guiraudie's account of cruising, instant sex and murder in *L'Inconnu du lac* (*El desconocido del lago*; *Stranger by the Lake*) (2013), Morel's portrayal of murder and prostitution in *Notre paradis* (*Nuestro paraíso*; *Our Paradise*) (2011) and Robin Campillo's story of prostitution, migration and exploitation in *Eastern Boys* (2013). More lyrically and elegiacally, Téchiné's *Les Témoins* (*Los testigos*; *The Witnesses*) (2007) presents a retrospective account, via a fictional narrative inspired to a degree by true events, of the first years of the HIV and AIDS pandemic in France. These films, which are studied in Chapter 3, endow their representations with an often challenging grittiness, gravity and directness. They have also attracted the attention of cinephile queers and of professional critics whose manner of addressing them compares interestingly with other responses that we have been able to gather (and this is explored in Chapter 5). In this, then, they differ from Pedro Almodóvar's second release during the project's timescale, *Los amantes pasajeros* (*Les Amants passagers*; *I'm So Excited!*) (2013), which uses the familiar Almodóvar device of provocation in its portrayal of gay men as camp and hedonistic.

All of these films combine to create our corpus, which means that the book takes an eight-year slice of contemporary representations, contemporary, more-or-less, with the life-period of the project, which was conceived in 2008 and completed in 2015. The corpus films have been selected because they are considered to be key interventions on LGBTQ cultures and issues, they have garnered a substantial following beyond LGBTQ festivals (including among broader audiences – both specialist and non-specialist, actual and online) – but also because they were screened at the LGBTQ festivals and special screenings at which we undertook our audience research. Chapter 2 explores these festivals, their distinctiveness and their audiences as emerging from the responses. We include one film that falls outside of the timeframe of our corpus – Pons's *Ocaña, retrat intermitent* (*Ocaña, portrait par intermitence*; *Ocaña, an Intermittent Portrait*) (1978) precisely because it was screened at the Festival Ecrans Mixtes in Lyon in March 2013, one of our key sites. The book thus considers a broad range of different genres, including documentaries, and films that have received critical acclaim or achieved notable success with mainstream audiences, activists, online viewers and cinephiles.

AN AUDIENCE'S PERSPECTIVE:
INDIVIDUAL AND COMMUNITY IDENTIFICATIONS

Festival programmes, one-off screenings and the buzz around films in cinema auditoriums and online largely determined our corpus and pointed us to the predominant motivational factor in determining the shape, scope and subject of this book: the audience. It is whether, how and why the depictions in our films 'matter' for non-domestic audiences that preoccupies us here. As well as pondering the 'translatability' of patterns and codings of LGBTQ identity and desires through cinematic media, performances and agencies, we also examine how the movement of films and filmmakers across national, cultural and linguistic lines feeds into the social construction of LGBTQ identities. It is from the point of view of the audience that we explore how individuals historically positioned at a slant to the mainstream might learn to make desire and difference the materials of self-development and social interaction, specifically through their engagement with 'foreign' films.

The focus on LGBTQ festivals and special screenings allows us to provide concrete examples of the distillation of these concerns through films and how they play out in the construction of self and community identity among LGBTQ viewers. To a degree, festivals play a role in audience formation or, to put it differently, in creating what Stanley Eugene Fish famously called interpretive communities (1980: 14). We take a flexible approach to this, though, that recognises the potential contribution of films and of festivals to individual and collective identity construction and projection, as well as the importance of a sense of community for how viewers respond to films, while, at the same time, paying due attention to a degree of agency in the strategies and subject positions chosen by viewers in their interaction with media texts. We say a degree of agency because, as researchers have noted (Buckingham 1991: 229–30; Seiter 1999: 29), as users of language, audiences can only select from those linguistic resources available to them (Buckingham 1991: 229).

We contribute, then, to a mapping of patterns of personal and group self-formation and affiliation, that may – or indeed may not – transcend or disrupt preconceived ideas of the local, national or global. Because many of our films engage with aesthetic approaches and activist stances that specifically set out to trouble and undermine the traditional homogeneous labels of lesbian and gay, this mapping necessitates a brief overview of the reception of queer debates in each country. The introduction of queer discourses and politics to debates on sexuality and gender in France has been 'laborious' (Foerster 2012: 187) – a paradox, perhaps, given that North American queer theory has drawn so heavily on so-called 'French theory' (including the work of Michel Foucault, Guy Hocquenghem, Gilles Deleuze and Monique Wittig). The academic and activist Marie-Hélène Bourcier has been pivotal in enabling the term 'queer' to enter political and scholarly vernaculars, via the Zoo seminars that she organised in 1997 and 1998, their ensuing publication (1998) and the three monographs that constitute the Queer Zones series (Bourcier 2001; 2005; 2011). While high-profile contributors to sexuality debates in France had either failed to engage with queer politics (Martel 1996) or expressed some scepticism (Eribon 2000: 107–8), Bourcier embraced their potential for challenging monolithic identity categories (such as lesbian and gay) and as a tool for contesting, exposing and even dismantling the assimilationist ideology of the French Republic (2001: 178). Queer has been seen, by Bourcier and others, as a means of challenging the conformist principle of 'indifférentiation' – the 'state of complete and unconditional integration of lesbians and gays within the French Republic' associated with Frédéric Martel (McCaffrey 2006: 293) – and of enabling a dialogue between same-sexuality and other forms of difference and dissent, around race, ethnicity, nationality, transgender and class (Bourcier 2005: 37–41; Rees-Roberts 2008: 5; Cervulle and Rees-Roberts 2010: 19). Bourcier's queer 'mauvais élève' (2001: 178) chimes with Denis Provencher's bad French sexual citizen, modelled on the author Jean Genet (Provencher 2007: 27) and has, in recent times, been taken up by trans activists, particularly members of the GAT (Groupe Activiste Trans'; Trans' Activist Group), in their direct action or 'zaps' that seek to denounce the preserve of a select group (of activists and intellectuals) (returned to in Chapter 4). Cross-cultural exchange between France and Spain in this area is evidenced in the collaborations between Bourcier and Beatriz Preciado (now Paul B. Preciado) – Preciado wrote the preface for Bourcier's first volume of *Queer Zones* (2001) and Bourcier did the same in Preciado's *Manifeste contra-sexuel* (2000) and both are interested in the queer potential of (lesbian) porn and post-porn, as Nick Rees-Roberts affirms (2008: 138). Moreover, Preciado 'paved the way' for Emilie Jouvet's 'lesbian/trans porn flick' *One Night Stand* (2006) (Rees-Roberts 2006: 138). The precise meaning and value of 'queer' within and for sexual politics in France is still a point of contention (as the panel 'Comment dit-on "queer" en français? Queer Theory in French' proposed for the 2016 Annual Convention of the Northeast Modern Language Association, Hartford, Connecticut, confirms).

Modern France is a key source for some crucial elements in the elaboration of queer feminist and lesbian theory in Spanish writing in essays that have a substantial presence on the physical and virtual bookshelves accessible to the Madrid (and wider Spanish) queer public and which have fed into everyday debates on issues such as same-sex marriage, parenting, and gender identity and the law (Perriam 2013a, 9–14; 92–5). As Vélez-Pellegrini's (2011) overview history of LGBTQ theory in Spain reminds us, Ricardo Llamas – influenced by the AIDS/HIV activist and cultural critic Philippe Mangeot – has Foucault's thinking on death, power and the body at the core of his work (37–46); the philosopher and queer activist Paco Vidarte worked with Derrida's ideas on deconstruction (50–2); the queer theorist and activist Javier Sáez is seen as joining with Llamas in a project of recuperation of psychoanalysis for queer theory (67–9), responding to the Foucault expert Didier Eribon's anti-psychoanalytic position; in his work on queer bodies, the radical art critic Juan Vicente Aliaga draws on Eribon, Mangeot and the public intellectuals Didier Lestrade and Elisabeth Lebovici (104–5); and Preciado, working between Paris and Barcelona, opened up Monique Wittig's work in French and English to Spanish radical audiences (183–4). In June 2003 Preciado organised the seminar (or 'Maratón postporno') 'Pornografía,

Pospornografía: Estéticas y Políticas de Representación Sexual' (Pornography, Postpornography: The Aesthetics and Politics of Sexual Representation) at the Museu d'Art Contemporani de Barcelona. The seminar included a keynote talk on Virginie Despentes and Coralie Trinh Thi's *Baise-Moi* (*Fóllame*; *Rape Me*) (2000) – already discussed by Bourcier (2001: 23–8) – and marked the beginning of a surge of post-porn projects in Spain such as Post-Op, Girls Who Like Porno and La Quimera Rosa as well as the individual work of Diana Pornoterrorista and the Barcelona-based Valencian activist-artist María Llopis. It was a defining moment in the development and consolidation of a strong Barcelona-based porn collective, further mapping the links between this city and France and, as the documentary *Mi sexualidad es una creación artística* (My Sexuality Is a Work of Art) (Lucía Egaña Rojas, 2011) shows, further establishes the Catalan capital as a transnational space for creative and activist work around sexuality and gender. We return to the radical scene of activism, theory and performance in Barcelona in Chapter 4, and in Chapter 1 explore some of the more ideas-based links between one sector of the Barcelona gay and lesbian community, French thinking on sexuality and French film.

WORKING WITH THE AUDIENCE: METHODS

There are many different ways in which the audiences that we encounter may affiliate themselves to a notion of community in its broader, more social sense. When we attend a screening at an LGBTQ film festival, as we look around the auditorium as other viewers take their seats and, perhaps intentionally, perhaps inadvertently, listen in to their conversations, we attain both a tangible sense of what unites us, as well as recognising those aspects that separate us from the crowd. A heightened awareness, or perhaps a timely reminder, of what makes us individuals as well as members of a community is thus facilitated by attendance at such events, but it is the impression of shared values and a collective outlook on the world that brings many of us to the festival and the screening in the first place. So it might be said that LGBTQ festivals foster a certain consensus or solidarity, in that we attend because of a desire to connect with like-minded people and because we expect to come into contact with values and sensibilities that we recognise and share and which can then be reaffirmed or challenged by the films being shown or the people we meet there.

Awareness of this ambivalence calls for a supple understanding of community identity, which at once acknowledges its power and its value as a unifying force, as well as its porosity and potential to homogenise difference and individuality. Here, we have found theoretical understandings of a 'sense of community' useful in thinking through these issues and have adopted the socio-psychological definition of this elaborated by McMillan and Chavis (1986). We are not concerned with applying this theory in a systematic way, which would, in any case, fail to embrace the multiple and shifting positions that the viewers we interview assume in response to our films, but some aspects of their theory have enabled us to locate and interpret the tensions between collective and individual identity formation as they are revealed to us through the responses of our participants.

McMillan and Chavis derive their taxonomy from Joseph R. Gusfield's (1975) categories of territorial communities and relational communities. The first of these is applicable to our work with festivals, in particular, in that their role and function have been to build a 'sense' of community affiliation by physically bringing people together in the same venue or venues (Gever 1990: 201; White 1999: 74; Pidduck 2002: 267). The second – a 'sense of community' in its more relational manifestations – interests us since the transient nature of our interaction with viewers at festivals, special screenings and online prevents us from having a real and meaningful understanding of the material ways in which they maintain community affiliations over time and through other cultural practices and pursuits. This relational 'sense of community' does not depend on physical location (Gusfield 1975: xvi; in McMillan and Chavis 1986: 8), which is clearly pertinent to our exploration of how a community affiliation can be expressed across physical borders. Of the four elements of community membership that McMillan and Chavis identify, membership (a 'sense of belonging and identification' (1986: 11) to a particular community with distinct boundaries) is vital, of course. How this membership is claimed, confirmed and reinforced through expressions of 'shared values' (13), a 'shared emotional connection' and a 'shared history' in our respondents' written and verbal responses to our films is, as will be seen in the chapters that follow, a central concern.

More crucially, given our interest in cross-cultural and transnational interaction with LGBTQ films, we are particularly keen to probe and reveal how that expression of collective shared experience and perspective is claimed as having been facilitated by encounters with foreign-language films. Such encounters have themselves played a key role in the identity construction facilitated and affirmed by LGBTQ film festivals, partly as a result of the paucity of representations of LGBTQ issues and concerns in any one national visual culture before the advent of the Web and subscription TV channels. LGBTQ film festivals have been described as fostering a 'cross-fertilisation of international images, ideas, and people' (Pidduck 2002: 268). Such cross-cultural exchange could be perceived as transnational in a formative sense; if some LGBTQ community and individual identities are (partly) constructed in and through attendance at festivals, the encounters those festivals encourage with foreign-language films feed into that construction.

However, some care is required when using the term 'transnational', because of the risks of overlooking what Higbee and Lim (2010) refer to as the 'specific cultural, historical and ideological contexts' in which films are produced and received (11–12). Foreign-language films obviously draw on local geographical, social, cultural, and political realities and contexts, and, for this reason, can elicit the curiosity of the nondomestic viewer seeking encounters with exotic and unfamiliar cultures from the safety and comfort of the cinema auditorium (see Nichols 1994). And yet, many nondomestic audiences often talk about how they prompt feelings of empathy, (self-) recognition and (self-) revelation. Moreover, they can be read as offering what is perceived to be lacking from the domestic culture of the viewer who watches them by furnishing alternative resources for self-making and social identity construction. In such cases, allegiance to one national domestic culture can be superseded by an alignment with worldviews associated with another, transmitted through its cinema. The discussion of responses in this book explores the extent to which such viewing and subject positions emerge from the responses to our films. It examines how respondents negotiate and transmit other cultures' interpretations of LGBTQ experience, sensibility and taste, and from complex, non-localised sociopolitical circumstances.

The expression of community affiliation that we are addressing in this study, then, tends to be malleable, blurred and negotiated, open to connections with other communities and predicated on allegiances to distinct sections within that community or to values or groups outside of that community. It exists in concrete ways, and in different combinations, for our respondents both territorially and relationally. It is conveyed and claimed through their value judgements, both on elements within the films and on the issues they raise, and in their affirmations of proximity, empathy and identification.

Such claims of correspondence between films and the lived realities of audience members are a strong feature of the ways in which audiences interact with media texts. Identification is 'part of the folk wisdom of responding to films' and 'the success or failure of a film partly depends on whether this identification occurs, and . . . the quality and strength of emotional responses depend on identification' (Gaut 1999: 200). And yet, by virtue of its emphasis on actual reactions to films, the concept of 'identification' has been highly contested within work on audience reception, as Martin Barker argues (2016). We approach expressions of identification, self-similarity, shared values and common perspectives on the world from a sociological perspective; that is, not as psychological processes, but as means of articulating pre-existing social affinities and/or spontaneous affiliations with particular personality types, communities and values. In an echo of some of the points made above, Barker (2016) asserts that 'as audiences we bring "interpretive frameworks" to our encounters with films and make associations with those elements that are salient and powerful to us owing to their coming from our relevant experiences, connections and communities' (153). Barker (2006) argues elsewhere that when we watch films we 'carry in' with us a 'sense of belonging to different discursive communities, some real, some imaginary, even as [we] may watch, listen, read alone' (28); and, with Mathijs, notes that 'cultural values and world views are used as active points of reference' and that 'people's sense of community, legacy, and affiliation . . . influence the longer term settling of the viewing experience' (Barker and Mathijs 2008: 2). Such affinities can often frame our readings of films, including foreign-language and documentary films, and how we evaluate them in front of our peers.

We have been careful to emphasise the fact that our work focuses on the social dimensions and functions of 'talk' about media products. Following a trend within qualitative work with audiences (Buckingham 1991; Seiter 1999; Thomas 2002; Austin 2002), we acknowledge that we can work with and make interpretations from only the materials available to us, which in this case is, broadly, responses, handwritten, typed and verbal. Hence, we seek to avoid the dangers of falling into the trap of assuming that what people write and say about films constitutes an accurate reflection of what they actually think (Seiter 1999: 28–9). This is not to instil suspicion with regards to the veracity or authenticity of the information provided in the responses we collect, which would be contentious and unethical, but simply to show that we gear our interpretations of those responses to the particularities of the contexts in which they are expressed (be that quickly after watching a film and on a set questionnaire form, in subsequent email follow-up, in a focus group discussion, or unprompted, in a blog, online).

In the light of this sociological premise that underpins our work, our approach is broadly underpinned by the work of Pierre Bourdieu (1979) on taste and distinction and its application in and adaptation for qualitative audience research (see, for example, Seiter 1999: 24–8; Thomas 2002: 13–26; Austin 2002: 20). In fact, echoes of Bourdieu's argument that our identity is constructed in and through our cultural tastes (1979) can be clearly seen in Seiter's justification for not taking talk about media at face value: 'media tastes do not simply reflect identity, but are actually constitutive of it' (1999: 29). In our book, we probe how the values, allegiances and sensibilities acquired as a result of tastes, identifications and affiliations in adulthood and with regards to sexuality and gender are invoked within and expressed through interaction with foreign-language LGBTQ films.

However, conscious that an overemphasis on sociological methods may lead us to ignore or downplay the ways in which our respondents affirm an affective and emotional connection to our films, we also consider what Barker describes as less '*routinised*' reception practices such as investment and surprise (2006: 39, italics in original). Barker (2006) defines investment as drawing 'attention to all the ways in which the audience *care* about the experience they seek [and] treats as crucial variables *how much* they care, and the *manner* of their caring' (39, italics in original). Surprise, according to Barker (2006), can be 'happy or unhappy' and 'can occasionally be life altering – an experience gained that breaches boundaries, opens new perspectives, wanted or not' (39). Hence, we remain open to those instances in which an encounter with a foreign-language film is described as having had such an emotional impact on a respondent that, they claim, it has influenced how they view and approach a particular issue, or indeed themselves. Affective and emotional connections have traditionally proved difficult to study (Plantinga and Smith 1999: 1; Staiger 2005: 89), though, in keeping with the sociological slant of our research, we are interested in how the expression of these feed into and shore up the sociocultural affiliations and allegiances claimed by our respondents.

APPROACHES TO DATA COLLECTION AND INTERPRETATION

We have gathered our responses via a mixture of direct and indirect formats, including written questionnaires distributed at festival and one-off screenings, focus group discussions and post-questionnaire follow-up emails. The standard questions used are presented in Appendix I. We are aware of the specific limitations of each of our methods – questionnaires can elicit fleeting responses and may not 'help to establish thick description or to understand process or social context' (Bertrand and Hughes 2005: 69) while focus group discussions can result in some participants feeling inhibited in responding or feeling pressurised to follow a group consensus, as well as introducing other relational factors (see Barker and Brooks 1998: 21; Schrøder et al. 2003: 151–4). However, we wanted to include a combination of individual and one-to-one methods with audience work with groups. Moreover, the problems of these methods notwithstanding, they still have their advantages: questionnaires allow access to a large number of respondents (Bertrand and Hughes 2005: 69) while group discussions provide instances of instantaneous observations and reflect the significance of relational aspects for the negotiation of self-identity and of social relationships (Frith 2000: 282–6). When combined, they can allow access to a rich variety of different reactions to films.

Continuing in a text-based tradition in audience research, we interpret the questionnaire responses and focus group discussions in close connection to the films on which they are based. Much existing cross-cultural audience research has been based on the transnational reception of individual film, televisual and/or radio texts or series (see among others Katz and Liebes 1990; Barker and Mathijs 2008) or on Hollywood (Austin 2002). Given that we survey and interpret responses to multiple films, all of which are not in the English language and most of which are recent to the time of writing, and that many will be obscure or unknown to the reader, some reference to narrative, genre and aesthetic features has been necessary. Hence, although our work contributes to a move away from a 'text-centric theory of spectatorship' (Reinhard and Olson 2016: 8), we are attentive to the importance of the 'text' for the audience–film encounter (Morley 2006: 109). This does not mean, though, that we subscribe to any outdated notion of textual determinism; we recognise the polyvalence of meanings within films and of the possible readings and viewing positions that viewers adopt in watching, digesting and talking about them. To mitigate the impact of our interpretations of our films on our analyses of the responses, we have included the synopses in programmes and uploaded online and film notes that have been and are still made available to our audiences – the *ancillary materials*' (Barker and Mathijs 2008: 11, italics in original) that many festival and special screening attenders encounter before the opening credits roll. Unlike some recent projects that combine qualitative and quantitative methods to get past 'snapshots' and generalise responses (9), use of numerical data in interpreting our responses is minimal. Again, this is partly due to the nature of our project as seeking to probe and reveal the importance of multiple foreign language films for individual and community identity formation.

Between 2012 and 2014, we gathered 416 completed questionnaires from nine festivals in France, Spain and the United Kingdom: the Festival des images aux mots in Toulouse (with no offical English name but roughly translated as 'From Images to Words'), Ecrans Mixtes in Lyon (again, with no offical English name but translated as 'Mixed Screens') and, in Paris, the Lesbian, Gay, Bi, Trans & ++++ Film Festival, Chéries-Chéris (a play on words that conveys the sense of 'Darling Girls, Darling Boys'); in Barcelona, the Casal Lambda Film Festival (Mostra Internacional de Cinema Gai i Lesbià, a.k.a. FIRE!!) and The Barcelona International Gay & Lesbian Film Festival (Festival Internacional de Cine Gay y Lésbico de Barcelona: FICGLB), Zinegoak, the Bilbao International Gaylesbotrans Film and Performing Arts Festival, and the Madrid International LGTB Film Festival (LesGaiCineMad); Flare, the London Lesbian and Gay Film Festival, and a POUTfest touring showcase in Manchester. We also polled LGBTQ screenings at two other seasons, the VIVA Spanish and Latin American Film Festival and an Instituto Cervantes series of LGBT films, both in Manchester. FIRE!! and Flare/LLGFF generated the highest number of completed questionnaires: ninety-seven for the former and 111 for the latter. The least productive were the Festival des images aux mots (two), the FICGLB (eleven), Ecrans Mixtes (thirteen), and Zinegoak (eighteen). We have received thirty-five follow-up emails, conducted one Skype conversation and facilitated five focus group discussions in Lyon, London, Barcelona, Salamanca, and Manchester, with twenty-four participants across all five. In all, then, the book is based on the reactions to our films by 440 respondents, and, in Chapter 5 particularly, comments and observations on online blogs and forums.

Despite a robust and hands-on campaign of publicity and follow-up in addition to our web presence (see, for example, Appendix II), we experienced some difficulties in recruiting volunteers for our group discussions, except for that in Salamanca (where we used an on-site research co-ordinator who was able to engage in informal follow-up of publicity and invitations). In Barcelona, an initially promising list of eight who committed to come dwindled to five on the day, and then three (none self-identifying as trans, for a discussion on a trans-themed documentary). For Lyon and London, we resorted to including, among our focus group participants, nine of our Research Assistant Ros Murray's acquaintances (made on various music and activist circuits in France, Spain and Britain). We were nervous about having people already known to one of the research team, given the potential impact that this can have on the data produced (Hollway 1989: 11; Seiter 1999: 37–8; Waldron 2009: 92–3).

However, both of the focus group discussions in question were led by Darren Waldron as the project's Co-Investigator, and the relaxed atmosphere that prevailed at these two events reassured us that their presence, as well as that of Ros, facilitated the generation of relatively free-flowing exchanges in which individuals seemed unrestrained in claiming particular subject positions. Their confidence, which was expressed through an affirmative delivery style and/or the display of specialist knowledge (the Lyon respondents variously claimed positions as feminist, anti-capitalist and/or queer activists), was undoubtedly reinforced by the presence of someone who, for them, formed part of their own political and social 'subculture'. While there were minimal signs that the confidence of some inhibited others, the quieter members were also Ros's acquaintances, and such disparities in contribution are a common feature of any group discussion, whether that group is composed of people known or unknown to the facilitators. Given that some of these people already had strong political identities that were known to the research assistant, they were arguably less likely to be swayed by the viewpoints expressed by others. While this might minimise the relational influences on talk produced in group discussions, it nonetheless offers us a glimpse of the social identity that they are likely to project outside of the contexts of the discussion.

Our aim was to maximise our potential of eliciting the 'natural vocabulary' (Barker and Brooks 1998: 24) of our respondents. However, we are aware that accessing pure, unmediated reactions is extremely difficult, given that responses tend to be expressed within the frames of available discourses, which might be influenced by the film and the contexts in which it is seen, as already noted in relation to language above. In our study, these contexts include the venue of the screening and any prescreening notes, presentations and publicity, the film's theme, the common vernaculars generally deployed in approaching that theme, similar films viewers may have seen, or texts on its subject, and so on. Moreover, the research event itself can also have a contextual bearing on the responses produced, given that respondents can mould their answers in certain ways because they are participating in a research project, something that Schrøder et al. refer to as the 'halo effect' (2003: 249) and Morrison, in relation to focus groups, labels 'moderator demand' (1998: 215).

We are thus aware of our own potential influences on the data we present and that our empirical evidence is produced within our own data-gathering and analysis frameworks (Ang 1989: 105). We also recognise the ambivalence of our own position as both members of the audiences and communities we study (attending festivals and special screenings is part of our regular social practices and has contributed to our own sense of self) and as academics specialising in Spanish and French and LGBTQ visual cultures, with access to 'specialist' knowledge (and, in the case of Chris Perriam, with some experience of serving on festival selection committees). Such specialism enables us to interpret comments and place them within a 'wider system of understanding' (Morrison 1998: 209), but it also risks influencing our interpretations of our data in that we read the responses according to traditional hierarchies that differentiate between the 'enlightened' and 'unenlightened'. Hence, while we do invoke scholarly, theoretical and aesthetic criticism in our interpretations of the data, we have been careful to do this when prompted by the response under discussion, in which awareness of those issues is implied or inheres.

However, we also recognise the dangers of 'interpretive paralysis' that can arise from excessive self-reflexivity and self-criticism (Austin 2002: 68). All of our questionnaire respondents attended the festivals and screenings of their own accord and prior to encountering us in the auditoria, many follow LGBTQ films and go regularly to LGBTQ festivals, and many too see themselves as forming part of LGBTQ – and other – communities. We thus strive to record and interpret prominent, sustained and recurring viewing positions and strategies in relation to our films while, at the same time, acknowledging that these are adopted within the parameters of our study.

Mindful of these issues we chose open-ended questions for both our written questionnaires and focus groups, and because of the dangers of ambiguity (see Bertrand and Hughes 2005) kept them as simple as possible. We formulated them along the lines of what we thought people would 'instinctively' discuss after watching a film, such as whether they liked or disliked it and why, and whether they found it 'true to life', as well as some more 'specialised' questions around the quality of the director's work and their approach to the subject of their films. The questions were translated from English into Catalan, Spanish, and French, and linguistic and idiomatic accuracy was assured by having native speakers verify the wording. Former and current postgraduate students were employed to input the questionnaire responses into a spreadsheet and to transcribe the focus group discussions, using the system of symbols created by Potter and Wetherell (1987) that record, on the written transcription, elements denoting verbal expression such as emphases and pauses. The responses we have selected in our publications reflect the most recurrent topics, and we have anonymised our data by using pseudonyms, which have been chosen by using both public and private websites from the country of origin of the respondent and according to equivalents in terms of the popularity of the original name.

Our initial contact with most of our respondents was, as mentioned, minimal given that they quickly collected the written questionnaires as they filed into the auditorium and then swiftly returned them to us once the film had finished. We invested much effort in publicising ourselves and thus making our project visible in the festival cinema foyers. We wore T-shirts emblazoned with the project's logo (see Appendix II for example of the logo as it appeared on the project's web pages) and stood in strategic positions at the entrance of the auditoriums. We always printed and distributed between seventy-five and eighty questionnaires, and an average of between fifteen and twenty were returned to us. We attributed this relatively low rate of completion to questionnaire fatigue, the physical length of our questionnaires (those distributed at festivals in Barcelona were translated into both Spanish and Catalan) and the busy schedules of festival attenders who, among other commitments, might also be rushing off to watch additional films. Contact with those who attended focus group discussions was obviously better and for this reason those events sometimes yielded more refined data. A few respondents continued the discussion via follow-up emails, and fewer still solicited further information about the project.

We conducted the focus group discussions in line with recommended practice (Morrison 1998: 207–23). Each discussion was preceded with appropriate 'stimuli' in the form of a screening of the particular film we wanted to examine and was based on the same set of questions that we used for the questionnaires (none of the focus group participants had encountered these beforehand). While we ensured that they were covered, we were less prescriptive about the order in which they were addressed, thus fostering a relative sense of ease, flexibility and freedom. Aware of the potentially restrictive impact of the 'leader effect' (Morrison 1998: 215), we kept direction and guidance to a minimum, allowed our interviewees the space to express themselves fully, engaged with each topic as it arose, including those that fell beyond the themes covered by our questions, and, given the nature of our study, drew out the 'affective and value-laden' implications of our respondents' comments (Morrison 1998: 213 based on Merton and Kendall 1946: 545).

Given the fleeting nature of our encounter with those respondents who completed questionnaires, we did not have sufficient time to go through the ethical issues related to our project verbally and so we included the information of the kind recommended by Schrøder et al. (2003: 247) – presentation of ourselves and our institution and details about the 'topic and purpose' of our study, why and how they had been selected, eventual uses of their answers in publications and assurances about anonymisation – on a separate sheet that we attached to the questionnaire. We also included a disclaimer that they were asked to sign giving authorisation for their responses to be used in the project, in accordance with the ethics procedures of the University of Manchester.

The Sample

Since the inception of our project, we have aimed to work with audiences likely to identify with one of the categories brought together under the LGBTQ banner. Aware of the dangers of predefining participants, however, and of pre-interpreting their responses, we decided not to ask them to declare their sexuality (although some volunteered this information), and instead chose to focus our recruitment on outlets we thought would boost our chances of reaching our intended audience, this being why we turned to LGBTQ film festivals. Our strategy of primarily recruiting respondents at LGBTQ festivals risked restricting our sample in terms of the type of viewers we were likely to attract, as having a strong sense of community allegiance, as mentioned, and – because of the historical significance of festivals within LGBTQ activism – specific, if various, political sensibilities. We attempt to counterbalance this, and to broaden and diversify our sample, to a degree at least, through our inclusion of responses gathered from elsewhere, including special screenings, but also online remarks, observations and comments in threads and blogs. Of course, many LGBTQ-identifying viewers are likely to see these films when they are on general release, or after. Similarly, many LGBTQ viewers may well prefer to watch them as part of everyday programming because they may feel daunted by the prospect of attending a festival. We have captured some of these responses from the online sources just mentioned; but it is for reasons of practicality that we have mainly focused on festivals as sites of recruitment. More recently, the purpose and audiences served by LGBTQ film festivals have evolved, partly because the Web and subscription TV channels have made images of LGBTQ issues and concerns more available, and partly due to a general perception that queer lifestyles are now more accepted, at least in Western societies. The remit of the bigger festivals has broadened, which has also been facilitated by the involvement of cultural institutions that cater to the general public, and, possibly, by the support of corporate sponsors. There is, of course, a danger of exaggerating audience diversification at contemporary LGBTQ festivals. Some greater diversity is inevitable, though, as the attention of the critical establishment and broader population increasingly turns to films with queer content, and as those same films are selected to headline at LGBTQ festivals held in mainstream institutions (Suárez 2006; Galt and Schoonover 2014). Consequently, while we believe our main method of recruiting our respondents among festival attenders has succeeded in reaching mainly LGBTQ viewers, our sample also includes non-LGBTQ-identifying respondents.

We asked all of those who completed questionnaires and took part in our focus group discussions to answer a selection of sociocultural questions in order to allow us to construct a picture of the overall constitution of the group (see Appendix I). At the beginning of the project, we omitted a question on gender, but added this later as we became aware of the importance of gender identity to some of our films and audiences. Hence, the respondents at the Paris festival were not asked to identify themselves in gender terms. Again, it should be reiterated that we are deploying a discursive notion of identity, that is, as it is constructed in the 'talk' based on our films. Consequently, the following socioeconomic profile is intended to give a general overview; more pointed issues with regards to identity will feature among the in-depth analyses of the responses in Chapters 3, 4 and 5. Each time a new respondent is cited, pseudonymously, in these chapters, their response is accompanied by a short description of how they identified themselves in response to these questions.

In terms of nationality, the main regions covered by our project, either within the films (France and Spain) or as locations within which the encounter with those films unfolds (France, Spain, including Catalunya, and the UK) are, as expected, the most prominent among our sample: twenty-eight per cent (122) identified themselves as Spanish (thirty-three of these, however, choosing Catalan for their responses), and a further five per cent (twenty) as Catalan, eleven per cent (forty-nine) as French and thirty-two per cent (142) defined themselves as British. Beyond those who did not provide any information about their nationality, the remaining participants came from a range of different countries (Argentina, Australia, Austria, Canada, Chile, Cuba, Denmark, Finland, Germany, Greece, Ireland, Italy, Mexico, Pakistan, Poland, Portugal, Puerto Rico, Slovakia, South Africa, Switzerland, Turkey, Uruguay, Venezuela, Vietnam and the USA), while some declared that they had dual nationality (American-British, British-Australian, British-German, British-New Zealand, British-Spanish, British-Trinidadian, Canadian-Greek, Canadian-Swiss, Colombian-Spanish, French-Algerian, French-Argentinian, French-German, French-Moroccan, Greek-Danish and Polish-Italian). The relatively low number of French-identifying respondents can be explained by the fact that relatively few LGBTQ films from Spain were being screened at festivals during the period in which we undertook our research, possibly because of the impact of the post-2008 financial crisis on film production within that country. By contrast, France continued to produce a high number of high-profile films with LGBTQ interest and which were included in festival programmes.

The balance in terms of gender among those asked is tipped towards men. Forty-four per cent (174 of 396) defined themselves as male and thirty-one-and-a-half per cent (139) wrote female, one respondent identified as trans MTF and four as trans FTM, while five defined themselves as genderqueer. Where genderqueer individuals are quoted in the book, neutral pronouns ('they', 'their', 'themselves') are used, as is also the case for those who chose not to indicate a gender identity. The general level of education is very high: seventy-one-and-a-half per cent (315) have completed undergraduate degrees, which includes twenty-six per cent (114) who have also studied to postgraduate level; six per cent (twenty-eight) left education after school and four-and-a-half per cent (twenty) have technical or vocational qualifications. On the basis of the International Standard of Occupations, almost half are employed in the top two categories of the professions (forty-four per cent or 192) and managers (five per cent or twenty-two). Six per cent (twenty-seven) are technicians and associated professionals, two per cent (ten) are clerical support workers, four per cent (nineteen) are service and sales workers, half a per cent (two) work as crafts and related trades workers and one per cent work (five) in elementary occupations. Among the remaining participants, eleven-and-a-half per cent (fifty) are students, seven per cent (thirty-two) are retired, three per cent (thirteen) simply wrote 'work' and three-and-a-half per cent (fourteen) defined their status as unemployed.

The combination of high level of education and higher employment positions enjoyed by many of our respondents might reflect the appeal of film festivals and special screenings of foreign language films to educated and professional audiences. Similarly unsurprising is the fact that the vast majority of eighty-four per cent or 371 live in large cities, with Barcelona, Madrid,

Paris, London, Lyon and Manchester strongly represented. The age range is broad, although the majority of respondents are above twenty-five and below forty-five. Thirty-seven (eight-and-a-half per cent) are in the fifteen to twenty-four range, 141 (thirty-two per cent) are between twenty-five and thirty-four, ninety-eight (twenty-two per cent) are between thirty-five and forty-four, seventy-seven (seventeen-and-a-half per cent) are between forty-five and fifty-four, thirty-seven (eight-and-a-half per cent) are between fifty-five and sixty-four, twenty-one (five per cent) are between sixty-five and seventy-four, and six (one-and-a-half per cent) are above seventy-five years of age.

Gauging racial and ethnic background was more challenging given that there is no tradition of asking for such information in France and Spain; in fact, in the former such questions can be deemed offensive in that they bring attention to difference within a society that actively compels people to publicly assimilate to a universal model of citizenship. However, as this book is based on a project conceived in the UK, in which such questions are asked and often viewed positively as recognising diversity (in the sense of ensuring that a voice is given to as broad a population as possible), we still included this question. Given the varied responses – many of those in Spain chose to write their region as their ethnic origin – it is perhaps only worthwhile stating here that eighty-three per cent of our respondents identified themselves as white or in similar terms, twelve per cent did not offer an answer and as few as five per cent described their race or ethnicity as other than white or as mixed; these include Arab-French, black-British, French-Malian, Irish-Jewish-Indian-Jamaican, white Indian Caribbean, white North African, Latin American, North American, Iranian, Indian, South East Asian, Sri Lankan, Filipino, Turkish and English-Jewish. The very high proportion of white respondents might well be a reflection of the continued appeal of LGBTQ film festivals to a mainly white (and, given the above data, middle-class and male) audience. It also alludes to perceptions around the place of people from minority ethnic backgrounds in LGBTQ visual culture. In fact, with the exception of one of our films, *Les Témoins*, all of them focus on the experiences of white LGBTQ people, which, given that we chose them on the basis of what was being selected at programmes, was not a conscious decision on our part. We are keen not be silent on race and ethnicity: for this reason we have decided to include the person's declared identifications in terms of race and ethnicity when introducing them before citing their responses, and we are particularly attentive to those moments where race and ethnicity arise in responses. As can be seen in the list of different ethnic origins, we use the terms that our respondents have chosen for themselves rather than placing them within predetermined categories.

Chapter Breakdown

Our first chapter focuses on what France and Frenchness means in dominant discourses that circulate in Spain and the values attached to Spain and

Spanishness in France. It offers a contextual and historical background to the kind of values (including stereotypes) attached to each culture, which, in many cases, resonate globally. We trace the historical background of such values and associations and, where possible, with specific reference to the perspectives of sexual politics and LGBTQ cultural exchange. The chapter thus focuses on the two-way traffic of cultural, political and historical exchange between France and Spain but, as mentioned, we are attentive to the risk of homogenising geographical and cultural spaces in simplistic and monolithic terms, and of ignoring the multidimensional identities and affiliations of people with regards to nationality. The chapter begins and ends with a discussion of the regional and diasporic affinities between the two countries, by way of illustrating some of the complexities of national and cultural identity and allegiances, particularly in France.

Chapter 2 includes an overview of the emergence and development of LGBTQ film festivals in France, Spain and the UK, covering the FIRE!!, Barcelona, LesGaiCineMad, Madrid, FICGLB, Barcelona and Zinegoak, Bilbao, as well as Chéries-Chéris, Paris, Ecrans Mixtes, Lyon, and Des images aux mots, Toulouse, the London Lesbian and Gay Film Festival – renamed Flare – and the annual series of queer films shown at Manchester's Cornerhouse cinema (now HOME) in connection with the city's lesbian and gay Pride celebrations and drawing on the touring season POUTfest, supported by Peccadillo Films. Some of our audience responses are used to finesse how these particular LGBTQ festivals fit into wider discourses on film festivals in relation to niche designing, space and locality, and responsiveness to community and individual spectators' needs. The chapter draws on our corpus of 416 written questionnaire responses to programming at all of the festivals, as well as interviews and correspondence with programming teams.

Chapters 3 and 4 turn to the audience responses, and to specifics of LGBTQ experience, in more detail. It is here that we consider whether and how representations from 'abroad' are brought to bear on the ways in which our respondents construct themselves and project their relationships with the outside world. Chapter 3 focuses on the responses to representations of ageing among lesbians, gay men and bisexuals and to images of same-sex desire and relationships. We show how viewers claim to relate to the images and narratives in the films. In Chapter 4, we interpret trans films and their reception by showing how they relate to broader political movements and debates in both France and Spain. A comparison between the data presented in these two chapters reveals that, while close proximity and self-implication recur prominently among the subject positions claimed by the viewers cited in Chapter 3, many of the responses analysed in Chapter 4 express a more distanced and negotiated form of empathy or solidarity that allows them to project their understanding while also maintaining their difference from the trans subjects depicted.

Informed by the outcomes of the analysis of audience responses in Chapters 3 and 4, Chapter 5 turns to critical reception. It is here that we focus on those films that have been the subject of substantial critical interest, as well as eliciting online interventions. We begin with a review of the general, semi-establishment, critical reception of *La Vie d'Adèle* and *L'Inconnu du lac* in Spain and compare it with the reactions of 'amateur' LGBTQ cinephiles and general audience members uploaded online and collected via our questionnaires. The chapter takes the same approach in its consideration of the responses among audiences and critics to three star filmmakers from France and Spain: Ozon (including Spanish responses to *Une nouvelle amie*. Téchiné, and Almodóvar. It finishes with a comparison of the online reviews and blogs among LGBTQ viewers to Almodóvar's *La piel que habito* and *Los amantes pasajeros* with the reviews of LGBTQ journalists and prestige film critics. We show how those details of fine response often displace the necessary generalities of the professional and semi-professional critics, or, on the other hand, offer more telling microscopic readings than academic writers or the quality media's star reviewers.

The conclusion reflects on the findings presented in the chapters and on the project as a whole, highlighting key points of convergence, and difference, between these audiences and published or established LGBTQ and general film cultures.

NOTE ON PRESENTATION

Film titles are given in the first instance and in section headings with their official title in the other language as relevant to the context of discussion; in cases where no official title appears to exist in the other language, we supply one only if the filmmaker's own website or publicity suggests it. In describing our respondents we have explicitly indicated where they have chosen not to supply certain details about themselves. In reproducing extracts of the transcriptions, of the symbols created by Potter and Wetherell (1987) for clarity we have retained only the use of (.) indicating a pause.

1. CULTURAL CROSSOVERS

It is a fruitful coincidence that, at the time of writing this section on the cultural and historical encounters, dialogues and diasporic flows between France and Spain, much is being made in the French, Spanish and Catalan press about the Spanish Catalan origins of the newly appointed French Prime Minister, Manuel Valls (born in Horta, Barcelona, 13 August 1962) and the Andalusian infancy of the recently elected Mayor of Paris, Anne Hidalgo (born in San Fernando, Cádiz, 19 June 1959), the second and third most powerful positions held by any politician or statesperson in France (Agencia EFE and Comas 2014; de Taillac 2014; Le Parisien 2014; Uría 2014). That both were born in Spain testifies to the enduring strength of the links between the two countries, whose histories, at least over the past five to six hundred years, are intertwined. In fact, their respective appointment and election constitute a fascinating evolution in these interconnected histories. It illustrates how some of the children of Spanish immigrant families have been successfully integrated within the higher ranks of French political life and revises – if this is the correct term – historical events that saw Spain being forced to endure rule by French aristocrats and politicians in the eighteenth and nineteenth centuries. With regards to this book's focus on the LGBTQ dimensions of these Franco-Spanish intersections, both Valls and Hidalgo have championed high-profile LGBTQ causes; Hidalgo served as First Deputy under Bertrand Delanoë, the first openly gay mayor of Paris, and she and Valls were public supporters of president François Hollande's gay marriage legislation, ratified on 17 May 2013 and which triggered what is widely interpreted as the most hostile reaction among conservatives of all Western European countries that have adopted similar laws (Chault 2013; Le Parisien 2013).

The account that follows traces the historical background of these flows by way of attempting to identify what 'Spain' and 'Spanishness' have tended to signify within political and public imaginaries in France and what 'France' and 'Frenchness' mean in the same imaginaries in Spain, including Catalunya. Such a wide cultural mapping of a broad array of meanings is of relevance to our study precisely because many of the responses to films discussed arise from festival screenings – festivals being sites that tend to attract audiences with an already contextualised, and sometimes specialised, set of expectations and responses (Harbord 2009; Loist 2012; Rouff 2012). As will be seen in the next chapter, too, some responses clearly show that these sub-fields and meanings are available to audience members in certain contexts (following on, for example, from the decision to go to a French film at a particular festival) and show how they are 'contingent . . . upon the tastes, values and life experiences of the spectator concerned' (Waldron 2009: 2). As was suggested in the Introduction, too, French ideas on sexuality and identity have informed the Spanish LGBTQ imaginary to some degree. Illustrations are drawn from films, where possible, and particularly those with LGBTQ interest.

Constructions of Spain and Spanishness

Despite broad awareness of the greater autonomy enjoyed by Spanish regions, certainly compared to their French counterparts, Spain still constitutes a largely homogenised entity within dominant and popular discourses in France. Hence, this account of the meanings attached to 'Spain' and 'Spanishness' uses the term 'Spain' in the singular, despite the plurality of what is now the Spanish State, comprised of historical nationalities and autonomous communities. However, the book attempts to engage, albeit partially, with plurality through its inclusion of festivals, films, filmmakers and audiences from most of Spain.

Historically, perceptions of Spain in France have fluctuated between antipathy and admiration (Angoustures 2004: 9; Pageaux 2007: 459–69). Whether Spain has been castigated or extolled has depended upon the particular period, the aspect of Spanish cultural life under consideration and the objectives of those who are doing the judging. Class, gender, sexuality, religion and regional identity have inflected, and continue to inform, the ways in which Spain has been apprehended in France. Middle-class intellectuals, encyclopaedists and philosophers engaged in 'hispanophobia' during the Enlightenment in a development of the 'Black Legend' (Ilie 1976; Hilton 2002; Powell 2008) while, during the nineteenth and twentieth centuries, aristocrats and their sympathisers looked to Spain as an example of a country that succeeded in retaining some of the values that French society was deemed to have lost (as, for example, in Henri de Montherlant's novel *Maître de Santiago* of 1947). For some in France, beyond the historical denigration of the Spanish as avaricious and deceitful, Spain today can symbolise something more popular and material, as the source of pleasures that contrast, in their perceived rawness and immediacy, with dominant conceptualisations of refined taste and the emphasis on reason over affect, and, by extension, as a country within which bourgeois patriarchy and heteronormativity have been more effectively undermined. Whatever form such images of Spain have taken, though, they clearly reveal more about France and how that country is perceived from within than provide insights into the realities of life in Spain and into the actual complexities of what has been taken as a Spanish national character.

Institutional enmity towards Spain burgeoned in the sixteenth and seventeenth centuries as the result of anxieties about France's more powerful southern neighbour, and was broadly promulgated at the beginning of the seventeenth century. Paradoxically, this antagonism is said to have been accompanied by a strong appreciation for the sophistication of the artistic creativity yielded by the Spanish Golden Age (1530–1640). Animosity heightened during the Spanish War of Succession (1701–14), which pitted Bourbons against Habsburgs and arose from Louis XIV imposing a French king, Philippe (Felipe) V – and 'a Versailles-oriented elitism' (Ilie 1976: 382) – on the nation in 1700. In the following century, Napoleon's occupation of Spain in the Spanish War of Independence (1807–14) – as later to be discussed from the point of view of France as seen by Spain – saw Spanish literary and theatrical works adapted for middle- and upper-class French audience preferences in an intensification of an existing cultural tradition of mild denigration of 'le "goût" espagnol' ('Spanish taste') and assertion of the superiority of 'le "goût" français' (Pageaux 2007: 463). Spain and its culture have been exoticised and subordinated to the status of an ornament via three processes, it has been argued: 'cultural fragmentation' in which specific elements are arbitrarily selected and valorised as representative of 'Spain'; 'cultural feminisation', in which Spain is projected as the 'feminine' other (as 'woman', as 'female dancer', as 'female singer', as 'femme fatale') to the 'masculine' and rational self (France); and 'cultural theatricalisation', in which Spain is seen as a decor that bears little connection to the material realities of Spanish life (Pageaux 2007: 463; 465). Through these processes, people who come from and live in Spain, with all their complexities, are excluded and Spain, the nation, serves as a springboard for the transmission of self-serving ideologies.

Through 'cultural theatricalisation', Spain serves as a decor that corresponds to the most prevailing of generalised images, whether based on no direct experience of Spanish cultural life at all (Ekman 1992: 49; Pageaux 2007: 466) or produced later by the simultaneously inventive and archaising expectations of Romantic travel writers finding otherness in geographically nearby places (Thompson 2012: 176–202). Such exoticisation has produced a dominant binary in which the supposed diligence, measure and reserve of the French are juxtaposed with the presumed laziness, pride and passion of the Spanish, already asserted at the start of the eighteenth century in the *Dictionnaire géographique universel* (Baudrand 1701: 411).

Oppositions of this type have over time projected inertia as a defining trait of the perceived Spanish character (except, notably, by nineteenth-century travel writers discovering dynamism, energy, turmoil and intensity – Thompson 2012: 176–202). This was a caricature that had been manipulated by proponents of the Enlightenment (such as Nicolas Masson de Morvillers) as evidence that Spain had contributed neither to its own cultural advancement nor to that of Europe (Eamon 2009). The association of the Spanish with pride can be traced back to the reception of the reign of Felipe II; it resounds through the War of Succession (Ilie 1976: 378–80) and permeates the French cultural imaginary well into the twentieth century, featuring at the beginning of the much reprinted comic book *Astérix en Hispanie* (René Goscinny and Albert Uderzo, 1969) in which Spanish fighters misconstrue their Roman enemies and admire their courage and valour. Forty-three per cent of those questioned about the Spanish character in a 1980 survey mentioned pride (Angoustures 2004: 53). The stereotype that equates the Spanish with passion is ubiquitous. It is transmitted through literature, including travel writing (Thompson 2012), the opera, most famously in versions of the Don Juan story, from Tirso de Molina's *El burlador de Sevilla* (1630), and most particularly Prosper Mérimée's novella *Carmen* (1845–7), 'adapted' to the opera by Georges Bizet in 1875, and set during the War of Independence highlighting a pointedly differentiating presence of France in Spain.

As Powrie et al. (2007) argue, Carmen 'does not embody a form of Spanish culture so much as the Spain of the French imaginary' (22). *Carmen* recreates and reinforces nineteenth-century interpretations of Spanish culture as the first romantic Orient; the confrontation between the 'voluptuous, but immoral' Orient and the 'austere, but moral' West 'reaches its height in *Carmen*' (Angoustures 2004: 59). This construction of Spain as the *first* Orient – or as 'an outpost of Africa and the Orient' (Thompson 2012: 162) – allows us to consider perceptions of 'Spanishness' through the prism of Edward Saïd's Orientalism. Despite Said's conflations that Britain plus France equal Europe, and that North Africa and the Middle East equal the Orient, Orientalism can offer productive ways of grasping the appeal of the foreign other particularly for a study that seeks to identify and reveal the lure of transnational representations (here of queerness) for actual viewing groups. Saïd defines Orientalism as 'the enormously systematic discipline by which European culture was able to manage – and even produce – the Orient politically, sociologically, militarily, ideologically, scientifically, and imaginatively during the post-Enlightenment period' (Saïd 1998: 873). In her queer phenomenological reading of Saïd, Sara Ahmed argues that the Orient points to 'another way of being in the world – to a world of romance, sexuality and sensuality' (Ahmed 2006: 114). This Orient is 'full of signs of desire in how it is represented and "known" within the West' and 'is also desired by the West, as having things that the "West" is assumed to be lacking' (114). Ahmed goes on to say that 'this fantasy of lack, of what is "not here", shapes desires for what is "there"' (114). The idea that the Orient symbolises ideas around romance, sexuality, sensuality and desire that are perceived to be lacking in the West can be mapped on to the ways in which Spain is apprehended within some dominant discourses in France, as wild, free, unorthodox and lubricious against its reserved, constrained, moral and prudish northern neighbour. This is portrayed in *Carmen* through the juxtaposition of the Basque soldier José, enlisted by the French in their endeavour to impose order on the Peninsula, with the threatening 'Oriental' female character Carmen. Her 'dangerously' disruptive existence may appeal to North European audiences precisely because it manages to defy, withstand and exceed middle-class and patriarchal moralities, legalities and aspirations. Although not queer in any literal sense, she nonetheless subverts the bourgeois values around gender identity and sexual desire promoted by, through and after the Enlightenment; she functions as a 'model for excessive and uncontainable desire' and, while she may be punished through death, that same fate allows her, particularly in the operatic version, to 'float free' (Powrie et al. 2007: 17–18).

The idea that Spain is brought into cultural and social life as filling a perceived lack is exemplified in French invocations well before Mérimée's novella and Bizet's adaptation, however. If Van Loo's famous paintings *La Conversation espagnole* (1754) and *La Lecture espagnole* (1755) revived an enduring representation of Spanish culture as synonymous with ideas of gallantry (Barker 2007: 590), in Hugo's *Ruy Blas* (1838) Spain conforms to the exoticised and ornamental image of a land of passion and valour, and of a culture that is lamenting the loss of its past glories. In the 1948 film adaptation, directed by Pierre Billon, Spain is invoked in the many visual references to Spanish art that Jean Cocteau, as scriptwriter, demanded (including allusions to the paintings of Goya and Velázquez) and the presumed valour of the Spanish is given a French inflection through the casting of Jean Marais as Blas and his rebellious double Don Cesar de Bazan, alongside Danielle Darrieux as Marie de Neuborg, the Bavarian-born queen of Spain. Elsewhere, Cocteau's 'queer' touch is pervasive in *Ruy Blas*, seen not only in the casting of Marais but also in his caricature of court dress, theatricalised emotions, expressive dialogues and acting, and feminised male characters (Blas's melancholy romanticism and Don Cesar's flamboyance). The highly successful parody *La Folie des grandeurs* (*Delirios de grandeza*; *Delusions of Grandeur*) (Gérard Oury, 1969), also based on Hugo's story, accentuates the ineffectualness, avarice and narcissism of the Spanish nobility in contrast to the chivalrous, brave and romantic peasants.

The idea that cinema – and especially its transnationally adored actors – takes up the association of Spanishness with distracting narratives about love and passion is illustrated and projected through the figure of the Spanish-born film and stage actor Maria Casarès (Casares in Spanish). In her three main postwar roles – as Nathalie in *Les Enfants du paradis* (*Los niños del paraíso*; *Children of Paradise*) (Marcel Carné, 1943–5), as Hélène in *Les Dames du Bois de Boulogne* (*Las damas del bosque de Bolonia*; *The Ladies of the Bois de Boulogne*) (Robert Bresson, 1945) and as the Princess/Death in *Orphée* (*Orfeo*; *Orpheus*) (Jean Cocteau, 1950) – she corresponds to various 'troubling' visions of female subjectivity that find their roots in some of the ideas about Spanishness mentioned above. Nathalie is problematic, if not disruptive; as the anti-heroine of Carné's epic, she serves as an allegory for traditional (some have said Vichy) France, with its emphasis on female servitude, devotion and maternity. By contrast, as Hélène, Casarès recalls the Marquise de Merteuil from Laclos's *Les Liaisons dangereuses* (1782), a jealous, but powerful, narcissistic woman who manipulates all those around her into playing out her fantasies. Similarly, as Death, she symbolises the lure of the illicit, tempting Orphée into an underground world of passion and pleasure. Hélène and the Princess/Death are at once nostalgically Spanish and troubling (perhaps queer) characters through their reconfiguration of the femme fatale. Casarès threatens to upset and undermine the values of love, monogamy and romance attached to other characters in the films (in the young cabaret dancer Agnès (Elina Labourdette) and Eurydice (Marie Déa). In these roles, she mediates uncontrolled desires and emotions, and can thus be seen, in part, as a queerly marked character. More recently, in the post-Franco and post-Transition period one critic observes how, on screen, actors like Marisa Paredes, Carmen Maura, Victoria Abril, Penélope Cruz, Miguel Bosé or Sergi López 'ont donné de l'Espagne une image tour à tour dramatique et drôle, mutine et séduisante' (Aubert 2002) ('have offered alternately a dramatic, amusing, rebellious or seductive image of Spain'); and another asserts that Abril and Rossy de Palma are 'absolutamente idolatradas en Francia' (Loureda 2012) ('absolutely adored in France').

The exoticising of Spain in France extends to the simplistic ways in which the Civil War and its aftermath have been received, as Pageaux notes (2007: 467); this is a point critiqued in *La Guerre est finie* (*La guerra ha terminado*; *The War Is Over*) (Alain Resnais, 1966) (mentioned below in relation to political exile). Semprún's screenplay has its central protagonist Diego/Domingo (Yves Montand) talk of the situation in Spain and express his frustrations with the double values of the French:

> La malheureuse Espagne, l'Espagne héroïque, l'Espagne au coeur : j'en ai par dessus la tête. L'Espagne est devenue la bonne conscience lyrique de toute la gauche: un mythe pour anciens combattants . . . L'Espagne n'est qu'un rêve de touristes ou la légende de la guerre civile. Tout ça, mélangé au théâtre de Lorca . . . L'Espagne n'est plus le rêve de 36, mais la réalité de 65, même si elle semble déconcertante.

> (Sad Spain, heroic Spain, the Spain in our hearts: I've had enough of it. Spain now symbolises the good lyrical consciousness of the broad left: a myth for veterans . . . Spain is but a dreamland for tourists or the legend of the Civil War. All that, mixed with Lorca's theatre . . . Spain is no longer the dream of '36, but the reality of '65, even if it seems disconcerting.)

Although the Spanish film industry since the historical moment of Resnais and Semprún's 1965 film has been prolific in the export of historical dramas both mythifying and demystifying the Civil War and the postwar period (as several essays in Feenstra and Sánchez-Biosca 2014 attest for French readers), it has been suggested that the overriding image of Spain as the locus of liberalising attitudes has led to three film directors in particular being selected and celebrated as projecting a quintessentially Spanish worldview in France: Luis Buñuel, Carlos Saura and Almodóvar (Angoustures 2004: 60). Buñuel and Almodóvar are considered, in French academic writings, as iconoclasts (Tesson 1995; Obadia 2002) (and hundreds of French-language Google results attest to a similar perception in popular journalism and among Web-based audiences). From the perspective of studying Franco-Spanish cross-cultural intersections, Buñuel's films are particularly illuminating, not least because his attack on the bourgeoisie and depiction of unconventional desires is inspired by his early appreciation of the writings of the Marquis de Sade (Buñuel 1994: 268–70). The sardonic studies of the constraints of bourgeois morality that he made in France, and in French – six films between 1964 and 1977, as well as *L'Age d'or* (1930) – arise out of economic, collaborative and political circumstances, of course (Baxter 1994: 276–303). Consequently, some of the characteristics of bourgeois tastes and values he critiques and satirises may seem, if Catholic, universal, with location and mise en scène being deliberately non-specific as well in *Le Charme discret de la bourgeoisie* (*El discreto encanto de la burguesía*; *The Discreet Charm of the Bourgeoisie*) (1972). *Cet obscur objet du désir* (*Ese oscuro objeto del deseo*; *That Obscure Object of Desire*) (1977), however, plays on the tensions between French and Spanish national identities and their concomitant images, and how they are connected to and wrapped up in distinct approaches to sexuality and affect. The central female character, Conchita, a femme-fatale figure who 'lures' the protagonist Mathieu (Fernando Rey) into a masochistic unconsummated affair, is played by two actors, Carole Bouquet and Ángela Molina who was later to have iconic roles in a run of Spanish films with queer narratives or by queer directors – *Las cosas del querer 2a parte* (*The Things of Love Part 2*) (Jaime Chávarri 1995), *Carne trémula* (*Live Flesh*) (Pedro Almodóvar, 1997), *El Mar* (*The Sea*) (Agustí Villaronga, 2000), *Sagitario* (*Sagittarius*) (Vicente Molina Foix, 2001) and *Piedras* (*Stones*) (Ramón Salazar, 2002). The character Conchita is constructed of two facets; on the one hand, she appears vivacious and free, when played by Molina, while on the other, she is remote and frigid, depicted through Bouquet. It is when she is played by Bouquet that Conchita is more threatening, since she represents the disruptive potential of instinctive desires that lie beneath a seemingly bourgeois veneer for bourgeois respectability.

As Julián Daniel Gutiérrez-Albilla writes in his nuanced and sensitive rereading of Buñuel's work from a 'queer subject position', 'conventional criticism has recognised the subversion of bourgeois values in his films, but has perpetuated the habitual association of his cinema with misogynist and homophobic attitudes' (Gutiérrez-Albilla 2008: 15). Indeed, non-straight subjectivities within these anti-establishment endeavours tend to be sidelined, as seen in Madame Anais (Geneviève Page), the bisexual madam of the bordello in *Belle de Jour* (1967) who attempts to seduce Belle (Catherine Deneuve). Gutiérrez-Albilla is more interested in Buñuel's Spanish-language films than those he made in France, but he nonetheless seeks to 'demonstrate how a queer rereading of these representative films . . . provides us with theoretical and methodological tools that challenge the conventional criticism of these five films or other films on Buñuel' (15). While the incorporation of a study of audience responses allows this book to extend beyond the theorised queer spectator of whom Gutiérrez-Albilla speaks (and who is very much related to himself as outlined in the preface) (vii), his sophisticated analyses enable us to see the recurrent queerness that can be found in Buñuel's films. Because these films articulate Buñuel's combative beliefs on middle-class morality and institutions, they project a worldview that is not so remote from some of the most counter-hegemonic drives of queer politics and theories.

Another discourse associated with Spanishness in France centres, unsurprisingly, on *la fiesta*. Much of this refers to the perceived abundance of religious-based festivals and fervour with which the local population is assumed to invest in them, but another equally important and more contemporary image relates to Spain as a place where nightlife thrives far more than in 'sleepy' France – which relates to the (proto-queer) youth- and pop-culture movement, the *movida* of the late 1970s to early 1980s and its self-conscious revamping of the experience of *fiesta* (Angoustures 2004: 69–70) – and as a tourist destination, not least for a gay and lesbian market (Madrid, Maspalomas, Sitges, Torremolinos; Barcelona, Bilbao, Calpe, Granada, Valencia). The liberalisation of morals that emerged after the end of the Franco dictatorship and through the period of transition to democracy (1975–82) was received with curiosity in France. Since then, Spain – during the dictatorship seeming closed and constrained – has come to symbolise for some in France a space in which different sexualities are accepted and the pursuit of pleasure takes precedence. Beyond the 'politics of pleasure', this is given political currency in that Spain is considered as more progressive than France in its perceived ability to accept and celebrate social changes including same-sex marriage and adoption by same-sex couples (Bardou 2015).

If, post-*movida* and in the wake of Barcelona-based radical queer politics of the 1970s (see below), Spain is constructed in France as a queer other to the restrained and stifled self, popular French LGBTQ cinema profited from and reinforced these connotations, with Spanish women, in particular, used to expose the hypocritically puritan and heteronormative values of the bourgeoisie. The major popular success *Gazon maudit* (*Felpudo maldito*; *French Twist*) (Josiane Balasko, 1994) casts the stars of *Tacones lejanos* (*Talons aiguilles*; *High Heels*) (1991), one of Almodóvar's most successful releases in France, Victoria Abril and Miguel Bosé, as representatives of a casual libertarianism that is projected as essentially Spanish, thereby consciously connecting Spanishness with queer sexual discovery. Elsewhere, in the acclaimed short that launched François Ozon's international career, *Une Robe d'été* (*A Summer Dress*) (1996), it is a Spanish woman, Lucía (Lucía Sánchez), who seduces Sébastien (Sébastien Charles), a bored and cynical gay man, on the beach. Through this act, Lucía reignites Sébastien's sex life with his boyfriend Luc (Frédéric Mangenot). Similarly, in Ozon's first full-length feature, *Sitcom* (1998), the Spanish maid, María (again Lucía Sanchez), calms and eventually seduces the anxious mother (Evelyne Dandry), unable to find adequate support during her family's sexual disarray, either from her husband (François Marthouret) or from her psychotherapist (Jean Douchet), precisely because both approach this issue through rational philosophical or medical terms. The anarchy and countercultural sentiment to be found in Buñuel's films and which offer a means of escaping the constraints of bourgeois culture (mentioned above) are, as seen, often associated with Spanish culture in France. This is underlined in *Sitcom*, which, beyond the character of María, adopts a similarly satirical, ironic and surrealist – though far more explicitly non-straight – take on middle-class morality. Again, these films are getting at that enduring image of Spanishness as equated with raw, free and uncensored desires, and which flags up the absurdity of the French middle-class's concern with keeping up appearances (*paraître*) and their intellectualism.

Many of the clichés of 'Spanishness' and broad discourses about the (queer) appeal of Spain in circulation in France persist in visual and filmic representations (and are explored in a wider European dimension, for example, through the film acting career of Sergi López, by Amago 2005). A particularly fruitful illustration – and one that contains a gay subplot in which 'Spanishness' is partly defined by Spain's presumed libertarianism – is *Pas si grave* (*Nada facil*; *No Big Deal*) (Bernard Rapp, 2003). The film recounts a trip to Valencia by three adopted brothers from Belgium: Max (Jean-Michel Portal), Charlie (Sami Bouajila) and Léo (Romain Duris). Spain is exoticised via a mixture of classic iconography (statues of the Virgin Mary, bullfighting, machismo, gypsy culture) and twentieth-century associations (a fascist police chief, played by Luis Hostalot, Republican veterans, strong women and emancipated gay men). While the film is set mainly in the Valencia region, specific regional identity and language are not mentioned. Familiar allusions to the Carmen story abound in Ángela (Leonor Varela), a free-spirited woman who has sex with both Max and Charlie. Knowing and somewhat clunky evocations of Almodóvar emerge through Ramón (Pep Munné), an openly gay captain of the Guardia Civil who performs in a bodega as a transvestite and who eventually seduces Léo. When Max, Charlie and Léo act surprised to discover that Ramón, now in his uniform, is the cross-dressing performer they have just witnessed on stage, he replies 'vous avez du mal à imaginer un capitaine de la Guardia Civil en bas résilles et talons aiguilles?' ('are you struggling to imagine a captain from the Guardia Civil dressed in stockings and high heels?'), thus mentioning by name the French translation of Almodóvar's *Tacones lejanos* before turning to Ángela and asking 'ils n'ont jamais vu les films d'Almodóvar, tes copains?' ('have your mates never seen Almodóvar's films?'). Spain predictably allows the three brothers to discover their 'true' selves, most obvious in Léo who remains in the country with his lover Ramón because it is the only place in which he can be himself and live out his sexuality.

Both Bouajila and Duris feature in famous road movies either with queer protagonists or which challenge French middle-class conventions around taste and conduct. One, *Drôle de Félix* (*The Adventures of Felix*) (Olivier Ducastel and Jacques Martineau, 2000), about a young HIV-positive gay man of North African origins, Félix (Bouajila), coming to terms with his place and status in France, was one of the most readily available titles on DVD in Spanish retail outlets during the 2000s. The other, *Exils* (*Exiles*) (Tony Gatlif, 2004), concerns a young man called Zano (Duris) and his girlfriend Naïma (Lubna Azabal) who journey on foot through Spain before catching a ferry to Algeria to reconnect with their North African roots. In *Exils*, Spain is depicted as enabling the characters to live out their already implied corporeal and visceral engagement with the world, and, while this too chimes with prevailing French stereotypes about Spanish culture, it can be said to achieve a depth of engagement lacking in *Pas si grave*.

An arguably more popular example is *L'Auberge espagnole* (*Una casa de locos*; *Pot Luck*) (Cédric Klapisch, 2002). Here Duris, again, plays Xavier, a Master's student in Economics who spends a year in the Catalan capital to study the Spanish economy and lives within a multinational household. Various clichés abound. The somewhat familiar image of Barcelona as a space within which people are encouraged to loosen up and experience their real desires emerges strongly, and the triggers of this derive firmly from the specifically Spanish aspects of life in the city. *L'Auberge espagnole* does portray regional separatism and identity; an Economics lecturer insists on teaching in Catalan and a local student states that Spain is not just 'olé' and 'flamenco', but it is a female flamenco teacher who seduces the film's only (token) non-straight character, Isabelle (Cécile de France) from Belgium. Consequently, although Barcelona provides the physical setting within which a certain liberation unfolds, it is the hackneyed clichés of Spanish culture in general that are shown to enable these temporary residents from elsewhere to shake off their inhibitions. The city is better constructed as a queer, diasporic hub in the coming-out comedy *Pourquoi pas moi?* (*¿Entiendes?*; *Why Not Me?*) (Stéphane Giusti, 1999) (briefly discussed below).

In the queer road movie *Plein sud* (*Going South*) (Sébastien Lifshitz, 2009), Spain – or more specifically the Navarran town of Tudela – is the final destination and the site of reconciliation between a queer son, named Sam (Yannick Renier), and his mother (Nicole Garcia). *Donne-moi la main* (*Dame la mano*; *Give Me Your Hand*) (Pascal Alex-Vincent, 2008), a homoerotic tale of jealousy and intimacy between two brothers, shows its two protagonists, Antoine (Alexandre Carrill) and Quentin (Victor Carrill), travelling to Spain for their mother's funeral. Early scenes in the successful autobiographical comedy *Les*

Garçons et Guillaume à table! (*Guillaume y los chicos ¡a la mesa!*; *Me, Myself and Mum*) (Guillaume Gallienne, 2013) sees its protagonist, Guillaume (Gallienne himself), going to La Línea de la Concepción in Andalusia to learn Spanish and mastering the feminine moves of La Sevillana choreography. This film offers an unusual approach to the theme of performativity – the acquiring, through imitation and citation, of gender codes from birth (Butler 1990); Gallienne identifies as a girl when growing up and so his family – in particular his mother (also played by Gallienne) – defines him as a gay man, but he ends up falling in love with a woman called Amandine (Clémence Thioly) and marrying her, much to the disappointment of his mother, who always wanted him to be gay to avoid a female rival for his attentions. Among the intertextual comparisons with the work of other directors that, predictably, pepper reviews, Almodóvar is the most recurrent (see for example Kaganski 2013 and Dalton 2013). A French film about gender nonconformity thus gives rise to intertextual comparisons with Spain's most famous auteur with a reputation for pushing the boundaries of normative conventions of gender and sexuality.

In terms of the industry, and of LGBTQ film festival success (see Chapter 2), the dynamism of such exchanges or transfers of meaning and the liveliness of these images have certainly sustained the flow of films between these audiences. An online survey conducted as part of the research project underpinning this book shows fifty-eight separate Spanish LGBTQ films listed on the websites of the four principal online retailers of LGBTQ films on DVD in France: Amazon, Virgin, FNAC and Les Mots à la bouche. According to available data, takings and market share of Spanish films in France fluctuate significantly; for instance, 2008 saw nineteen Spanish films as well as six Spanish co-productions distributed in France, thus making the French market the biggest for Spanish cinema that year, with 3.17 million tickets sold (Tertois 2009). Such a figure is remarkable given that no Almodóvar film had been released in France in 2008. However, 2007 had seen only 390,000 tickets sold (Tertois 2008) while the figure was 3.23 million in 2006 (Cinespagne 2007), although 2,290,000 of these were for Almodóvar's *Volver* (2006). By 2010, France had once again become Spain's biggest overseas market with Spanish films making a profit of €18.18 million at the box office (Ríos Pérez 2010). Almodóvar films have remained, predictably, the most successful in terms of ticket sales; *La piel que habito* managed 735,732 while *Los amantes pasajeros* sold 533,232 – both roughly three times as may as in the UK (248,487 and 129,606 respectively (as of May 2014). In terms of festival screenings of short films, France remains a particularly attractive location for directors from Spain: forty shorts were shown at the Chéries-Chéris, Cineffable, Bordeaux, Grenoble and St Etienne LGBTQ festivals. Beyond Pathé, Almodóvar's distributor in France, Epicentre distributed *80 Egunean* (Jon Garaño and Jose Mari Goenaga, 2010) (11,290 tickets sold) and *Krámpack* (*Nico and Dani*) (Cesc Gay, 2000) (23,249 tickets sold) and ARP films distributed *Reinas* (*Queens*) (Manuel Gómez Pereira,

2005) (38,298 tickets sold). (A similar account of the case of French films in Spain comes at the end of our next section).

Perceptions of France and Frenchness

French ideas have long been seen from a traditionalist Spanish point of view as threateningly progressive. The term *afrancesado* – Frenchified – is rooted in the Spanish eighteenth century as a way of signalling a move towards modernising, enlightened, free thought. It came again to the fore during the War of Independence to refer to those Spaniards loyal to Joseph Bonaparte; and it became shorthand for unpatriotic liberalism, or, in patriotic popular and middlebrow drama in the early nineteenth century, for example, perfidiousness (Gies 2008: 8–11). During Franco's dictatorship, the notion of the French as the other against which true Spanish patriotic values are formed came back into use. In the 1940s a series of films on the War of Independence emphasised the superiority of the Spanish 'race', and the crusade for national unity and spiritual integrity (Larraz 1984: 246–50). During the years of the Franco dictatorship, Spanish cinematographic apprehensions of the French were shaped by a nationalist desire to promote the glories of Spain and its people. As Seguin (1994: 43) argues, although the xenophobia towards other cultures included the Flemish – as in *Locura de amor* (*Poignard et trahison*; *Love Crazy*) (Juan de Orduña, 1948) – it was above all directed towards the French. This was achieved by invoking and portraying various heroic narratives from Spain's past, including that of Agustina de Aragón, whose story of martyrdom was depicted in *Agustina de Aragón* (*The Siege*) (Juan de Orduña, 1950). Approximating the epic, the political imperative to glorify Spain by depicting the apparent indiscriminate brutality of the French is expressed via shots of Agustina (Aurora Bautista) shouting her defiance of the brutal and barbaric Napoleonic forces as she lights cannons. Agustina herself is constructed in similar ways to the patron saint of France, Jeanne d'Arc; and the Iberian David versus French Goliath mytheme had also been deployed, in a Catalan context, in *El tambor del Bruch* (*The Drummer Boy at Bruch*) (Ignacio F. Iquino, 1947) (Seguin 1994: 43).

By the time of the 150th anniversary, in 1958, of the start of the War of Independence, historiographical interpretations that might put a positive value on the French influence were duly being erased (Ramón Solans 2008: 6–7). Even in the post-Franco period the ghosts of older mistrust are still used as narrative props. In a later version of the iconic Carmen story, for instance (where the presence of the French is, we recall, a key plot motif), Vicente Aranda's *Carmen* (2003) has the voiceover narration (a version of Mérimée's narrator) privilege French neo-Imperial rationality over raw Andalusian affect and pities the French-affiliated Basque soldier José as failed on the fronts of sex, gender and honour (Powrie et al. 2007: 184; 188). In *Goya's Ghosts* (*Los fantasmas de Goya*; *Les Fantômes de Goya*) (Miloš Forman, 2006), sadism, fanaticism and self-interest, in the character of Brother Lorenzo (Javier Bardem), carry over to become a stain on the principles of the French Revolution which Lorenzo, espouses, having betrayed the cause of the Inquisition.

In part, the long Francoist project of erasure had to do quite simply with an association in the reactionary and traditionalist Spanish mind between France and support for the wrong – that is, the Republican – side during and immediately after the Civil War of 1936–9. France was a bad neighbour for a regime which famously had in place elaborate mechanisms for the censorship of cinema and the oppression of queers (Melero 2010: 11–46). The country harboured and protected Spanish republican exiles with loud public voices – most famously Jorge Semprún, whose script for *La Guerre est finie* feeds later into a gay-themed subplot in *En la ciudad sin límites* (*The City of No Limits*) (Antonio Hernández, 2002), linking homosexuality both to political resistance to Franco and to resistance to matriarchal and patriarchal oppression (Perriam 2013b). Paris, through the middle third of the twentieth century, was a focus (and home) for Spanish-language dissenting intellectuals, notably (from 1955 to 1996) Juan Goytisolo, a lifelong sexual dissident whose writing and intellectual affiliations (including Jean Genet: Goytisolo 2009) construct a radically un-gay and un-Spanish homosexual identity – writing from France (and latterly from Marrakech) – which makes him one of contemporary Spain's queerest points of cultural reference.

A reference point with strong French, dissident connections for part of one of the audiences at the core of our study is Barcelona's Casal Lambda (Lambda Centre) – a community, volunteer-run LGBT organisation, with charitable status, established in 1976 (as the Institut Lambda). It runs FIRE!!, to which we return in detail in Chapter 2. Its advice, support, and cultural activities are complemented by an open archive, the Centre de Documentació Armand Fluvià. Fluvià was one of the founders, in 1972, of the Movimiento Espanyol de Liberación Homosexual (MELH), and had in 1970 begun to correspond with, and then met, André Baudry, editor of the French homophile magazine *Arcadie* (giving a name to an Association and then a venue) (Jackson 2009: 58–95). The magazine began to focus on the Spanish cause and the continuing (and recently revised) systems of repression and demonisation of homosexuality in these last years of Franco's regime; and Arcadie (the organisation) printed and arranged for distribution of MELH's periodical pamphlet *Aghois* (Huard 2014: 325–31; Jackson 2009: 208).

The French connection in terms both of political ideas and of cinema is regularly made in the magazine of the Casal (initially as the *Revista Casal Lambda*; from March 1994 as *Lambda*). Fluvià himself contributes to the second issue a two-page piece celebrating the 'curiosa i bona coincidència' ('the happy and interesting coincidence') of the bicentenary of the French Revolution and the twentieth anniversary of 'la Revolució Gai', with the creation of MELH as starting point, and the participation of the group in an event organised by Arcadie in Paris, November 1973 (Fluvià 1989: 6). When the original members of the MELH began to form the Front d'Alliberament Gai de Catalunya (FAGC) (Catalan Gay Freedom Front) after Franco's death, it was, argues Huard (2014: 277–8), under the influence of the Argentinian Frente de Liberación Homosexual and the French Front Homosexuel d'Action Révolutionnaire (FHAR), the latter in part freighted with theories of desire of Gilles Deleuze and Félix Guattari, Guy Hocquenghem and François Lyotard (338; 298–305). In the effectively inaugural 1977 'Manifest del FAGC', from another theoretically engaged angle 'es feia una anàlisi althusseriana completa de la situació soferta pels gais' ('a complete Althusserian analysis was done of the situation being lived through by gays') (Petit 2004: 114). France and Catalunya are joined, then, by signs of militancy from these queer-politically formative years in the pages of this community magazine. As late as issue 27 (Autumn 2010) *Lambda* devotes its Editorial and six further pages of interviews (one with Fluvià) to further developing an account of the early 1970s. Similarly, though from a different political direction, the anti-normalisationalist queer collective Brot Bord (meaning 'Bastard Offshoot') invokes the 1970s spirit of *revolució* to support its 2013 anti-Pride campaign, as part of a historic, and ongoing 'estratègia de lluita per l'alliberament LGTI al nostre país' (Sarita 2013) ('strategy of struggle for LGTI [Lesbian, Gay, Trans and Intersex] liberation in our country').

It is not just to the 1970s that the magazine and its audience consistently turn. Issue 14 has a summary essay on Michel Foucault's radical thought (Azo 1994). Issue 23 remembers Genet's days in Barcelona (1932–4), and how, in the 1920s and 1930s 'els francesos baixaven a Barcelona per allò d'anir al sud. Ara solem fer-ho anant a Marràquex' ('the French would travel down to Barcelona as a way of going south. Nowadays we tend to go to Marrakesh to do so') (Díaz 1996: 38) – here 'south', obviously, signifies forbidden desire); and, accordingly, the second Mostra Lambda (October 1996; later to be named FIRE!!) organised a homage to Genet, including showings of *Un chant d'amour* (*A Song of Love*) (1950) and Kenneth Anger's *Fireworks* (1947), with its brawny sailors and transgressive form – a pairing picked up on in detail ten years later, in issue 57 of the magazine, in a contribution to a series on Gay Cinema History (García 2006). Issue 58 devotes a double-page spread to Gilles Deleuze, as being closer than Foucault to the cause of the early gay movement and more influential in the militant sexual politics of liberation (Carbonell 2006a: 28). This short essay's concluding summary – 'Deleuze ens convida a vigilar . . . esdevenir sempre minoritaris i no acontentar-nos mai de ser-ho' (29) ('Deleuze invites us to be vigilant . . . always to be becoming minority and never to feel satisfied that we are') – is one which conflates a number of complex ideas (and Guattari with Deleuze), but is nonetheless one that has substantial resonance for considerations of Catalan cultures and contemporary, revolutionary identities framed by those cultures, as Fernàndez (2000) and Vilaseca (2010: 18–63) have demonstrated. Just two issues later (number 60), a similar essay on Simone de Beauvoir points up her pioneering, if brief, treatment of lesbian lives and culture, her anti-pathologising stance on homosexuality and something of the complexity of her responses to André Gide and to Truman Capote (Carbonell 2006b: 27).

The magazine's coverage of the first LGBT festival, as mentioned, sets the scene by noting that it is a watershed for those who 'recorden bé un temps en què calia creuar els Pireneus per a veure cinema' (Lambda 1995) ('remember well those days when you had to cross the Pyrenees to see cinema'). The trans-Pyrenean perspective of the magazine can be, on the one hand, starry-eyed, with France lauded for the realism in cinematic matters LGBTQ which Spain is implicitly deemed to lack. 'Els nostres veïns de la França . . . potser són més realistes' (Salom 2003) ('our neighbours the French . . . are perhaps more realist'), suggests one critic, where being realist means recognising the need for diversity in casting and plot, and 'ja se sap, el cinema francès sempre tan realista' (Salom and Herranz 2003) ('French cinema, of course, being so realist always') another piece feels able to assume. In a similar vein, *Presque rien* (*Primer verano*; *Come Undone*) (Sébastien Lifshitz, 2000) is seen as 'un film gai allunyat de les pel.lícules gais de sempre' (Gil 2002) ('a gay film that is set apart from the usual ones'), which gives this French product, then, a certain distinction for the reviewer's supposed audiences. *8 Femmes* (*8 mujeres*; *8 Women*) (François Ozon, 2002) is seen as stylishly, and stylistically, marked as French (Gil 2003), in another attribution of distinction. On the other hand, views are balanced, with Balasko's *Gazon maudit* seen as predictable, but amusing 'malgrat els tòpics' ('despite the clichés') (Daniel 1996) and *A toute vitesse* (*Sin respiro*; *Full Speed*) (Gaël Morel, 1996) held up as an exception to French cinema's scarce concern with certain issues (such as teenage homosexuality, class and race) (Daniel 1997: 41).

For a different audience than that comprised of the members of the Casa Lambda and the readers of its community magazine – the obvious cinephilia of some of the writers quoted above notwithstanding – a far more solidly cinematic connection to France and radical filmmaking comes through looking to the French New Wave. Discussions of the new auteur directors and iconic films of the 1960s and 1970s in Spain habitually make reference to the French cinematic tradition – for example, in relation to Carlos Saura (D'Lugo 1991: 8, 39; Kinder 1993: 90–2) or Basilio Patino (Faulkner 2013: 11–12, 18) – and Luis Buñuel's work in France famously consolidates these connections. This most iconic of French film movements exerted a very strong influence over experimental filmmaking practices in Catalunya, where the directors associated with the so-called Escola de Barcelona sought to distinguish themselves from the state-sponsored New Spanish Cinema (Nuevo Cine Español) (Larraz 1986; Galt 2010; Epps 2013). This grouping of filmmakers of the second half of the 1960s is of particular interest because of its proximity to the early years of gay political mobilisation in Spain, its importance to Catalan (high) cultural resistance to the Franco regime in its last decade and its subversive qualities (Vilaseca 2010: 129). The Escola, suggests Vilaseca, 'drastically transgresses the "regimes of the normal" of its time and ... can therefore be labeled "queer"' (129). A similar effect is at play in the more marginalised but more radical – and in places more queer – independent Valencian cinema of the late 1960s and early 1970s (Muñoz 1999: 27–9, 65–79).

As an 'elitist, bourgeois, cosmopolitan, and Parisian response to the Madrid-Based ... New Spanish Cinema' (Epps 2013: 69; citing Román Gubern), the Escola de Barcelona had a particular veneration for Jean-Luc Godard and drew on elements of New Wave practice (and those of other European leftist cultural projects – Galt 2010) in technique and in the casting of foreign actors, including Jacques Doniol-Valcroze and Mijanou Bardot (Riambau and Torreiro 1999: 188, 199, 247–8). It was sidelined by Madrid-based establishment critics, suggest Riambau and Torreiro, in part because of its cosmopolitan use of French 'como segunda lengua' ('as a second language') despite dialogue in Castilian (187); there are relatively extensive voiced quotations, textual citations, song and monologue – all in French (187–8). Indeed, in the words of the critic Miguel Marías, in 1968, this was an 'escuela pseudofrancesa' ('a pseudo-French school') (in Riambau and Torreiro 1999: 191), and its films drew critical attention in France, in *Cinéma* 66 and 67, *Positif* and *Cahiers du Cinéma* (302-–5). Many of the films of the Escola examined (though not systematically) philosophical concerns associated with the New Wave, namely around existentialism and the idea of *ennui* or disaffection (Aubert 2009: 254): and, as was the case for many of the New Wave filmmakers, conceptual reflection and debates about filmmaking fed into or flowed alongside the actual making of films (129). The legacy of the Escola persists as a question of form and of politics. This may be seen, for example, in the conceptual (non-queer) films of Albert Serra, or Marc Recha, but also, earlier, in Ventura Pons's (queer) *Ocaña, retrat intermitent* (1978) which, despite showing signs of Pons's later mastery of 'narrative-driven cinema in Catalan' (Epps 2013: 70), takes liberties with documentary form, perspective, ambience, expectations of taste and narrative logic.

The mark on individual queer viewers in France and Spain of such exchanges of ideas, images and approaches is evidenced in various of the responses which are at the core of the following chapters. Memories include first viewings of *Les Roseaux sauvages* and the emergence of Ozon's films on Spanish screens large and small; and many respondents are alert to and have recourse to talking in terms of the typical qualities of French film as laid down by film history but in relation to their own LGBTQ experience. In the period under analysis in the rest of this book, there has been a considerable influx of French LGBTQ films on DVD. Our project's survey of the four principal online LGBTQ-customer-targeted retailers in Spain showed forty-one separate French lesbian and gay titles, although this finding is enormously complicated by the scale of digital piracy in Spain, at least until 2014 (Donaghue 2014). For different generations and a range of audiences French cinema and French films form a substrate of their lives. The presence of the French film industry in recent Spanish culture can be roughly gauged by searches on the Spanish Ministry of Education, Culture and Sport (MECD) database on France as country of production of films screened on Spanish territory. The ten years 2002–12 show 375 French titles, with 2009 showing thirty-four, 2010 twenty-eight, and 2011 forty-eight (compared to 316, and twenty-three, twenty-one and twenty-nine respectively for UK productions in those same periods). Spain was the third largest consumer worldwide of short French films in 2009 in terms of box office takings and of sales (despite a globally impelled seventy per cent decline from 2008 figures on all sales); in all film genres, sales of French productions rose back up by thirty per cent in 2010 and had reached 5.5 million admissions by 2012 (UniFrance Films 2009; 2011; 2013). Among the twenty active distributors of French films at the end of the first decade of the 2000s, Vertigo Films is noteworthy since it had taken *Les Roseaux sauvages* and *Les Témoins* (2007) as well as Ozon's *Le Temps qui reste* (*El tiempo que queda*; *Time to Leave*) (2004), Lifshitz's *Presque rien* and Morel's *A Toute vitesse* among other queer films.

Diasporic Flows, Geographical Proximity and Regional Affinities

So far, this discussion has focused on the cross-border exchange of cultural discourses and constructs between France and Spain. Yet, diasporic migration, geographical proximity and regional cultural empathies and affinities shift the debate beyond an appreciation of one country's significations within the imaginaries of the inhabitants of another. When individuals have a familial attachment to a country beyond the borders of their place of residence or birth, the form that country and its culture take cannot be understood in simple terms as having been 'shaped by the outsider' (Ilie 1976: 376). Such people are ambivalently positioned; neither internal to nor external to a given culture, they occupy a space between the two. Conceptualising their recourse to certain cultural products can be complex, for what they may seek is not to satisfy their curiosity for the exotic but to find tastes, values and cultural practices that they recognise and with which they empathise. For many young LGBTQ people born and resident in France with Spanish heritage, for example, Spain and Spanishness can form an integral part of the education and socialisation they acquire from their family, in which strong links with Spain are maintained, via relatives who continue to live in Spain and through the recounted histories of their parents and grandparents.

The main direction of the migratory flows between both countries has been northbound, from Spain to France. At the end of the nineteenth century and throughout the First World War and its aftermath, Spanish migrants moved to France in search of temporary work in agriculture, in the Midi, and agriculture and industry in the south-west of France (Lillo 2009: 11–12). Having increased from 106,000 in 1911 to 255,000 in 1921, the Spanish population represented the third largest minority in France, rising to 352,000 in 1931 (14).

Seventy-five per cent of these people lived in the south-west, with 100,000 (thirty per cent) residing in the departments of Languedoc Roussillon, most from bordering Spanish regions (Spanish residents of Perpignan constituted a quarter of the whole city's inhabitants (14)). Successive policies introduced in the 1920s facilitated immigration into France to increase numbers of workers after the devastation wrought by the First World War. The Spanish tended to live together in designated urban areas including 'La Petite Espagne' in Saint Denis and Saint Michel in Bordeaux and did not mix.

After a decrease due to the economic crises of the 1930s, migration increased significantly during and after the Civil War; 500,000 Spanish refugees arrived between 1938 and 1940 (including the father of Manuel Valls, with whom we began this chapter) to escape persecution and hunger (Lacroix and Bouhet 2004: 11; Lillo 2009: 21). Most lived in poor conditions, many in camps (Cate-Arries 2010) and many more continued to cross the Pyrenees during the dictatorship, with a particular concentration in Toulouse and its surrounding region (Guilhem 2005). The establishment of the Instituto Español de Emigración in 1956 as an instrument of Francoism's migration policies contributed, though in a small part, to an increase in migration to France from 1960 (including Anne Hidalgo's family). By 1968, the 607,000 people of Spanish origin represented the largest foreign community in France, with many now settling in northern cities, mainly Paris (145,000) (Lillo 2009: 21; 25).

Many migrants were women who worked in the domestic service industry (Oso Casas 2009: 79–98), as depicted in two films, one contemporary to events, the other nostalgic: *Españolas en París* (*Des espagnoles à Paris*; *Spaniards in Paris*) (Roberto Bodegas, 1971) and *Les Femmes du 6e étage* (*Las chicas de la 6a planta*; *The Women on the Sixth Floor*) (Philippe Le Guay, 2010), whose cast includes, alongside Carmen Maura, another Almodóvar favourite, Lola Dueñas. Following the economic crisis of 1973 and various anti-immigration and repatriation policies and changes introduced by the French government, the numbers of Spanish people living in France decreased significantly (Lacroix and Bouhet 2004; Lillo 2013).

The end of the twentieth century and the years leading up to the economic crisis of 2008 saw some migration of young French people of Spanish origin back to Spain, due to the perception that the Spanish economy was more vibrant than the French, and frustrations with the perceived failure of the integration of minorities in France. After the crash of 2008, this flow was stemmed, although, according to the French Museum of Historical Migration, Spain was the sixth most popular country to which French people migrated in 2010, with 89,391 expats (Musée de l'histoire de l'immigration 2013).

The links between the people of the southern regions and Spain also take shape in a perceived shared cultural and historical heritage, evident, most obviously, in languages spoken in both countries such as Catalan and so-called minority and regional dialects, such as Occitan. For some inhabitants of the French Basque country, the south-west (or former Occitania) and French Catalunya, which have been subsumed in the metropolitan regions of Aquitaine, Midi-Pyrénées and Languedoc Roussillon respectively, aspects of Spanish culture can seem very familiar. In Languedoc and the Basque country, cultural affinities with Spain are expressed in obvious ways via popular festivals, including the *ferias* of Nîmes and Dax, in which French revellers watch bullfights and party in the streets. In terms of film culture, residents of Toulouse are able to engage with Spanish cinema through the Cinespaña festival that has taken place in Toulouse each year since 1992. The mixed heritage of some of the inhabitants of the south-west can be observed in André Téchiné's Franco-Spanish co-production *Alice et Martin* (*Alice et Martin*; *Alice and Martin*) (1998), in which one of the characters, Benjamin Sauvagnac (Mathieu Almeric), is gay and much of which is set in the Cahors area of south-west France; Martin Sauvagnac (Alexis Loret) is born to a Spanish mother (played by Maura) and flees the constraints of his obstinate and domineering father Victor (Pierre Maguelon) by escaping to the city of Granada and its nearby coast.

On the Spanish side of the border, recent independent films attest to transcultural and polyglot linguistic realities of areas of Catalunya, which construct different kinds of links – for example, in Marc Recha's *L'arbre de les cireres* (*L'Arbre aux cerises*; *The Cherry Tree*) (1998), *Pau i el seu germà* (*Pau et son frère*; *Pau and His Brother*) (2001) and *Les mans buides* (*Les Mains vides*; *Where Is Madame Catherine?*) (2003) (Epps 2013: 76). At a more classically transnational and commercial level, co-productions with Catalan and French stakeholders include Recha's *Les mans buides* and *Petit Indi* (2009), which marked the start of a strategic campaign by the consortium Catalan Films & TV backed by the Generalitat de Catalunya – including a special day event on 30 April 2009, at the Palau de Mar, Barcelona – to develop co-production possibilities with France as its second largest market after Spain (Televisió de Catalunya 3/24 2010).

With specific relation to the LGBTQ communities living in the South-West of France, Barcelona can serve as their queer hub. The Catalan capital is where many go to escape a humdrum, provincial lesbian and gay scene, and, in some cases, where they eventually migrate. Barcelona's status as a queer hub, not only for Catalan and Spanish people but for the French also, is illustrated in the coming-out comedy *Pourquoi pas moi?* (*¿Entiendes?*; *Why Not Me?*) (Stéphane Giusti, 1999). While the film is set in the city, it stars French or Francophone actors, the dialogues are all in French and the car number plates are registered in France (in fact the Hérault department which is part of the Languedoc Region). According to Smith (2000), *Pourquoi pas moi?* constructs a pan-European space from which 'Latin queers, more secure in their sexuality than in their nationality, speak in their own voice', through its emphatically generic Mediterranean locations (including the recognisable Barcelona settings) and its unusual insistence, for the 1990s, on queer identity and community as part of the narrative of everyday life in Latin or Mediterranean as much as in Anglo-Saxon or northern societies.

Concluding Remarks

The above outline furnishes an overview of the cross-Pyrenean connections between general and minority queer French and Spanish cultures. An interesting paradox emerges; on the one hand, France can be upheld as the origin and site of an avant-garde – and arguably queer – culture in Spain because of the artistic expression and political and philosophical reflection it has given rise to; on the other, Spain can thus be apprehended as disruptive and therefore queer – in its symbolisation as the source and location of a rawer, more immediate affect that, in some ways, furnishes an emancipated alternative to the perceived restrictions of so-called French *bon goût*.

It is crucial to warn against oversimplifying the issues, however. The degree to which individuals identify with dominant constructions of French or Spanish culture varies and is contingent upon temporal, spatial, emotional and affective factors. What we are interested in knowing, though, is whether, and in what ways, the images mobilised within the LGBTQ films emerging from one of these two countries are brought to bear on the ways in which people in the other construct their social selves and negotiate their relationships with the outside world. How, that is, do these images and narratives of pleasure, affiliation, political commitment or identification cross over between countries, communities, viewing habits, languages and lives?

2. LGBTQ FILM FESTIVALS AND THEIR AUDIENCES

Je vais au festival 'Des images aux mots' depuis 3 ans. Et vois tous les films. Je ne participe pas aux gay pride. Voisins, entourage savent que je suis lesbienne. Je tiens la main de ma pétite amie maghrébine depuis 20 ans. Et l'embrasse dans la rue [depuis] avant le PACS.

(I have been going to the Des images aux mots festival for three years and I watch all the films. I do not participate in the gay pride. [My] neighbours and entourage know that I am lesbian. I have been holding my Maghrebi girlfriend's hand for twenty years. And I have been kissing her in the street since before the PACS (civil partnership)) (Daphne, 40-year-old French female, volunteer with WWOOF International, on the LGBTQ film festival in Toulouse)

I've visited all 27 LLGFF festivals! (Malcolm, 65-year-old British white retired male, attender at the London Lesbian and Gay Film Festival, March 2013)

The above responses are testament to the resolute investment of some of our participants in their 'local' LGBTQ film festival. Declarations of longstanding patronage are utilised by the second of these respondents as proof of his commitment, while the first cites her consistent presence over a shorter period as a marker of her self-affirmation as lesbian. This particular respondent makes a series of illuminating suggestions in which attendance at the LGBTQ festival is aligned with broader political acts in her life (longstanding openness about her sexuality to her peers and the people she encounters in her everyday life, and habitual public displays of affection for her partner, which predate the formal legalisation of same-sex partnerships). Gay Pride emerges, via implication, as enabling a much less committed display of lesbian identity than a film festival, given her apparent keenness to deny any participation in that particular event.

Daphne's response, though, may also be said to paint a certain picture of the 'typical' LGBTQ film festival-goer as having a strong sense of LGBTQ political identity and community affiliation. As such, her remarks could illustrate the point that we made in the introduction that our use of festivals as principal sites of recruitment for our research may limit the breadth and diversity of viewers that we access and consult. Of course, Daphne's viewpoint is unlikely to be shared by all attenders at such events, but, given that LGBTQ film festivals tend to assume a sociopolitically committed viewing public and, indeed, one that has a certain degree of film literacy, it is important to note and acknowledge such issues. Moreover, Daphne's confidence and eagerness in asserting her commitment to the festival provides a fruitful example of how the expression of cultural tastes and practices aids in the formation of social identities; Daphne projects outwards to her audience (in this case the researchers and eventual readers of the publications) the extent and intensity of her political self-identification as a lesbian, one who is open to unfamiliar cultures and experiences, given that she claims to have watched all of the films, the majority of which are from overseas. Her remarks arise in response to the Catalan- and Spanish-language co-production *El sexo de los ángeles* (Xavier Villaverde, 2012), which portrays a three-way relationship between two bisexual men and one heterosexual woman in Barcelona. Daphne claims to have enjoyed the film, highlighting its emotional candour as one of the features that she prefers, which therefore reaffirms the impression she creates of herself as relatively free-thinking while, at the same time, not undermining her political identification as lesbian. That she emphasises the ethnicity of her girlfriend – particularly in France where such public identifications are uncommon and officially discouraged – further contributes to this impression that she is a liberal with strong political values (and which are not defined in traditional terms of left and right).

As outlined in the Introduction, we visited a number of different festivals in France, Spain and Britain in order to distribute questionnaires and recruit people to participate in our focus group discussions. All of these festivals were selected for practical reasons as well as relevance: they screened recent French and Spanish films and we were able to attend them. They are thus not offered as a definitive word on the French and Spanish films shown at festivals in France, Spain and Britain during the period in which we undertook our research, but we can nonetheless say that they furnish a snapshot of what was selected and being watched in festival auditoria at the time. Our focus on cross-cultural responses in France, Spain and Britain to French and Spanish LGBTQ films informs our overviews of the festivals we visited and their reception by their audiences is illustrated via both comments made by our own participants and those uploaded online in social media websites. We recognise that Facebook likes (and indeed followings or tweets on Twitter) may not be the most reliable barometer of the size and breadth of a festival's following, or of the intensity of its popularity. There are many variables, including the demographics in terms of the size of the potential audience and national and international exposure of the event, and, as Rodríguez Ortega (2013: 544) states in relation to the social media pages devoted to Pedro Almodóvar, Facebook walls can be '*infiltrated* by a variety of users whose goals, preferences, and sense of belonging have little to do with' the subject of the page or the original object of appreciation (emphasis in original). However, they do constitute an active investment – though requiring minimal effort – on the part of the user who clicks on the 'like' or 'follow' icon which then automatically broadcasts that preference to fellow users, including friends and family.

The chapter begins with a general discussion of the functions served by LGBTQ festivals in sense of community formation and which includes an analysis of a documentary on festivals entitled *Queer Artivism* (Maša Zia Lenárdič and Anja Wutej, 2013) and an overview of countercultural feminist and trans festivals in France and Spain. It then examines the Spanish festivals, followed by those in France and Britain, that we attended.

LGBTQ FILM FESTIVALS: PURPOSES AND PARAMETERS

Film festivals are established and privileged sites for the projection and reception of LGBTQ tastes, values, fantasies and desires, and continue to have a particular resonance for many LGBTQ viewing communities (Gamson 1996; Loist 2012; 2013), as the responses that open this chapter reveal. They bring together 'political needs', certain means to 'identity formation', senses of 'community' and 'belonging' (Rich 2013b: 162) and, particularly in the cases to be looked at here, 'invite' – or sometimes simply re-show – 'films in which other languages are spoken and other cultures are made tangible' (163). For many viewers there is a particular importance to the LBGTQ festival, as it is situated within a wider politics of programming and event-making whereby 'programming decisions amount to an argument about what defines [a] field, genre or national cinema', and as part of such an 'argument' 'queer festivals help define what gay, lesbian, bisexual and transgendered cinema is' (Czach 2004: 85). The majority of the festivals to be discussed in this chapter are 'nodal points' (Pidduck 2002: 268) in a specifically plotted, transnational network; and they are special zones (de Valck 2007: 27) whose 'spatial and temporal dimensions channel certain flows' (18), albeit not the much wider range of 'flows in contemporary cinema culture' discussed by de Valck in her globally positioned argument (18). The smaller festivals particularly (some of which we simply mention, but were not able to visit and explore) are events of the sort which Elsaesser (2013) reminds us are the 'self-celebration of a community' (82) – a community which is also an audience.

Our festival case studies are not of a size and weight sufficient to make them 'international' in the globally networked sense (de Valck 2007) or in the sense of being events standing in relation to the marketing and aspirations of the global city (Stringer 2001), even though they are used to promote the cultural scene of the cities that stage them. They bring together mainly local audiences, in local spaces of significance temporarily transformed, helped (in good times) by local money, and concentrate into three to ten days a flow of films from afar (subtitling capacity allowing) or, for our case, from neighbouring countries. Lead-in publicity, the gentle flow of comment on social media, opening and closing parties (especially in the Spanish cases), the buzz around audience prizes based on voting on individual films (a particularly high-profile feature of Madrid's LesGaiCineMad film festival) and gala awards (as in the festival Chéries-Chéris in Paris), all add aura, excitement and significance. The glamour that comes of programming mainstream films such as those by Almodóvar or Ozon discussed in Chapter 5 is usually beyond the reach of these financially constrained festivals; their value and prestige is built up in these other ways.

The documentary *Queer Artivism* collates several testimonies which directly corroborate expert studies of these sites, their attractions and their qualities (Gever 1990; White 1999; Pidduck 2002; UNWTO 2012). Interviewing organisers and audience members at Inside Out (Toronto), OMovies (Naples) Queer Lisboa, Queer Zagreb, the Entzaubert Radical Queer DIY Uncommercial Film Festival and Zinegoak (Bilbao) – one of our own case studies – the directors of this film also place striking visual emphasis on place, positioning the discussions and the festivals and their audiences in a clear act of cinematic making visible which inflects such comments as that by Zvonimir Dobrović, artistic director of Queer Zagreb, about festivals being 'very important for a local scene', also illustrated by Daphne's response cited above. 'Scene' in its sense of community implicitly coincides with scene in its sense of site here. In Lisbon, artistic director João Ferreira emphasises the festival's centrality there to the city's culture and how it creates a 'social and cultural experience around queer film'. From a more social perspective, Jen Markowitz (lead singer, Dance Yourself to Death) talks in Toronto of how the festival there 'normalises' and makes queerness visible to society, as well as to younger queer people for whom (she implies) the history of struggle is unseen; in Bilbao, the producer John Badalu also focuses on consciousness-raising and building knowledge, 'of queer movements in other parts of the world'; director Slavica Parlov in Zagreb talks in terms of connection. Again in Bilbao, the visiting film director and video artist Juanma Carrillo talks of how a mix of passion and activism make the organisation of the Zinegoak film festival so special.

In common with the North American and German festivals that predate them, our French and Spanish festivals have mixed heritages where activist, issue-based and low-budget independent priorities affect programming and audience composition. As Gamson puts it (1996: 238), such festivals can be thought about in ways that '[bring] collective identity theorising face-to-face with organisational analysis', and we will see in this chapter how these festivals as organisational phenomena have evolved, as so too have their audiences and sponsoring environments. They are all, in Gamson's terms, 'homes or

Figure 2.1 Gaël Morel collecting his honorary award, Zinegoak festival 2013. Photo by Miguel Ángel Chazo (official festival photographer). Reproduced with kind permission of Pau Guillén for Zinegoak.

warehouses for collective identity; they involve ongoing and self-conscious decision making about the content and contours of the "we" [the collective identity] being made literally visible' (Gamson 1996: 238) in their programming, the siting of their events and screenings, and their convocation of audiences and participants (not least the filmmakers themselves, whether simply submitting work or, just as often, there in presence introducing it or receiving modest prizes or accolades for it). Some of the festivals expand to embrace a semi-commercial ethos, like the New York Lesbian and Gay Film Festival in the early 1990s, 'largely a combination of activism and entrepreneurship' (Gamson 1996: 252) or – as in the case of LesGaiCineMad – they have to adapt to meet the exigencies of matched funding arrangements (or, post-2008, the diminishment of these) with local and regional authorities.

Other festivals, again in line with global tendencies, continuously constitute and are constituted by 'interventionist counter-publics' (Loist and Zielinski 2012: 50), remaining close to activist and countercultural values and practices. This is the case in the Festival International du Film Lesbien & Féministe de Paris (aka Cineffable), which began as a week of screenings of films made by lesbians in April 1989, but which, in its latest manifestation, was reduced to four days, and which announced its twenty-fifth festival as an explosive cocktail, 'rétif à la bien-pensance et générateur d'idées différentes' ('resistant to convention and a generator of different ideas') (Cineffable 2014). Similarly, Zinentiendo (whose name combines the ideas of a -zine, of cinema, and of being lesbian, gay or bi), in Zaragoza, has traditionally included much 'identity-disruptive content' (Gamson 1996: 242) and in 2014 used a highly self-reflexive presentation citing Deleuze and Foucault to question and amplify the meanings of 'sexuality' (Zinentiendo 2014); and the off-festival Muestra Marrana (Girl Pig Showcase) at Zinegoak, Bilbao (since 2008), highlights post-pornography and feminist direct action. The first dedicated Spanish trans and intersex film festival, to take another of these counter-publics, was MosTra'ns, organised by the Guerrilla Travolaka group and other trans groups in Barcelona in 2009. It screened the French documentary *L'Ordre des mots* (Cynthia Arra and Mélissa Arra, 2007) alongside other self-produced and independently distributed films from around the world. The festival's declared aims were to be 'un exercici de visibilitat i d'activisme audiovisual' ('an exercise in visibility and audiovisual activism') aimed at 'apropar aquesta realitat a la societat barcelonina per així trencar tòpics i estereotips' (MosTra'ns 2009) ('bringing the reality [of trans lives] closer to people in Barcelona so as to break down clichés and stereotypes'). The festival also screened *Test de la vida real* (Real Life Test) (Florencia P. Marano, 2009), which gives exclusive voice to trans people in Barcelona.

In France, IdentiT was the first film festival for trans people and boasted Marie-Pierre Pruvost (Bambi – the documentary about her is discussed in Chapter 4) as its guest of honour at its first event. IdentiT combined issue-based priorities with an aspiration to reach out to broader audiences. It sought to tackle 'l'absence de représentations respectueuses de l'identité et de la culture trans' ('the absence of respectful representations of trans identity and culture') and it aimed to 'susciter un intérêt collectif pour la *transidentité*' (Calphi 2008) ('create collective interests in transidentity') (emphasis in original). In an interview with *L'Humanité*, the organisers Jihan Ferjani and Catherine Oh spoke of their aim to 'mobiliser avec pédagogie le public le plus large possible' (Kirschen 2008) ('mobilise through education as big an audience as possible'). The themes it set out to examine range from the scholarly and communitarian to more activist concerns: the links between gender, body and sex, minority belonging, the relationship between trans identity and queer and feminist emancipation, employment, immigration and identitarian activism (Calphi 2008). The organisers aimed to galvanise support for the removal of transsexuality as a pyschiatric condition according to the World Health Organisation and to foster an environment in which changes to civil status are easier for trans people, irrespective of whether they have undergone surgery or not (in Bourgeois 2008). In its second year the festival was even more political in its aims, although the organisers still seemed keen to forge connections between trans identity politics and other social movements; in an interview for *Têtu* magazine, Ferhani argued, for example, that 'il est temps de redonner toute sa place à la mobilisation politique. Pour les trans bien sûr, mais aussi pour les minorités visibles, le féminisme, et le mouvement social dans son ensemble' (Kirschen 2009) (' it is time to give political mobilisation back its place. For trans people, of course, but also for visible minorities, feminism, and the social movement in its entirety'). Such broadening of issues addressed could be said to have weakened the political impact and appeal of their festival, which ran in only two years (2008 and 2009), although the organisers implied in 2009 that its eventual demise would ultimately be caused by the extraordinarily difficult climate for securing funding for minority cultural and political initiatives (Yaggvideo 2009).

Madrid, Barcelona and Bilbao

LesGaiCineMad in Madrid (from 1996), the Mostra Internacional de Cinema Gai i Lesbià (from 1995; subsequently Mostra Lambda, and later, from 2008 branded with the tag FIRE!!, as we have seen) and FICGLB (from 2000 as a breakaway festival from the Mostra) form part of a second wave of Western European gay and lesbian film festivals clustered in the early to mid-1990s and which includes Chéries-Chéris, Paris (1994) (Loist 2013; Rhyne 2007). Zinegoak, Bilbao, to which we turn last in this section, has run since 2003 and is perhaps closer in ethos to the first wave of lesbian and gay festivals with a distinctive political and community-oriented edge to it.

The annual Madrid LesGaiCineMad is one of the bigger events in this field, boasting in July 2014 of having become, with more than nine thousand 'likes', the second most followed LGBT film festival on Facebook worldwide, after Outfest (LesGaiCineMad 2014a). By 2005 LesGaiCineMad was running a ten-day programme from 4 p.m. until late across three or four venues, a framework which was largely sustained at least until 2015. The 2013 festival saw some twelve thousand tickets issued on a commercial basis within the main programme (Gerardo José Pérez Meliá in interview with Chris Perriam 2 July 2014). By 2009, it had gathered sufficient momentum and cultural capital to set up a Spanish Lesbian and Gay Film Market (SFM) initiative (truncated by the global recession's effects on Spain). This consisted of: an event which was planned to be repeated annually (coinciding with the festival) and designed to connect producers and companies with distributors, facilitate bookings for programmers and offer professional training; a digital, catalogued archive of films; and (less commercially) the CineLGBT Network facilitating resource and information sharing among festivals in Spain (as detailed below) and Latin America. Organisationally, the surviving CineLGBT Network forms part of the national campaigning and welfare charity the Fundación Triángulo dedicated to 'la igualdad de derechos políticos y sociales para gais, lesbianas, bisexuales y trans' (Fundación Triángulo 2010) ('the equality of political and social rights for gays, lesbians, bisexuals and trans people'). The Fundación Triángulo also provides advice, contacts, distribution, advertising co-ordination and, to a certain extent, an agenda regionally at Fancinegay (since 1997: Badajoz, Cáceres and Mérida: part funded by the Junta de Extremadura), Cinhomo (since 2000: Valladolid), Andalesgai (since 2005: Seville and four other provincial capitals in Andalusia) and CanBeGay (since 2014: Santa Cruz de

Tenerife). LesGaiCineMad is operated as one of the Fundación's six key areas of activity (along with International Co-operation, Health, Education, Youth, Women). It is run by a core team at the Madrid headquarters of the Fundación Triángulo with a substantial volunteer base (fluctuating around twenty) both at the event proper and at the viewing-and-selection stage; recognition of and thanks for the team's efforts frequently appear on the festival's Facebook and Twitter pages.

The conception of an associated film market enterprise (even if it did not survive), Fundación Triángulo-branded festival events in other parts of Spain, and the wider social and welfare actions of the Fundación Triángulo (which have very much survived) mean that this particular festival is not only the classic 'specific, intense and fleeting happening' discussed by Harbord (2002: 68) which '[invokes] the presence of experience' (68) but is also both a constantly replenished and re-registered archive and an activism in progress, present for much of the year in various publics' minds. There were 626 followers on Twitter (tagged for the 2014 festival) as at 11 August 2014, and 2058 YouTube subscribers to the page for the 2013 festival.

The outreach initiative to Latin America which was part of the original SFM project has been maintained and considerably expanded, with one of the Fundación's team effectively seconded to these activities and with the network pages offering a news feed on festival activities in, principally, Latin America and comprehensive information for programmers on available Spanish- and (some) Portuguese-speaking LGBTQ films, filmmakers, distributors and producers. In 2014 the network's webpage reported festival programmes running for ten out of the twelve months of the year (2013) in fourteen countries, and with seventeen affiliated organisations (CineLGBT 2014). The initiative thus takes its place in a history going back to the 1970s of 'specialised thematic programming' allowing events such as LGBTQ festivals to 'maximise their agenda-setting effect' (de Valck 2013: 103).

This level of international outreach, which combines both sociopolitical motivation and pragmatic commercialisation, and the organisation's agility with resources and cross-funding, bring LesGaiCineMad closer than the other Spanish LGBTQ festivals to being like the 'mixed spaces crossed by commercial interest, specialised film knowledge and tourist trajectories' studied by Harbord (2002: 60) in her investigation of the contribution of festivals to the range of 'film cultures'. The short-lived festival of short films, MiMi (Barcelona 2011 and Sitges 2012), also came close to being such a mixed space, although such was the strength of the motivation of the gay business sector and the obviousness of the touristic target that these arguably eclipsed film knowledge as such, and even films themselves (it being difficult via some channels to see if this was a festival or a rather expensive party). On a much larger scale, the FICGLB – although with strong backing from the Generalitat de Catalunya and close association with the Filmoteca de Catalunya (Catalan Film Archive) (in whose premises it has been staged since 2009) – has increasingly moved in the mixed space of commerce, specialism, and tourist attraction (as the 2012 spot set entirely on the Barceloneta beach emphasises).[1] While the brochure programmes yearly offer profiles of the impressive and diverse line-up of judges for the different prizes, the 2014 advance Web publicity, for example, displays none of the prestige cultural and political connections (save the presence of the Filmoteca as the main site for the Barcelona programming) and instead has images and links for three prominent commercial sponsors Axel Hotel (who also backed MiMi), Castro Restaurant and Revista G[ay] B[arcelona] Men's Lifestyle Magazine (FICGLB 2014).

FICGLB's core ideals, nonetheless, are social (with an annual main prize and high-profile expert jury, for the category of 'diversity') and film educational (with involvement of students from the film and media schools ESCAC, Escola Superior de Cinema i Audiovisuals de Catalunya, the CECC, Centre d'Estudis Cinematogràfics de Catalunya, EMAV, the Escola de Mitjans Audiovisuals and the cultural association 'El cine secreto') (see, for example, programme brochures and festival web pages for 2011 to 2014). A statement on the 2013 web pages recapitulates a particular position on social issues in its attention to repressive laws worldwide, introducing examples of films fighting repression from twenty different countries, and noting 'també altres temàtiques' ('other issues too'), such as homophobic bullying, adolescence and identity uncertainty, and lack of social awareness (Viera 2013). This emphasis on social commitment and awareness is underlined by Xavier Daniel, the festival's director (and former chief programmer for LesGaiCineMad). In a local television interview (gayles.tv 2013) he also points out that several sessions in the 2013 festival sold out. This had also happened in 2012, for a change delighting one audience member on Twitter (25 October 2012) who presumably was forearmed with a ticket: 'Que bé veure el cartell d'entrades exhaurides en la interessant doble projecció de documentals d'aquesta nit al @ficglb' ('great to see the "sold out" sign for tonight's interesting double programme of documentaries'). The festival has had travelling showcases of international titles regionally in Terrassa, Sant Adrià de Besòs and Castelldefels, as well as (since 2011) Girona. In social media FICGLB had 504 followers on Twitter and 525 subscribers on YouTube, as at 11 August 2014. Rather than use Facebook, it has its own basic website.

FICGLB's 2013 programming of just nine feature films but thirty-five shorts was representative of a then growing tendency in Spain, in part due to the fallout from the post-2008 recession years and in part due to a traditional audience preference for a format well suited (when not hermetic or poetic) to address specific, immediate or local sociopolitical issues. The older-established Mostra (later FIRE!!), Barcelona's other annual LGBTQ film festival, has also both been forced to become more compact (and since 2014 it has begun to rely on crowdfunding to maintain its range) and been consistently and strategically focusing its programming of films and events on what it calls 'educational' issues, compared to FICGLB's 'social' issues. Antoine Leonetti, the French- born and

French- and British-educated co-programmer of the Mostra, interviewed by the festival director Joako Ezpeleta for the 2014 festival, remarks on the twin distinctive aims of the Mostra – to match high cinematic quality with a wide educational impact (Ezpeleta 2014: 12). A regular educational outreach programme of films and talks has been established (on Transphobia and Homophobia in 2014; Diversity, Trans Health Issues and Fighting Homophobia in 2013; a sequence of shorts about homophobia in France, sponsored by the French Ministry of Health in 2010); and since 2009 there has been a section Som Família (We Are Family). This programming shares the festival frame with a less obviously thematic and more ethos- and image-building occasional focus on iconic figures (David Bowie in 2014; Tilda Swinton in 2013) or on themed retrospectives (notably, The Look of French Cinema, in 2013). The aim behind the concluding statement in the 2009 'Manifesto FIRE!! 2009', placing value on quality, distinctiveness and engagement, still stands:

> Només volem fer una Mostra de cinema i documental d'autor sense etiquetes i sense concessions. Una Mostra que ens ajudi a no 'escapar', sinó a mirar de cara aquest cartell per a dir: sóc jo. (Ezpeleta 2009)

> (Above all we want to create a festival of auteur cinema and auteur documentary where there are no labels and no concessions. A festival that will help us not to 'escape' from ourselves but to look right at the image on the poster and say 'that's me'.)

This question of visual identification – 'that's me' – has become more complex since 2009, when Ezpeleta was making these remarks. That year's image for the festival was of a geometrically composite male–female human face and upper torso (followed in 2010 with a portrait of paint-daubed embracing bodies and smiling faces), clearly meant to evoke a relatively straightforward recognition by the general festival-goers of themselves. By contrast, for its 2013 event, FIRE!! opted for what could be described as an avatar, assembling an odd figure from a bright yellow and black pen and ink drawing of the body of a Renaissance queen (most probably Queen Elizabeth I based on either Isaac Oliver's drawing of c. 1592–95 or Marcus Gheeraerts the Younger's *The Ditchley Portrait* of c. 1592), with a red artichoke globe as its head (see front cover of this book). In his analysis of the choice of non-human forms in the poster imagery of a number of international LGBTQ film festivals, Karl Schoonover sees such images as:

> part of an old-style liberal humanism in which difference and variety challenge the viewer to remember that we are all human, no matter how different we may look to each other, while at the same time trying to accommodate the instability of the category 'queer'. (Schoonover 2015: 122).

Schoonover proposes three 'iconographic subsets' in the promotional images on festival posters in which a move away from human forms is effected – avatars, objects and animals (124). FIRE!!'s combination of drawing and primary colour scheme endows the image with a certain naive charm, as do London's LLGF cupcakes (2011) and Outfest's (Los Angeles) two attached rainbow-coloured rocket-shaped ice lollies (2013), of which Schoonover writes (2015: 124–6). And yet, the image might also seem so far abstracted from the focus and target audience of the festival (save for the resonance of Elizabeth I as a potential transgender icon for some) as to appear perplexing at best to most viewers. As well as referencing the title and content of the festival publicity spot 'No Kings, No Queens, Just You' (an elegant, camp pastiche of elements of Derek Jarman's *Edward II* (1991), by Juanma Carrillo), it also functions as a symbol (of power and presence, dressing up and taking down a peg or two) that is meant to be recognisable for both local and international audiences. The artichoke globe that serves as the figure's head is polysemic (associated in ancient Greek metamorphic myth with the alluring Aegean Cynara, in Renaissance Europe with regeneration and sexual desire and in modern-day rural Valencia and Catalunya with popular religion and festive cultural identity). It simultaneously serves to reduce the 'particularities of the

Figure 2.2 Festival banner for Mostra FIRE!! 2014 displayed on the Institut Francès building, Barcelona. Photo by Darren Waldron.

body to universalise the identity of the queer' (Schoonover 2015: 124) and to imply the diverse and multiple kinds of identity and sexualities embraced and addressed by the festival.

The festival itself is, year on year, just as layered with meanings and tonalities as that disrupted iconic image of the artichoke queen. Where FICGLB's physical association with the Filmoteca de Catalunya, and its institutional backing, give it gravitas and a sanctioned cultural distinction, FIRE!! has the advantages of lying topographically and ideologically in a less defined, more relaxed, though equally serious cultural field. The hosting of the main programme at the Institut Français (Institut Francès de Barcelona), since 2010, has given the festival a distinctive atmosphere. The position of the Institut's building, in the quiet Carrer Moià but only a hundred metres from the wide and busy Avinguda Diagonal and the Via Augusta, gives a special accessibility and mood to the festival. The building is functional but chic. It has a smartly designed garden area to the front, and a tall, prominent façade given over at festival time to the season's commissioned banner image. An inviting café-restaurant with shaded terrace area greatly enhances pre- and post-screening meeting and mingling, as do the garden's benches and scattered deck chairs and an offshoot bar from the café serving beers, enticing snacks and sandwiches late into the evening. The Institut was set up in 1931, according to its current website, to be '[un] lloc d'intercanvi cultural entre França i Catalunya, i de manera més general Espanya' (Institut Francès 2013) ('a place of cultural exchange between France and Catlaunya, and more generally Spain'). It is thus typical of this sort of cultural institution, forming part of an external cultural policy, linked to national ambitions of linguistic expansion and conservation (Paschalidis 2009: 284). Moreover, along with Antoine Leonetti's own personal and past academic-professional connections with France, the Institut has supplied to the festival a strong connection to both the historically prestigious and the resistant traditions in French cinema and culture. That first year of the festival being held at the Institut, and with a gala opening of François Ozon's *Le Refuge* (*El refugio*; *Hideaway*) (2009), Leonetti introduced the sequence of shorts about homophobia in France, mentioned above, by noting how this new connection would 'mark' the festival (Leonetti 2010). When *Les Témoins* (André Téchiné, 2007) was shown at the 2012 festival, with its setting in 1984–5 at the outset of the AIDS epidemic in France, the programme brochure suggested to the audience that 'Els testimonis som nosaltres, espectadors, lectors i oients d'una història que vam tenir la fortuna de viure per poder-la explicar gràcies a aquests altres testimonis' (FIRE!! 2012) ('We are the ones who are the witnesses, spectators, readers and listeners, in a story that it was our lot to live through and – thanks to those other witnesses – to be able to make some sense of it'). The programme note drew attention, indirectly, to the ways in which AIDS in France (as elsewhere) became the catalyst for a certain community formation, which Martel (1999: 351–2), with his support for republican 'indifférenciation', found problematic. Indeed, one audience member, Julia, a thirty-three-year-old white female NGO worker and journalist self-identifying as bisexual, cites as one of the things she liked about the film 'la visión realista de la homosexualidad y el VIH, de la manera de reaccionar ante el SIDA' ('the realistic picture of homosexuality, of HIV, and of ways of reacting to AIDS'), as well as 'la naturalidad con que se aborda la homosexualidad' ('the natural way in which homosexuality is approached'). The festival, then, facilitates for Julia a recognition of wider issues, linking Paris with Barcelona, the present of viewing with the past of queer history.

FIRE!!'s twin affiliation with the activist and welfare group the Casal Lambda (as we have seen in Chapter 1), however, takes the films and events back into the heart of local community specifics. The festival is, essentially, the Casal Lambda's own – at least historically – and on the logistical front it is staffed and prepared for by volunteers working at the Casal (as in the case of LesGaiCineMad and the Fundación Tríangulo). In a double-page spread on the volunteers, in the Casal's magazine *Lambda*, the team co-ordinator emphasises how, over and above the cultural value of the festival, '[el] voluntariat és testimoni i exemple de participació i d'implicació en aquesta transformació social que, amb la cultura i el cinema, reclamem des del Casal Lambda' (Samsó 2014: 16) ('the volunteers are a testimony to the Casal Lambda's contribution to, and an example of its involvement in, [work towards] the social transformation that through culture and cinema we fight for'). In their short testimonies in the feature, volunteers Charly Lay and Jordi Font home in on the idea of making a contribution, Carles Suay and David Bachiller Canal mention their fulfilment and self-affirmation, Adriá Manzano links hard work, know-how and 'alegria' ('joie de vivre'), and Xavi Montserrat associates 'cultura i amistats' ('culture and making friends') with the 'positive' benefit of collaboration with the Casal (Samsó 2014: 17).

In a more cinephile direction, in 2014 the festival entered into a partnership with Filmin, the pay-for-view online channel backed by the Spanish Ministry of Culture, providing access to a range of foreign titles, of which the French ones were *L'Amour fou* (*Yves Saint-Laurent*; *El amor loco*) (Pierre Thoretton, 2010), *Bambi* (Sébastien Lifshitz, 2013), *Chroniques sexuelles d'une famille d'aujourd'hui* (*Sexual Chronicles of a French Family*) (Pascal Arnold and Jean-Marc Barr, 2012), *Les Invisibles* (Sébastien Lifshitz, 2012), *Presque rien* (*Primer verano*; *Come Undone*) (Sébastien Lifshitz, 2000), *Les Témoins* (André Téchiné, 2007) and *Wild Side* (Sébastien Lifshitz, 2004). Of these, *Les Invisibles* and *Les Témoins* registered the highest number of online votes in favour (170 and 249 respectively, as at 31 August 2014) but the whole selection has attracted its own micro-community of commentators online, seventeen of whom also assiduously list their other French film likes.

Zinegoak (Bilbao, since 2003) – like LesGaiCineMad – has had a city-wide presence in the venues used. By 2013 two main and five (six in 2014) subsidiary venues were in play, with the two main ones being very high-profile on two rather separate cultural scenes. The one, Cinema 1 in the Golem multiplex in

Figure 2.3 Official poster of Zinegoak 2014 (artist Petrina Hicks). Image reproduced with kind permission of Pau Guillén and Petrina Hicks.

the basement of the flagship high-spec mall Alhóndiga (once a massive wine warehouse and an iconic reminder of the city's wealthy commercial foundations); the other, the deconsecrated church and now music, performance and recording venue Bilborock, overlooking the river Nervión (with all its industrial and port-related history) and the bohemian and studenty old town district on the other side. The one mixes the festival with the heterosexual, cinemagoing middle-aged middle classes as well as younger heterosexual couples and consumer youth (a curious mix of queers, fur coats and popcorn); the other blends the festival more readily with a relatively alternative and later-night scene (although this venue too is curious in making a visual mélange of venerability and zippiness, and combining older with newer rituals of adoration).

The festival has a high profile, despite its relatively modest 1700 likes on Facebook and a following of 115 on Twitter (very possibly far superseded by WhatsApp, not monitored) as at 11 August 2014. This is enhanced by its particularly strong element of activist commitment – for example, screening *Mi sexualidad es una creación artística* (*My Sexuality Is a Work of Art*) (Lucía Egaña Rojas, 2011) and *Vides transsexuals* (*Transsexual Lives*; *Vidas transexuales*) (Maria Popova, 2011) in 2012 – programmed alongside films with a strong and more or less conventional narrative or aesthetic appeal. The English-language version of the Zinegoak website and brochure presentation for 2014 explains that it is 'a festival about film, arts and culture, but it is also concerned with social issues' (Zinegoak 2014); like FICGLB, the festival, it says, would '[pay] attention to productions dealing with childhood and adolescence' and, in a link up with Amnesty International, would show 'works [about] the rights of LGTB people [who] are suffering in places such as Cameroon, Russia, or Morocco'. An Honorary Award was presented in 2014 to the Bok o Bok (Side by Side) LGTB International Film Festival, St Petersburg, and Tanya Shmankevich, the Bok o Bok project manager, was invited to the festival to receive the award (and was a generally visible presence for much of the time, on and off programme). Prizes include a Youth Prize, funded by the Equality and Citizens' Rights department of the Biscay Regional Council, and a prize for the best film on 'Lesbianism and Gender' funded by the Department for Women of Bilbao City Council.

Not all of those responding to the festival's position statement are convinced by the overall argument (in Czach's sense: 2004) on identity and commitment: on the Zinegoak Facebook page, one commentator noted angrily (16 January 2013: since transferred to undated Reviews) how the 2013 programme has allowed in cisexist and transphobic language – including text on *Bambi* describing Bambi as having been 'once a boy' (Ruiz 2013). Striking the balance between arts and cultures on the one hand and social commitment on the other proves characteristically difficult.

As we have already seen, the festival features in the documentary *Queer Artivism* where it is made clear how it is part of a wider sub-network driving programming and selection processes as well as informing ideological and aesthetic decisions. The latter set of decisions in particular gives the festival its necessary marks of distinction to aid its survival and success. At the national level of networking, the festival's new director Pau Guillén (from 2014) came to Bilbao (in 2010) from Alicante in the Spanish and borderline-Catalan southeast and had worked for Valencian television channel Canal Nou (Gara 2014), whereas the outgoing director Roberto Castón (Galician born) had cemented links with Basque cultural and media institutions through his writer-director-associate-producer role on the ground-breaking Basque- and Spanish-language *Ander* (2009).

Paris, Toulouse, Lyon

Although the first Paris 'lesbian and gay' film festival (retagged Chéries-Chéris from 2009), held at the American Center in Paris in 1994, is described as fostering a 'community of spirit, values and gazes' and at which a particularly convivial atmosphere is said to have reigned (Chéries-Chéris 2001), promoting the event as a serious film festival soon became a key priority. Hence, by the festival's tenth anniversary in 2004, the organisers inform us that 'Paris privilégie les auteurs, quitte à déranger, à surprendre, à bousculer les idées reçues' (Chéries-Chéris 2004) ('Paris privileges auteurs, even if this means disturbing and surprising [the audience] and shaking up preconceptions') and, seven years later, they boast that the 2011 event will be presented 'à la couleur de l'audace, de la créativité' but which will also 'défend une cinéphile LGBT rigoureuse plus que jamais au delà des clichés' (Chéries-Chéris 2011) ('in the hues of audaciousness, of creativity'; 'defend a rigorous LGBT cinephilia [which] is more than ever beyond clichés'). Perhaps unsurprisingly, then, given the image of Paris as a capital of film-literate culture (one of the City of Paris's 'actions pour le cinéma' includes training young Parisians to read films: Ville de Paris 2015), the Paris festival anticipates a film-literate audience.

Familiar terms strongly associated with dominant discourses affirming French cinematic sophistication, with regard to both output and appreciation, recur in the presentational forewords (or *éditoriaux* – editorials – as most of the French festivals call them): 'auteur', 'innovation', 'avant-garde', 'cinéphile', 'artistes' and 'européen' (French cultural institutions, we know, having played an instrumental and structural role in supporting European cinema). That the French Ministry of Culture and Communication has occasionally featured as one of the festival's listed sponsors (alongside the Forum des Images, the regional authority of the Ile de France and the Regional management of cultural affairs, the City of Paris authority, the National Institute for Health Prevention and Education, the US embassy, online magazine Yagg and Pink TV, as well as other smaller organisations, associations, magazines, bookshops and local restaurants) might inform this reiteration of an attention to 'quality' through film selection; according to the Ministry's catalogue of subsidies published in May 2014, money is available to groups wishing to organise festivals via a fund for cinema and the protection of cinematographic heritage, which prioritises festivals with a regional remit that promote cinematographic art, education and cultural diversity, and which undertake actions to promote cinema throughout the whole year. Structural and organisational issues (see below) may have prevented Paris from securing such support each time the festival was held, but the continued importance of public institutions in sponsoring the event appears to have saved it from relying so heavily on collaborations with corporate partners and multinational companies (although its status is arguably less robust than, say, London's Flare as a result).

Chéries-Chéris embraces experimental as well as activist and independent films, and portrays itself as an event that assembles a community of professionals and cinephiles, and which allows fruitful collaborations to flourish. Presenting the 2013 programme, Pascale Ourbih, the festival president, informs us that Sébastien Lifshitz met Marie-Pierre Pruvost (aka Bambi) when they served on the jury of the 2010 event and that this encounter led directly to Lifshitz making his documentary about her in 2012 (discussed in Chapter 4) (Ourbih 2013). For Jacques Martineau, in a 2005 interview with *Le Monde*, it is its predilection for films 'hors normes' ('unusual') that distinguishes the festival from its peers, including Toronto, San Francisco and Los Angeles (Regnier 2005). Paris claims to defy consensus and to challenge the preconceptions of its assumed audience; the 2004 selection, we are told, is 'plus riche, moins consensuelle, voire plus risquée' ('richer, less consensual, riskier') because it is 'moins immédiatement évidente' (Reilhac et al. 2004) ('less immediately obvious'). The festival's endeavours to cultivate an image as a 'serious' film event include offering an increasingly wide range of awards (which, from 2014 onwards, include three Grands prix and three separate jury prizes for full-length feature films, documentaries and short films).

If 'quality' and experimental cinema are perceived and promoted as among the festival's unique selling points, the presentational forewords nonetheless strive to claim that social commitment remains key to its mission. The significance attached to both aspects is evidenced in the 2009 'editorial', although catering to a cinephile audience is once again, if obliquely, to the forefront:

> nous avons voulu que cette édition 2009 joue sur ces deux dimensions aussi essentielles l'une que l'autre, car complémentaires. Celle qui s'ouvre sur un public qui aime d'abord le cinéma, d'où la présence dans notre programmation d'oeuvres de premier plan, remarqués à Cannes, Berlin ou Sundance ... et celle qui n'oublie à aucun moment de s'adresser aux spectateurs LGBT à travers des films, des rencontres, des débats qui les interpellent. (Roth-Bettoni et al. 2009)

> (we wanted the 2009 festival to operate on these two levels, each one as important as the other – one that opens up to a public that loves cinema above all, which explains the presence in our selection of high-profile productions, noticed at Cannes, Berlin and Sundance and the other that never forgets to address LGBT spectators through the films, encounters, debates that speak to them.)

Prioritising non English-language films in its selections was an early core ideal of the Paris festival that, it is implied, distinguished it from its peers – which, according to the long-time organiser Florence Fradelizi, in interview, were 'très anglo-saxons' and 'passaient peu de films européens' ('too Anglo Saxon'; 'screened very few European films') (Monnot 2001). The 'cross-fertilisation of international images, ideas and peoples' (Pidduck 2002: 268 – see Introduction) is modified in this case to favour films from countries other than – principally – the USA, but possibly also the UK (although offerings from both countries feature prominently in later years). A desire to bring together films from all over the world within one festival informs the selections each year. As the festival has developed, input has been sought from LGBTQ filmmakers from countries in South America, Africa and Asia, although French films unsurprisingly represent the majority. The number of films from Spain is relatively limited (under twenty full-length feature films and short films in the past nine years, for example), which may be explained by the impact of the economic crisis of 2008 on film production in that country. This said, heading the jury in 2012 was the Almodóvar fetish actor Rossy de Palma. The brochure highlights the association between the actor and her 'Pygmalion', despite also mentioning her roles in films from other countries, thereby obliquely and indirectly alluding to his importance as a reference for attenders at this LGBTQ festival (the assumption being that they will have seen *Mujeres al borde de un ataque de nervios* (*Femmes au bord de la crise de nerfs*; *Women on the Verge of a Nervous Breakdown*) (1988) (see Chapter 5 for more on Almodóvar's image in France).

Like other festivals of its kind, Paris has invested in global LGBTQ politics. In 2002, it invited the Beijing 'gay and lesbian' festival to show some of its Chinese films because the authorities in China had banned it in December 2001. In their critique of such engagements, Loist and Zielinski note the 'potentially . . . problematic neoliberal and neocolonial tendencies' of involvement of Western LGBTQ festivals in non-Western LGBTQ film events (2012: 55). While it would be wrong to suggest that the organisers of the Paris festival have sought to promote a neoliberal or neocolonial agenda, their originary emphasis on European and global cinema implies a subscription to the view that Paris is uniquely placed as a privileged site for the showcasing of queer films from countries outside of the English-speaking world and from Africa, Asia and South America. In his otherwise upbeat presentational statement for the 2012 festival, at which we conducted our audience research, Director General Hervé Joseph Lebrun emphasises the festival's political aims to shine a spotlight on repressively homophobic regimes, mentioning films from and about Cuba, Nepal, Russia and Uganda in particular, but then states 'mais au-delà de leurs provenances, c'est quand même ici que ça se passe, avec les débats qui animent la société française, homoparentalité, mariage, hétéronorme' (Lebrun 2012) ('but beyond their origins, this is where it is happening, with debates on the subjects that animate French society, gay parenting, marriage, heteronomativity'). Lebrun undoubtedly has local audiences in his sights here, but he nonetheless promotes the international reach and significance of his festival.

While, as mentioned, quality and social commitment have been core ideals, the presentation of the 2013 programme implies a concern with broadening the festival's appeal (Labory 2013; Legann 2013; Ourbih 2013; Quet 2013; Vives 2013). The length of the event was reduced from ten days in 2012 to five in 2013, although unspecified difficulties are suggested as the cause and not necessarily lower ticket sales, which had in fact risen seventeen per cent compared to 2011 (Ourbih 2013). Ourbih's lead piece in the presentations page resonates with obvious attempts at attracting non-cinephile audiences: 'il y aura, encore et encore, du muscle, des poils, des rasés, des imberbes, du cambouis, du cuir, de l'acier, de l'amour et ++++' ('again and again, there will be muscles, hair, shaved heads, smooth bodies/faces, grease, leather, steel, love and ++++') and adding sex, blood and passion to the usual genres of drama, comedy and thrillers (Ourbih 2013). Ourbih is engaging in a crude but arguably necessary compromise, if it was conceived that way, with each category indexing erotic subcultures that double up as object groups on online dating apps (Grindr had become ubiquitous on the Parisian gay scene in the three years preceding 2013). The use of recognisable promotional images could also be said to serve this purpose of reaching out to broader audiences by enhancing the festival's appeal. In fact, if, as Schoonover suggests, the turn to the non-human is a recent global trend in how LGBTQ film festivals promote themselves visually, then Chéries-Chéris bucks this trend, by continuing to depict actual people – albeit mainly celebrities – in its posters. Although in 2009 and 2010 it opted for an elaborate rainbow-coloured tubular image in the form of a heart, in 2011 it featured gay male photographers Pierre et Gilles as if posing for a wedding photograph, in 2012 it showed an image of the New York drag artist and performer Joey Arias in Z *Chromosome*, in 2013 it sported a drawing of a woman brandishing a gun with two men, one naked, one dressed, cruising in the fields behind her, and which makes an instantly recognisable nod to the poster of *L'Inconnu du lac* (Alain Guiraudie 2013) and in 2014 it depicted the actor Arielle Dombasle astride the American burlesque performer Dita von Teese on a bed.

Ourbih is an MTF transsexual actor and former model, and was President from 2008 to 2013. It was under her leadership that the festival added the tag Chéries-Chéris, thus reflecting what has been observed as a recent trend in global LGBTQ film festivals in moving away from identitarian names: 'in an attempt to remain relevant to people no longer identifying simply as L, G, B, or even Q' (Galt and Schoonover 2014) (for more on this see discussion of the London Lesbian and Gay Film Festival below). Chéries-Chéris indeed sought to highlight breadth and diversity by including the expression LGBT++++, although its tag is bound by the binary masculine/feminine structure of the grammatical gender system of the French language (it is difficult to identify precisely how Chéries-Chéris's tag embraces those attenders who identify as intersex or genderqueer, for example). This was not the first time, though, that trans issues had been addressed: 'transversales' sections had already been included, the 2007 event offered an 'intersexe/intergenre' section, which featured *L'Ordre des mots* (the activist trans documentary discussed by our respondents in Chapter 4) and the 2013 event boasted an Existrans section – Existrans being the title of an annual Parisian trans march (also discussed in Chapter 4). Diversity in terms of community has long been central to the Paris festival's declared remit, even if the title 'gay et lesbien', which it used from 1994 until 2008, appeared restrictive; part of the presentation of the 2002 event sets out its aim to 'tenter de balayer la diversité des modes de vie, des sexualités et des images' (Chéries-Chéris 2002) ('try to provide an overview of diverse lifestyles, sexualities and images'); and the subtitle 'festival de tous les genres' ('festival for all genders/genres' – gender and genre being the same word in French) was added for 2007 and 2008. Hence, while Chéries-Chéris targets a broad audience and, as outlined, claims that it caters to divergent lesbian and gay "taste" populations' (Gamson 1996: 244), it does not 'assume . . . and advance . . . a stable and recognisable us' (244) and like New York's experimental lesbian and gay festival seeks to 'build a consciousness in which the oppositional "we" [is] always under question' (243).

Chéries-Chéris has nonetheless endured a somewhat troubled history. Having enjoyed an increase to circa fourteen thousand spectators in 2004 (twenty per cent rise compared to 2003) (Chéries-Chéris 2004), by 2006 numbers decreased to circa seven thousand (Chéries-Chéris 2006). It has had to change venues frequently, from the culturally prestigious space of the Forum des Images at Châtelet-les-Halles to the more intimate establishments of, for example, Le Rex, on the edges of the second arrondissement, Le Latina in the 'gay quarter' of the Marais and the MK2 cinemas, adjacent to the Centre Pompidou and in the twelfth arrondissement. Crucially, it has been forced to renew its organisational committee and has built a reputation for tensions between its various members; in a declaration uploaded on the festival's Facebook page on 5 December 2014 (since removed) Ourbih described in detail what she terms a 'putsch' that ended in her presidency being 'illegally' revoked and her being implicated in accounting problems, which she strongly denied. Fluctuations in its success could be a result of a too narrow, a too broad or even an unclear mission. Hence, although the separation of New York festivals in the early 1990s into two with distinct remits had 'not only reduce[d] conflict between the festivals, it allow[ed] each festival to go about its own business without tremendous internal conflict' (Gamson 1996: 244), just such conflicts have continued to beset Chéries-Chéris, although *Yagg* webzine cautiously announced a stabilising new departure, in August 2015 (Le Corre 2015). It is perhaps a reflection of such issues, and possibly some confusion about its role, remit and target audience, that its uploaded trailers and events on YouTube and Daily Motion have received limited responses from an online public. Moreover, the Chéries-Chéris Facebook pages equally received a relatively small number of likes when compared to those of its peers (see LesGaiCineMad above and Flare below): 2,253 (at 2 September 2015). The festival also only has 1,148 followers on Twitter (at 2 September 2015). Giving us a scaled-down sense of frequency of attendance, of the twenty-nine respondents who completed our questionnaires at the 2012 event, ten replied that it was their first visit, while two more stated that they attended rarely, eight affirmed or implied that they come regularly and two wrote that they have attended three times and one four times.

If the ethos of Chéries-Chéris has historically been to shine a spotlight on films from abroad but which are not in the English language, Des images aux mots, the annual LGBT film festival in Toulouse that began in 2008, similarly emphasises, through its programming, the importance of films from other countries. Spanish films screened at the festival include two that are studied in this project – *80 Egunean* (Jon Garaño and Jose Mari Goenaga, 2010), which won the public prize in 2012, and *El Sexo de los ángeles*, which won the jury prize at the 2013 festival. Moreover, the Instituto Cervantes has occasionally featured as a sponsor since 2000, alongside the Goethe Institut, the Cinémathèque, the ABC and Utopia cinemas, the lesbian and gay group Arc-en-ciel (Rainbow) and the Toulouse city council. The organiser Laure Faghol states that the contribution of the Instituto Cervantes extends to the costs of screening one film at its premises (in interview with Ros Murray 7 February 2013); in this way the festival was able in 2012 to screen *80 Egunean*, which was attended by the two principal actors, Itziar Aizpuru and Mariasun Pagoaga, and followed by a debate. The festival is run by a group of twelve volunteers from Arc-en-ciel in Toulouse, of whom five are paid organisers and the remaining seven volunteers. It is part of the ARC network of LGBTQ film festivals in France and Belgium, which share costs including subtitling and which includes some French festivals, but not Chéries-Chéris and Ecrans Mixtes. Programming decisions are informed by the content and tastes of the team – Faghol mentioned, for instance, that she chose not to screen *Habitación en Roma* (*Room in Rome*) (Julio Medem, 2010) because she felt that it was uninteresting as a representation of LGBTQ identities (interview with Murray) – and whether the film had already been seen in France, partly as further justification for their existence and relevance and because they aim to offer films that audiences would not normally see. Attendance figures are high, according to Faghol, and opening nights tend to sell out in advance, which she explains as the result of choosing to screen films only once and in the evenings and at weekends (interview with Murray). Like FICGLB in Barcelona and Zinegoak in Bilbao, Des images aux mots reaches beyond the city walls and into its suburbs, satellite towns and the broader region. In addition to the city centre picture houses of the ABC, located in the bohemian area of Arnaud Bernard, and Utopia, in the St Georges' quarter, as well as the cinémathèque on the studenty rue du Taur, screenings of its films are held in cinemas in the suburbs (Auzielle, Blagnac, Muret, Tournefeuille and Ramonville) and beyond, and in rural centres (Auch, Carbonne, Cahors, Mirande, Montauban, Rodez and Saint-Gaudens). Via its programming choices and screening locations, Des images aux mots encourages cross-cultural encounters with foreign language films among suburban and rural audiences, as well as urbanites.

The selections include contemporary and older films, and range from the radical and political (*L'Ordre des mots* was screened in 2008) to the more mainstream – *Cachorro* (*Bear Cub*; *Le Gamin*) (Miguel Abaladejo, 2004) was shown in 2011 (the Grenoble Gay and Lesbian Film Festival had been quicker off the mark, showing it in April 2005). Moreover, Des images aux mots includes exhibitions (including one on the work of the photographer and filmmaker Emilie Jouvet) and, as mentioned, debates. It links into other similar festivals, including Les Rencontres du cinéma italien (Italian film festival), Kinopolska (Polish film festival), Cinelatino (a Spanish-language film festival that specialises in films from Latin America) and Cinespaña (the city's

Spanish film festival). In fact, in collaboration with the 2014 Cinespaña event, it organised a special event entitled 'sexe, genre et identités' ('sex, gender and identities') and screened eight Spanish films including *80 Egunean*, *Krámpack* (*Nico and Dani*) (Cesc Gay, 2000), with a younger gay male theme, *La mala educación* (*La Mauvaise Education*; *Bad Education*) (Pedro Almodóvar, 2004), on themes of memory, identity, sexual abuse and transvestism, and *Ignasi M* (Ventura Pons, 2013), on HIV/AIDS, ageing and identity (and presented by the director). Des images aux mots also organises out-of-season events, which include screenings of some of its films; *Bambi* was shown at the imposing Médiathèque José Cabanis on 17 May and was followed by a debate. Des images aux mots so far has a limited number of likes on Facebook (543) and only sixty-five followers on Twitter (at 1 July 2015).

Ecrans Mixtes, Lyon's LGBT film festival, on the other hand, boasts a comparatively high number of Facebook likes (1700) and followers on Twitter (326 as of 1 July 2015), despite having begun only in 2011. In its first year, the festival emphasised the importance of safeguarding a community past by proclaiming that 'il est urgent de prendre soin de notre mémoire collective' (Barbe 2011) ('it's urgent that we take care of our collective memory'). Thus, the community addressed by the organisers appears unified, although, as the event's organisation and programming reveals, that very same imagined collective is inclusive, incorporating those who identify with the lesbian and gay mainstream as well as those who embrace more alternative identities and lifestyles (Ecrans Mixtes' 'off' events feature a mini queer festival entitled La Chatte s'étire – 'the cat stretches') which questions fixed identity categories, and which included a lecture and debate by MartinE de Montpellier, a self-identified 'queer' and 'feminist' collective that, according to its entry on Montpellier's lesbian and gay pride website, welcomes lesbians, gays, bisexuals, trans and those without a label (Montpelliergay 2015). Moreover, Ecrans Mixtes promotes itself as 'le festival du film queer et LGBT de Lyon', implying that those who affiliate themselves with alternative identities and defy normative categories are particularly welcome. As with the festival IdentiT, Marie-Pierre Pruvost, alias Bambi, was the guest of honour at the 2014 festival. This, as well as her collaboration in the Chéries-Chéris festival and her guest appearance at the screening of *Bambi* at FIRE!! in Barcelona, illustrates her significance as a representative of LGBTQ culture at recent festivals in France and Spain.

The accent on LGBTQ historiography recurs in Ecrans Mixtes, with retrospectives featuring prominently. In 2013, incidentally the festival at which we carried out our research, Ecrans Mixtes acquired the subtitle 'Sweet Transvestite' and included such seminal films as *The Rocky Horror Picture Show* (Jim Sharman, 1975) and *Ocaña, retrat intermitent* (Ventura Pons, 1978) (discussed in Chapter 4). In an interview for the online magazine *Yagg* (and reproduced on the festival's blog site), the director Rémi Lange, who had been Co-Programmer at the Paris 'gay and lesbian' festival in 2007 (and thus before Ourbih's presidency and its change of name), defends the continued relevance of LGBTQ film festivals.

Lange describes such events as 'laboratoires de découverte' ('laboratories of discovery'), which offer films that cannot be seen elsewhere (Martet 2014). Recognising the potential impact of the Web for such events, Lange emphasises the pleasures offered by physical encounters with films and their makers, including foreign films, arguing that a successful festival 'nous présente les homosexualités des pays étrangers, nous amenant ainsi à réfléchir sur la nôtre, sur ces [*sic*] évolutions et ses interconnections avec la mondialisation des modes de vie LGBT et des représentations de ceux-ci' (Martet 2014) ('presents us with homosexualities from foreign countries, which in this way make us think about our own, about those evolutions and its interconnections with the globalisation of LGBT lifestyles and the representations of them'). Again, broadcasting LGBT film history is highlighted as a significant contribution of LGBT festivals, which Lange frames as a collective heritage ('patrimoine'). Elsewhere, as with the other festivals mentioned above, alternative visions of LGBT lifestyles and images that disrupt expectations are given precedence by Lange, who also warns against allowing festivals to be dictated by market concerns: 'certains festivals s'enorgueillissent de faire le plein de spectateurs, et j'ai peur que cette optique commerciale (projeter des films qui plaisent au plus grand nombre) étouffe la création LGBT novatrice' (Martet 2014) ('some festivals are proud of the fact that they fill up their auditoria with spectators, and I'm afraid that this commercial perspective – screening films that please the highest number [of spectators] – will stifle LGBT innovative creativity').

In a city with a reputation for conservative thinking (its biggest annual festival, la Fête des Lumières, Festival of Lights, enacts a kind of mini pilgrimage in which the city's inhabitants offer thanks to the Virgin Mary), it could be viewed as surprising that its LGBTQ film festival receives the public support of high-ranking city officials. The Deputy Mayor Georges Képénékian writes in his editorial for the third run of the festival: 'depuis sa première édition, la Ville soutient le Festival pour toute la diversité de la création qu'il représente, en dédiant sa programmation à la valorisation des cultures gays et lesbiennes' (Képénékian 2013: 3) ('since it was first held, the City has supported the Festival for all the diversity of creativity that it represents, in dedicating its programming to the valorisation of gay and lesbian cultures'). Describing the festival as one of Lyon's most important spring cultural events, Képénékian notes, in his presentation for the fifth event, that Ecrans Mixtes 'permet la découverte de la richesse et de la diversité des cultures gays et lesbiennes' (Képénékian 2015: 3) ('enables the discovery of the richness and diversity of gay and lesbian cultures'). The city authority and the regional council of Rhône Alpes, of which Lyon is the capital, back up their verbal enthusiasm with funding and are listed as the only two organisations that financially support the festival (in Spain, CinegailesAST in Gijón/Xixón and the Muestra de Cine LGTB in Murcia (LGBT Film Showcase) are cognate examples of small festivals integrated into local government's wider cultural offering). Ecrans Mixtes also has a range of partners, including Yagg and Pink TV, and local HIV/AIDS groups. The Ecrans Mixtes association runs the festival, with a team of twenty-one: eight members of the organising committee and thirteen volunteers. Of the thirteen respondents to our questionnaires, nine stated that they attend the festival regularly, a relatively high proportion when compared with the attenders at Chéries-Chéris. One claimed that it was their second time while three declared that they had never before attended.

LONDON, MANCHESTER

Having provided outlines of the Spanish and French LGBTQ film festivals at which we undertook our audience research, we now turn to the two British events that we also used to distribute our questionnaires and recruit our participants: the London Lesbian and Gay Film Festival (now tagged Flare) and Manchester's POUTfest, an event held each year to coincide with the city's Pride celebrations. Since the focus of this book is mainly on the cross-cultural exchange of images of LGBTQ desires and identities, and transnational mobilisation of values and tastes between Spain and France, discussions of these two events will be brief, focusing specifically on their role in facilitating encounters among their audiences with French and Spanish LGBTQ films and any broader similarities with and distinctions from the French and Spanish festivals discussed above.

Flare enjoys a privileged position as one of Europe's (and indeed the world's) leading and most high-profile LGBTQ film festivals; it boasted 21,949 likes on Facebook and 3376 followers on Twitter (as of 22 July 2015) and Galt and Schoonover refer to Flare as 'one of the oldest' festivals and 'in a sense the most institutionally grounded' because it is organised 'under the auspices' of the British Film Institute and (now) held at London's National Film Theatre (2014). London's festival was used as a point of comparison by the Paris festival when it was started, thereby reflecting its perceived standing among European LGBTQ festivals as early as 1994. London officially predated Paris in holding a bona-fide lesbian and gay film festival by eight years, having launched with its first event in 1986, although embryo mini-festivals occurred before this date; a one-off week of screenings, entitled 'Gays and Film' which examined mainstream representations of homosexuality in cinema, was organised in 1977 while the London Filmmakers' Co-operative held London's first Festival of Gay Film and Video in June 1981 (Clews 2013). This early festival illustrates the historical importance of France as a source of depictions of homosexuality that resonate across national borders: among its eight evenings of screenings and debates featured the biographical *Le Testament d'Orphée* (*Testament of Orpheus*) (Jean Cocteau, 1960), followed by a workshop, *Un chant d'amour* (Jean Genet, 1950) and Lionel Soukaz's retracing of homosexual emancipation movements, in collaboration with Guy Hocquenghem, in *Race d'Ep* (*The Homosexual Century*) (1979), which had its UK premiere at the event. The festival's thirteenth iteration, in 1999, included a section devoted to a series of French film comedies about queer desires, many of which were screened at the Ciné Lumière cinema at London's French Institute (see Waldron 2009: 4). Although by 2015 the Institut Français was no longer named as a sponsor, French companies and institutions have been well represented among the many supporters of the London festival: car manufacturer Renault as a general sponsor, banks BNP Paribas and Société Générale funding special screenings, and international promoters of French cinema worldwide uniFrance films (supported by the CNC, the National Centre of Cinematography and the Moving Image, and the Ministries of Culture and for Foreign Affairs) contributing to the event.

It is a marker of the festival's success and prestige that it has been able to move away from independent cinemas and into such a prestigious cultural institution as the National Film Theatre. However, this transition in locale and profile risks engendering demographic changes in the constitution of its audience. The same can be said of the locating of the Chéries-Chéris festival in Paris's equally distinguished Forum des Images, although the relationship between festival and institution there is less permanent than for its London counterpart. As Suárez (2006: 602) has remarked, though, the involvement of non-queer institutions in Spanish LGBTQ film festivals, prior to the post-2008 financial crisis at least, meant that they have tended 'to draw a mixed audience'. The BFI's involvement in Flare similarly inevitably has an impact on the audience of LLGFF, opening its films up to the attention of critics and cinephiles, the kind of audience drawn to more general festivals. The participation of corporate sponsors no doubt encourages this broadening of its appeal through the programming of high-profile films, but which have queer content or focus. In their review of Flare 2014, Galt and Schoonover (2014) argue that recent evolutions in terms of the subjects and themes addressed by films have blurred the traditional distinctions between 'queer cinema', 'world cinema' and 'art cinema'. Citing *La Vie d'Adèle* (Abdellatif Khechiche, 2013) and *L'Inconnu du lac* (Alain Guiraudie, 2013) as examples, they conclude that the 'apparent success of queer cinema suggests that they already had access to art cinema release channels and were buoyed by significant attention from mainstream cultural criticism' (Galt and Schoonover 2014). Both headlined at Flare in 2014 and are discussed in Chapter 5.

London was a relative latecomer in the shift from an identitarian name to a more abstract tag, rebranding itself as 'Flare' in 2014 after a process of consultation that included a suggestions board at the 2013 event and campaigns on social media and via email (Galt and Schoonover 2014 and Schoonover 2015). Flare, of course, implies the same sort of burst of bright, urgent images as Barcelona's FIRE!!; it was selected also, though, because it was deemed 'inclusive and welcoming to all audiences' and could embrace the festival's physical event on London's South Bank as well as its new channel on BFI player. BFI player streams many of the LGBTQ films it showcases for online subscribers, thereby (according to its website) helping to bring 'even greater visibility to queer cinema and expanding the access for LGBTQ-interested audiences'. By contrast to Chéries-Chéris but like FIRE!! via Filmin, this service endows the festival with a more permanent, year-long presence both beyond the event itself and beyond text-based social media. Subscribers are alerted to new content via email and Facebook updates and are sent various top ten lists – one such list assembles what the team label '10 Great French Gay Films', authored by the digital producer and former curator of the BFI National Film Archive Alex Davidson, and which includes *Les Invisibles* (2015).

The London festival's rebranding, much like FIRE!!'s in Barcelona discussed above, contributes to the growing trend away from human figures in the visuals utilised to promote queer film festivals (Schoonover 2015: 121). Flare's promotional images correspond to part of Schoonover's second 'iconographical subset' of 'nonhuman forms' – here, 'objects' (125) – with its brightly coloured orange shapes that, according to Galt and Schoonover, writing elsewhere (2014), resemble 'jellyfish, fractals, or chandeliers'.

If queer culture is only obliquely alluded to in the London festival's name Flare, it is indexed via a reference to camp posture in Manchester's annual POUTfest festival. This event is not an LGBTQ film festival in its purest sense since it represents the Manchester screenings of a UK nationwide tour that includes a range of British towns and cities, and which is organised by Peccadillo Pictures, a UK-wide distributor of 'art house, gay and lesbian, and world cinema titles' (Peccadillo Pictures 2015). The screenings that make up Manchester's participation in the event, which has existed since 2013, are presented in association with the Sexuality Summer School at the University of Manchester and with Manchester Pride, and they are often introduced by academics from the University. Among our films, the event has so far shown *Les Invisibles*, *La Vie d'Adèle* and *L'Inconnu du lac*, and we distributed questionnaires at each of these showings. POUTfest has accrued a relatively limited amount of Facebook likes (600 at 2 September 2015), although its page has been updated only sporadically, and 164 followers on Twitter (at 2 September 2015). Audiences tend to be small, probably because the screenings are often scheduled in the afternoons or coincide with other Pride events, and because they are not broadly advertised. Motivations for attending are varied, and the audience is diverse; in fact of those who responded to the questionnaire we distributed at the screening of *La Vie d'Adèle* in August 2014, many wrote that they came because of its polemical reputation (due to its long sex scene between two women and also because of the public spat between director and actors in the press) and some of these spontaneously identified as heterosexual. In Manchester, only half of those responding to the question 'Do you regularly attend LGBTQ film events/festivals or is this your first visit?' say that they do so, suggesting that in the context of a city highly sensitised to the lure of alternative cultures a specialist film festival as event in itself has a certain pull for some, regardless of the LGBTQ content; four respondents, additionally, had attended because of word of mouth recommendation and two out of a sense of duty to more assiduous or enthusiastic friends attending (one writing a PhD on foreign films).

Concluding Remarks

At a practical level, all these festivals are homes, or nodes, for information. The questions about why respondents chose a particular film, whether they had any previous knowledge of the film and whether they regularly attended LGBTQ festivals elicited 172 questionnaire responses saying that festival publicity had been used to guide choices and thirteen citing convenience of timing and/or venue as a reason. The festivals are also attended out of commitment, need, loyalty or habit. 207 responses indicated regular attendance at the festival being polled, and thirty-six occasional attendance. Michel, a forty-four-year-old French university teacher resident in Madrid describing his ethnicity as European, says of his regular attendance 'lo veo necesario' ('it seems necessary to me'); Marc, a fifty-five-year-old white worker resident in Barcelona, says he comes as a 'voluntari i persona compromesa amb la causa LGTBI' ('volunteer and someone with a commitment to the LGBTI cause'). Five others write that they have come to an LGBTQ festival for the first time but state their intention to come again. And, as seen in the opening comments of this chapter, Daphne describes her attendance at Des images aux mots as a prominent feature of her lesbian identity and manifestation of her public self-affirmation.

The overview of the festivals at which we distributed our questionnaires and alongside which we held focus group discussions reveals important similarities in aims, aspirations and remit, as well as significant distinctions in funding, scope and perceived success of the event. These accounts serve to give context to many of the responses that we engage with and analyse in the next two chapters. Though, as mentioned, our project did not only use festivals to recruit participants and collect data, it was at these high-profile cultural events that the majority of our respondents encountered our corpus films. Thus, as mentioned in the Introduction, the programming decisions of the festival organisers have a constitutive effect on the kinds of images these viewers – and LGBTQ festival-going audiences more broadly – come into contact with, as well as, by extension, influencing the type and range of discourses produced in their 'talk' about them. Moreover, the prescreening materials, issued mainly by the festivals, more often than not feed into their readings of the films. In the focus group discussions, which also feature in the next two chapters, our selection of those films that we deem pertinent to our study similarly set parameters on the readings, viewing strategies and subject positions that we, as researchers, encounter.

Note

1. Available at <http://vimeo.com/50701700> (last accessed 11 August 2014).

3. LGBQ THEMES AND RESPONSES

The director presented 'us' as normal, and our experiences as normal. We are passionate, eloquent and aware of our experiences. (Sarah, a forty-two-year-old white British security officer after the screening of *Les Invisibles* at Flare, London, March 2013)

Respecto a la representación de la sexualidad en el cine francés, pienso que en general suele ser tratada de forma más sutil y más delicada que en otro tipo de cine, como pueda ser el americano o el español.

(As to the representation of sexuality in French cinema, I think in general it's dealt with more subtly and delicately than in other sorts of cinema, American or Spanish for example.) (José María, a forty-two-year-old white Spanish male researcher in a follow-up email to his response to a screening of *Notre paradis* at the LesGaiCineMad, Madrid, November 2012)[1]

Two viewer responses, about two different films that explore two different issues – ageing among lesbians, gay men and queers in *Les Invisibles* (Sébastien Lifshitz, 2012), and the treatment of (homo-)sexuality in *Notre paradis* (Gaël Morel, 2011) – expressed in two different locations, in two different languages and in response to two different genres of film, one documentary, the other fiction. Two different stances, also; yet they both suggest that the film's modality, its interviewees or characters, their actual or portrayed lifestyles and experiences, serve as comparative resources for understanding sexuality. These are 'our' experiences, alleges Sarah, and French cinema is in some ways a better way of representing a core aspect of them, according to José María. The ways in which viewers claim such representations from abroad as having particular resonances with their own sense of selves and experiences, or apprehend them as distinct from themselves and their encounter with the world, and what this means in terms of cross-cultural reception and affiliations, will be the focus of this chapter.

Three dominant themes emerge in the films discussed: ageing among lesbians, gay men and bisexuals; gay male, and, to a much lesser extent, lesbian and bisexual desires and identities; and a sense of shared experience, which manifests variously as a stake in community history or as a more personalised mark of identity. These are approached via both documentaries (one French, one French-Spanish, one Spanish) and fictional films (one Basque, one Brazilian-Catalan-Spanish, three French), which allows this chapter, as also the next, to transcend simplistic oppositions between the 'real', most often attached to documentaries, and the 'invented', most often associated with fictional films; as will be seen 'truth' is almost as much a contested quality of documentaries, including by our respondents, as it is of the thrillers and melodramas that we also cover. As mentioned in the introduction, we interpret the questionnaire responses and focus group discussions (here, two) in close connection to the films on which they are based, but also recognise the potential polyvalence of possible readings and viewing positions. Additionally, to counterbalance our own readings of the films, again as mentioned in the introduction, we begin the discussion of each film with extracts from the synopses or write-ups provided by the festivals. These texts, as well as film notes, which are often reviews by critics or members of the organising committee, are important because they can feed into the respondents' declared opinions of the films (as suggested at the end of Chapter 2). Such texts can also serve as a cross-cultural filter in that they are often written by reviewers from the country in which the film is received rather than the one in which it was produced.

APPROACHING OLD AGE:
LES INVISIBLES (*LOS INVISIBLES*; *THE INVISIBLES*) (SÉBASTIEN LIFSHITZ, 2012), *LAS VENTANAS ABIERTAS* (MICHÈLE MASSÉ, 2014) AND *80 EGUNEAN* (*80 JOURS*; *FOR 80 DAYS*) (JON GARAÑO AND JOSE MARI GOENAGA, 2010)

According to its director, *Les Invisibles* highlights the courage, freedom and happiness with which a range of older interviewees (whom he refers to as heroes) have lived their homosexuality in France, despite the challenges and traumas they have faced (Odicino 2013). *Les Invisibles* broadly traces a trajectory from past oppression to present emancipation. Though the general mood is reflective, *Les Invisibles* is mainly light and jovial. Realist *cinéma-vérité* aesthetics are rejected for a more romantic style: a fixed camera and a wide-angle lens are preferred over close-ups and handheld filming equipment (Rees-Roberts 2015: 445–7). Pauses separate interventions, consisting of static long shots showing gently rolling green hills, the hues of the vegetation occasionally transformed by the passing of clouds, or of the interviewees themselves in deep reflection or caressing and caring for domestic animals. The interviewees are resilient, amiable and effervescent. Their familiar and humorous style of delivery softens the more radical aspects of their pasts, recounted and referenced in archival footage.

To a degree, *Les Invisibles* – and indeed *Las ventanas abiertas* and the trans documentaries discussed in Chapter 4 – approximate 'oral history', which seeks to include 'within the historical record the experiences and perspectives of groups of people who might otherwise have been "hidden from history"' (Perks and Thomson 2006: viiii). Lifshitz gives voice to those marginalised, not only by dominant histories of postwar French society but also by LGBTQ visual culture: older lesbians, gay men and queers. Contrary to what Nichols identifies as the dominant tendency in the use of oral histories in documentaries – 'as pieces of argumentation' – verbal testimonies are used in *Les Invisibles* as its 'primary source material' (Nichols 1991: 252). While elements of form and style do index additional voices beyond those of the interviewees, these devices work dialectically in order to bring attention to the subjective nature of the oral histories presented, serving to accentuate their poignancy. In a sense, the involvement of the filmmakers corresponds to the participation of oral historians in the production of their own sets of data (Abrams 2010: 59) and echoes our contribution, as audience researchers, in collecting the responses elicited by this film and the others in our corpus, and interpreting them for our readers.

All of the write-ups, reviews and film notes that were offered to attenders at the three festivals at which we collected responses and to future viewers via their websites recognise the film's potentially life-affirming message or impact. However, each one takes a slightly different approach, and either highlights or downplays its specificity as an examination of life for queer people in the French provinces. For instance, the writer of the notes for FIRE!! – which, we recall, is held in the French Institute in Barcelona – immediately establishes for the audience that 'Sébastien Lifshitz posa davant de la càmera 11 homes i dones francesos de més de 70 anys' ('Sébastien Lifshitz puts eleven French men and women of over seventy years old in front of the camera') before asking how the film's subjects coped 'quan la societat, en la seva joventut, rebutjava plenament la seva manera de viure' ('when society, in their youth, completely rejected their way of life') and how they found partners in the absence of 'referents socials positius' ('positive points of reference socially') (FIRE!! 2013b). Despite the generalised use of 'society' here, the context and the interviewees are presented as clearly French, and the discourses alluded to are presented as implicitly so. The writer notes that 'si bé en el fons podien viure lliurement les seves vides, l'escandalós per aquell temps no era tant ser homosexual, sinó dir-ho' (FIRE!! 2013b) ('though they were mostly free to live as they wanted; the scandalous thing back then was not being homosexual, but saying so'). Dominant French approaches to social integration are, indeed, broadly understood as actively discouraging public displays of difference in favour of a collective allegiance to a neutral, universalised construction of the French citizen (Martel 1999). It is thus not difficult to see why this writer locates the trauma depicted in *Les Invisibles* in its interviewees' supposed inability to be publicly open about their sexuality.

Another image of French cultural specificity emerges from the notes that accompany the streaming of *Les Invisibles* on the BFI website connected to Flare. Perhaps not surprisingly, the 'Frenchness' that emerges here evokes 'foreign' and British abstractions:

> French gay men and women in their 60s and 70s talk about their lives and loves. While some tell stories of repression, family estrangement and catholic guilt, all are out, proud and inspiring, from the infectiously enthusiastic lesbian activist to the octogenarian bisexual shepherd unrepentantly recalling his many sexual conquests. (BFIPlayer 2014)

Beyond the national identity qualifier, the mention of 'Catholic guilt' and the 'shepherd' align with common representations of rural France in Britain (but also registered by the Barcelona-based festival notes) as a haven of bucolic tranquillity, steeped in pre-industrial traditions. Such an image has been shaped by popular French films with British audiences, including, most obviously *Jean de Florette* (Claude Berri, 1986) and its sequel *Manon des Sources* (*Manon of the Spring*) (Claude Berri, 1987), as well as the later documentary about life in an infants' school in rural Auvergne, *Etre et avoir* (*To Be and To Have*) (Bertrand Philibert, 2002); indeed, one of our participants, Margaret, a fifty-seven-year-old retired white British physiotherapist, makes this very same intertextual comparison.

Neither note emphasises the film's potential resonances across borders. However, the notes that accompanied the announcement of *Les Invisibles* for POUTfest at Cornerhouse (and are archived in the web pages of Cornerhouse's successor organisation HOME) omit any reference to its status as a French documentary or to the fact that it is about French lesbian, gay and queer lives and experiences:

> *The Invisibles* explores the lives of men and women born between the World Wars who have nothing in common, except their sexuality and decision to live openly at a time when society rejected them. They've loved, struggled, desired, made love. Today they tell us about their pioneering lives and how they navigated the desire to remain ordinary with the need to liberate themselves in order to thrive. (HOME 2015)

The qualities that are said to unite the interviewees are universal (and, of course, presented in English-language translation): sexuality, defiance, love, desire, struggle and liberation. According to this author, then, *Les Invisibles* presents a depiction of queer life that can invoke feelings of recognition by people with similar experiences, irrespective of their national identity.

The vast majority of the 120 respondents who completed the questionnaires on *Les Invisibles* at FIRE!!, Flare and POUTfest pinpoint the film's optimism as having elicited their enthusiasm. Few mention its more sombre moments,

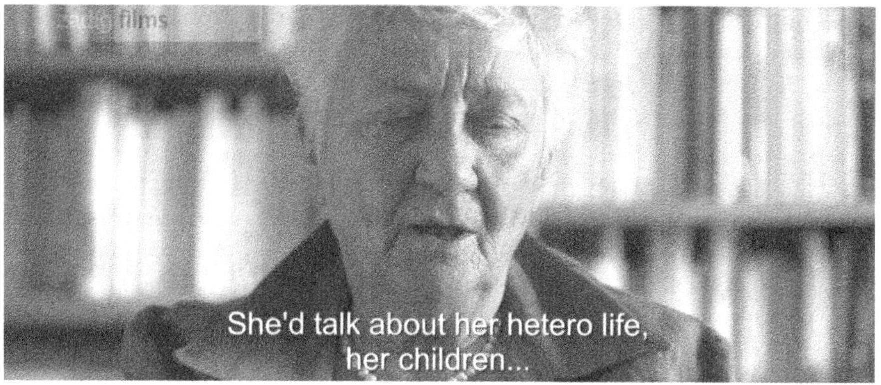

Figure 3.1 Monique Issele recounting a coming-out experience in *Les Invisibles* (Sébastien Lifshitz, 2012). Image © Courtesy of Zadig Films.

with almost all of them focusing their attentions on its 'feel-good' story of defiance and self-affirmation. Most eagerly convey how much they care about *Les Invisibles* and its interviewees, and thus project intensified investments in its subject matter (Barker 2006: 39). Many state that they chose *Les Invisibles* precisely because it was about older lesbians, gay men and bisexuals. The care they display thus transcends the imagined and real borders that separate and distinguish between peoples. Their investment might be described as a politically informed commitment to the film's values, but it is via their enthusiastic and candid projections of their affective attachment to the film and its interviewees, and their emphatic endorsements of what they characterise as the director's sensitivity, that the respondents align themselves with its perceived message about the need to give older lesbians, gay men and bisexuals a voice in visual culture.

A fuller analysis of the questionnaire responses has been published elsewhere (Waldron 2016), but it is worth bringing some of this out in this discussion. In response to *Les Invisibles*, Sarah, the forty-two-year-old white British security worker cited at the beginning of this chapter, affirms the power of community affiliation in transcending national, cultural, regional and linguistic borders in answer to the question about whether the director did a good job (see above citation). Sarah implicates herself within the community that she claims is depicted in *Les Invisibles*. Her choice of adjectives ('passionate', 'eloquent' and 'aware') conveys the intensity of her assertion of a 'shared emotional connection' with the interviewees in the film. Sarah thus exemplifies how films can be received from a position of perceived collective affiliation (as we saw in the case of *Les Témoins* in the context of its FIRE!! screening, in Chapter 2) although the quotation marks that hang around the term 'us' may convey some awareness of the dispersed, contingent and porous nature of that collective. Sarah's affirmation of community pride is neither impeded nor qualified by the film's setting, language, nor by the nationality or personal experiences of its interviewees. Transnational and transcultural LGBTQ community allegiance is the bond claimed as binding British viewer to French film.

In other cases, elements characterised as having prompted feelings of self-recognition are more intimate and less community-based. Personal experiences and romantic and erotic attractions in common with the film's interviewees are highlighted as reasons for expressions of self-similarity among some. Andrew, a sixty-six-year-old white British retired NHS manager living outside London, recalls 'I was born in 1946 and my (deceased) life-partner of 34 yrs in 1921 [so I] could identify with much of the "good-feel-factor" in the film as well as some of the negative aspects of growing up gay in 1960/70s'. Although he subtly criticises the portrayal of ageing among queers as 'utopian' he nonetheless claims to identify with the elderly male couple: 'one stated that as a young man he was only attracted to older men with grey/white hair . . . my partner was twenty-five years older who, in his eighties, needed help attaching his braces to trousers, which made me chuckle as that scene was played out in the film'. Intergenerational relationships and their impact on lived experience later on are thus framed as the nodes of identification, and these, once again, supersede any affiliation on national identity grounds.

In one instance, the encounter with *Les Invisibles* is portrayed as triggering an unanticipated engagement with a very intimate aspect of a respondent's own character and identity:

> I have never heard someone talking about falling in love and felt it could be me talking. I saw myself in these people. Whenever my parents would try to talk to me about sex I got embarrassed, but when these people spoke it felt natural, comfortable, and I wanted to hear them speak! I hated straight people trying to tell me what love would feel like one day.

This respondent declined to give a name, did not define themselves in gender terms or identify their occupation, although they did state that they were twenty-four, American and living in London. As this intensely personal response reveals, it is the candour with which the interviewees recount their romantic and sexual lives that is pinpointed as having driven their feelings of (self-)recognition. What is particularly striking is that, as this account suggests, the interviewees' frankness appeared to come as a surprise. The 'breaching of boundaries' and 'opening of new perspectives' that Barker describes as the consequences of such surprise in audience encounters with films (Barker 2006: 39 – see Introduction) are welcomed by this respondent, who writes that they recognise in this French-language film a crucial facet of themselves that they claim to have repressed while growing up. A French film is thus heralded as distinct from those coming from a respondent's culture of origin, but that difference is highlighted as the factor that facilitates their feelings of self-similarity or recognition. This viewer thus illustrates precisely how foreign-language films can offer people from 'elsewhere' alternative resources for understanding themselves, including their most intimate selves.

Others, however, pinpoint the perceived cultural specificity of *Les Invisibles* as the feature that attracted them. Paul, a fifty-year-old white British IT worker, states that he chose it because it was 'French and [a] documentary'. Nathan, a sixty-year-old white British retired lecturer, claims that he selected it because of his 'interest in French life'. Abigail, a seventy-year-old white British retired community worker from London, states that she loves 'French films' style'. Caroline, a sixty-four-year-old white British multimedia tutor, affirms that she is 'English, studying French, and attracted to French films'. On the surface, these responses might illustrate the lure of the 'foreign', the appeal of France as the home of specific cultural values and of a peculiar film culture. And yet, France and French cinema do not emerge from these responses as categorically 'other' because, while these viewers appear to seek out French films to encounter a different reality from the one they experience in their day-to-day lives, it is one that they claim represents a particular attraction for them, and, in some cases, aligns with their 'sense' of self. To express a particular liking for or interest in French cinema or 'life' projects a certain image in terms of (middle-)class status and (high) level of education, consonant with the profile of film festival attenders and of those who choose to watch documentaries but such responses also illustrate how the lines between the domestic and the foreign can be blurred in the reception of foreign-language films (and social identity formation), with the contexts of reception (including the localised and translated promotion of a film) and elements of the sense of LGBTQ community playing their part in this productive blurring.

An aspect that received almost unanimous praise from our respondents is the film's portrayal of LGBTQ history. In her work on memory and the Holocaust, Marianne Hirsch seeks 'to uncover and to restore experiences and life stories that might otherwise remain absent from the historical archive' (Hirsch 2012: 15). She is interested in '"post-memory"', which describes the relationship that the '"generation after"' bears to the 'personal, collective, and cultural trauma of those who came before' (5). There are obviously crucial differences between the history of LGBTQ emancipation and the experiences of Holocaust survivors and their offspring. Yet, young LGBTQ people, and those who have recently decided to define themselves as such, might be described as a 'postgeneration' (4) in that they are believed to assume their LGBTQ identity after periods of hardship, in which people were criminalised and pathologised because of their sexuality. However, members of this 'postgeneration' are commonly criticised for living out their sexuality in a vacuum, ignorant of the battles undertaken to secure their freedoms. The dangers of forgetting the traumas of past repression and the struggles of previous generations to secure the freedoms enjoyed today are thus recurrent concerns within community debates.

Implicit, though, within such views can be found a form of reversed ageism, in which younger LGBTQ people are framed as living for today, and lacking the political awareness and commitment of their community elders. Steve, a forty-nine-year-old white British town planner from Manchester, strongly articulates such an opinion, praising the fact that *Les Invisibles* 'made older LGBTQ people visible in a society that often marginalises older people and where the commercial gay scene is focused on the "young and beautiful"'. He commends the film as a 'reminder of the struggle by older LGBTQ people that has resulted in freedoms today, which are so often taken for granted by many'. Steve's reading evokes local tensions around the lifestyles and perceived priorities of LGBTQ people in his home city. He watched *Les Invisibles* at POUTfest (as discussed in Chapter 2), one of the few cultural events that constitute Manchester's annual Pride celebrations, which culminate in a three-day ticketed party centring on music stages and the many bars of the well-known 'gay' village. Here, then, we have a further example of how a film about queer identities and lifestyles from 'abroad' is taken up by a viewer 'elsewhere' as offering something they imply is unavailable to them in their home culture when they watch it and as offering a resource for self-making in political terms with which they distinguish themselves from other members of their community. Through his tenor and choice of vocabulary, Steve claims that the issues *Les Invisibles* raises – the invisibility of older queer people and need to record and recognise their pioneering advances and achievements – have significance well beyond France. His use of the term *reminder* nods to the perceived or alleged universality of the struggle; both the past and the need to represent it are characterised as affecting all LGBTQ people.

Similar issues arise in relation to a Spanish documentary, *Born Naked* (Andrea Esteban, 2012), on which we were able to gather responses from audiences at the London Lesbian and Gay Film Festival (on 23 March 2013) and the (non-LGBTQ) Manchester VIVA Spanish and Latin American Film Festival (on 15 March 2014), and it is worth briefly turning to this case before resuming our discussion of *Les Invisibles*. Here the focus is on a younger generation, as the synopsis for the London event (and the majority of responses) flags up:

> Twenty-something Spanish filmmakers Andrea and Paula [Alamilo] present a fascinating look at the lives of young queer women in Madrid, London and Berlin – cities they have both lived in and experienced first-hand. Using personal histories, beautifully animated sequences and interviews with the lesbian, queer and trans artists, activists and journalists they meet along their travels, the women present a picture of a vibrant and exciting European scene that takes in clubs, bars, magazines, art zines, Ladyfests and queer feminist squats. Through intimate interviews in parks, kitchens and basement bars, the women talk about shared experiences of coming out, falling in love, community building, challenging society's expectations, and how they feel about the label 'lesbian'. (BFI 2013: 21)

Of the thirty-six responses (from seventy-five questionnaires distributed) at the London event, twelve refer directly to the emphasis on younger women, two of these (who gave no names or consent to be quoted, but one fifty-eight years old) from a position of disappointment. The Manchester event, with twenty responses (from sixty questionnaires distributed) was not targeted at an LGBTQ audience; however, it was attended by eight respondents who explicitly self-identify as lesbian, gay or queer in their responses. All these, and three other respondents – so eleven out of twenty – comment on the emphasis on younger women, with four (all over forty-seven years old) regretting the absence of an older lesbian perspective. In London, Helen, a thirty-six-year-old white British nurse, says that she was surprised that 'things are similar for those much younger than me'; Patricia, a fifty-one-year-old white British management consultant, expresses identification with aspects of the film 'from when I was younger', while Rupah, a forty-two-year-old mixed white-Indian-Caribbean charity worker, says, 'I remember that time in my own life – twenties – these discussions'; and from a more political, less personal, perspective, Ronald, a fifty-five-year-old white British-New Zealander who gave no occupation, writes that he identified with the film through seeing 'a different generation facing the same issues'. In Manchester, Mary, a fifty-three-year-old white British retired nurse who identifies as gay, writes that she was surprised by 'younger lesbians encountering same prejudices as me'. These responses show the presence of a historicised sense of community and of continuity and solidarity, underlying the 'vibrant and exciting' elements rather conventionally highlighted by the programme note, and channelled through generational difference. The transgenerational identification and the surprise of these older LGBTQ people that those younger than themselves still suffer discrimination today illustrates the disparity between expectations and reality. There is a strong contrast between what these viewers anticipate and what the lives of the younger LGBTQ people depicted in *Born Naked* are actually like. Their implied assumptions appear to coincide with Steve's view, but their responses challenge any received idea that intolerance is confined to another time (and, indeed, space).

To pursue some of these issues further and via more interactive methods, we conducted a focus group discussion on *Les Invisibles* at Manchester's Lesbian and Gay Foundation on 11 March 2015. This was an activity linked to a season of LGBTQ films from Europe that we had been screening for users of the Foundation since October 2014. Although many people signed up to the event, only five turned up, and one left before the film had finished. The four participants included: Brenner, a thirty-seven-year-old white Danish genderqueer PhD student from Copenhagen; Damla, a twenty-seven-year-old Turkish female PhD student living in Manchester; Tom, a thirty-year-old white British male lobbyist, also living in Manchester; and Tariq, a thirty-three-year-old Pakistani unemployed male living in Rochdale. Tariq was a regular user of the Foundation, unlike the other three participants, and disappeared for a while during the screening to attend one of the Foundation's social groups. The group's general level of education is very high; beyond thesis students Brenner and Damla, Tom has a Master's degree and Tariq is educated to degree level. A surface interpretation of their comments might suggest that their level of studies informs the ways in which they talk about *Les Invisibles* and is reaffirmed through their responses. And yet, closer inspection of the focus group interventions reveals a more complex interplay between objective discernment and expressions of subjective self-proximity.

On two occasions, Brenner mentioned the fact that their PhD is on 'different people's accounts of their experiences' and specified the identities of those people as 'trans'. At the same time, Brenner also declares, again twice, that this was their third viewing of *Les Invisibles* and enthusiastically hails it as 'really extraordinary'. This ambivalence between expressing specialised knowledge and articulating the film's emotional effects returns throughout Brenner's responses. They tactfully dismiss the question asking whether the film is true to life and add 'I think it's not so interesting about if it's accurate, if it was really what they were feeling or experiencing or something like that, but er (.) but more exactly like . . . what kinds of stories are they telling and how, what are they feeling now that they are telling it, what do they want to do with the way that they're telling it and what does the director want to tell us'. Brenner then mentions, without being prompted, the significance of the film's form to its meanings, which, Brenner alleges, is 'as important as, er, as the question about like er how, how close is it to their experiences'. Here, Brenner refers to some of the scenic pauses mentioned above and shows awareness of what John Corner, drawing on Nichols (1991), terms the 'logics of exposition' (including 'direct and indirect' address, synchronised and non-synchronised sound, 'narrative and expositional development' and 'strategies of sequence construction and linking') (Corner 2008: 17).

Corner's interest is in revealing the 'illusionism' (16) with which documentaries tend to address audiences or how they create an impression of 'truth' and 'reality' through those 'logics of exposition'. Brenner's attention to form, however, does not translate into a critique of the film's truth claims. On the contrary, Brenner projects intense investment in *Les Invisibles* and its interviewees (Brenner maintains at one point that they were not bored even though it was their third viewing of the film). Brenner describes the personal histories of the individual stories as 'really touching' and highlights how 'you can kind of . . . mirror your own experience . . . and be inspired' and adding 'I love . . . that it's so many old people'. In response to the question asking whether they had been surprised by anything in the film, Brenner talks about having 'really enjoyed . . . the whole story about the housewife and then in her forties suddenly she has this er, er flourishing love life'. Brenner's comments exemplify how an 'aesthetic disposition' (Bourdieu 1979: iv) – perhaps informed by their studies and specialism – and an emotional connection can merge in audience responses. Although not a fan in the purest sense, Brenner illustrates Henry

Jenkins's observation that 'it is exactly those moments where the language of aesthetics allows fans to talk about feeling or emotion that breaks down . . . Bourdieu's notion of aesthetic distance as bound up in high art' (Jenkins 2006a: 23). This diverges from Tom, who tends to adopt a more fixed external perspective. While he qualifies the film's optimism about love as projecting a 'really powerful image', he does not implicate himself in the issues raised by *Les Invisibles*, preferring, in answer to the question on identification, to limit his declared empathy to unspecified universal emotions. Moreover, Tom postulates that the director's personal/political agenda is discernible, thus displaying a degree of awareness of the 'illusionism' to which Corner refers: 'maybe the agenda comes more when you're cutting it together and, er, the director starts creating a bit of a narrative er through the editing process'.

Brenner's enthusiasm may well be related to their investment in their field of research; while they do not confirm that they work in oral history, their description of their thesis strongly suggests that this is the case. Moreover, they describe *Les Invisibles* at the beginning of the discussion as a 'kind of oral history of the LGBT history'. This may be why Brenner nuances their response when talking about whether the film is true to life: personal accounts of the past are the very subjects of oral historians' research, as mentioned. Brenner is not alone in defending personalised memories of completed events; Tom claims that he initially questioned the veracity of the accounts presented in *Les Invisibles*, but then observes: 'as you get older your memories do tend to simplify . . . as time passes, the, what was a very complex situation tends to boil down into fairly clearly defined feelings or situations'. Yet, Brenner does not seek explanations in the same way that Tom does, and, perhaps more importantly, Brenner's expression of emotional connection could be a means of affirming and reaffirming their allegiance to a sense of a transnational collective LGBT identity: Brenner is the only respondent who really emphasises LGBT issues (twice) and who highlights the importance of 'the' LGBT history, and, as mentioned, they define themselves in non-normative gender terms and work with trans subjects. In Brenner's responses, then, cross-cultural political affinities, in terms of the politics of both gender and desire, merge with the projection of a strong emotional connection and a declared intellectual investment in a specific approach to history and identity.

This is not to argue, though, that Brenner claims to identify with the interviewees. On the contrary, Brenner is careful not to give this impression, although Brenner cites differences in lifestyles rather than national identity or culture as reasons. Brenner mentions France only once in relation to the LGBT history depicted and implies that this history forms part of a shared transnational past. Interestingly, though, Brenner, perhaps inadvertently, makes the implicit distinction between a progressive West and a regressive East. After referring to the different challenges depicted in *Les Invisibles*, Brenner recalls 'I started thinking also about some of my friends . . . from different parts of the world, like er Iran or Turkey or China . . . what kinds of lives people can have in these different kinds of . . . settings also if they are er, LG, LGBT people'. Where the film portrays closeted lives as part of the past in France and in the French provinces, Brenner implies that similar repressions are now unfolding in the countries they mention. Brenner's allusions to Iran, Turkey and China as places in which LGBT – and we could add queer – people are still repressed today could be said to illustrate, as Jon Binnie and Christian Klesse remark, that 'contemporary discourses around transnational LGBTQ politics within Europe frequently reproduce Orientalist discourses' (Binnie and Klesse 2012: 584). For Binnie and Klesse, focusing on how Central and Eastern Europe are perceived within Western LGBTQ political collectives, such discourses 'construct countries and regions . . . as backward and temporally delayed' (584). Beyond what might be perceived by some as an oversimplification of sexuality as it is experienced in non-Western countries, the problem with the view that discrimination and repression now belong to other national spaces is that it assumes a linear genealogy of LGBTQ emancipation that can be universally applied in the West, something that the anti-same-sex marriage demonstrations in France, which occurred around the time *Les Invisibles* was being made and released, contradicts.

However, a tangible sense of greater hardship attached to certain cultures, both foreign and diasporic, exists. A material awareness of this actuality perhaps informs the comments of Damla, who, as mentioned, comes from Turkey, one of the countries Brenner lists. She affirms some 'political identification' with Thérèse's story about performing clandestine abortions in the France of the 1960s and 1970s because 'something similar' is unfolding in her native city of Istanbul. In fact, Damla conveys envy, aspiration and even projected identification, both in relation to Thérèse's political determination and will – 'I told myself that I . . . I wanna have that sort of story to tell um when I'm at that age' – and of Pierrot's relaxed attitude towards life and sex: 'I wanna be that man'. For Tariq, who, we recall, is from Pakistan, the engagement with LGBTQ history in *Les Invisibles* serves as a 'great lesson' because '[the interviewees] faced so many difficulties' and 'nobody helped [them] so they tried to stand up for [themselves]'. Tariq frames the interviewees as other, but nonetheless nods to the transnational pertinence of their experiences by emphasising the didactic qualities of the film.

Early on in the discussion, Brenner alludes to the film's impact in potentially breaking down barriers in terms of physical intimacy and sex among older people, commenting that it 'speaks to the taboo [that] old people don't have sex or I mean they can't be, have alternative sexualities or like main, not mainstream lives'. *Las ventanas abiertas* (see Introduction) also features, among a range of different themes (including nursing or residential care for LGBTQ people as mentioned), frank talk about sex among two of its four interviewees. *Las ventanas abiertas* appeared on the festival circuit after we had completed our empirical research (it was shown at the LesGaiCineMadrid in November 2014 and Des images aux mots in February 2015 and we received a reserved copy in April 2015). Combining testimonies from two older lesbians in France with those of two in Spain, *Las ventanas abiertas* provides accounts of ageing and of past experience from both of our core countries. LesGaiCineMadrid provides the following synopsis:

> In Madrid and in Paris, Boti, Empar, Micheline and Jocelyne, four lesbian women in their seventies, tell of their fears, their desires, their differences . . . They are still active, or activists, and will not give in to the passage of time; they refuse to be pushed aside because of their age. They look at others, and at society, with curiosity. They live their everyday lives to the fullest, taking advantage of all opportunities. They show us their world, their experience, and their problems, and talk about their relationship with age. Beyond the taboos, they reflect on their loves, past and present, because their love-lives and sex-lives are not yet over. (LesGaiCineMad 2014b)

The French couple Micheline and Jocelyne (Joss) articulate in the most candid terms their continued pleasures in physical erotic exchange well into their old

Figure 3.2 Poster for *Las ventanas abiertas* (Michèle Massé, 2014) designed by Emmanuelle Janvier. Image reproduced with permission of Java Films and Michèle Massé).

age. Micheline recalls her desire, at the age of sixty-nine, to have sex with another woman: 'je veux crier, je veux qu'on me griffe dans le dos ('I want to scream, I want to feel someone's nails digging into my back'). She talks of the pleasures and power that can be gained from bringing her partner to orgasm and jokes about approaching the various sexual positions that she and Joss had witnessed in watching *La Vie d'Adèle* (Abdellatif Kechiche 2013; discussed in Chapter 5). Boti (García Rodrigo), by contrast, says she no longer has an active sex life (and in this recalls Monique in *Les Invisibles* who talks about how she relinquished love at the age of fifty because of fear that she could no longer seduce women). She talks about the necessity of coming to terms with no longer feeling able to flirt, and about the importance instead of the activist work she shares with other younger volunteers and workers (the legacy of her earlier presidencies of COGAM, the Lesbian, Gay, Transgender & Bisexual Collective of Madrid, and now of FELGTB, the National Federation of Lesbian, Gay, Bisexual and Transgender Associations). Empar (Pineda), perhaps drawing on her long history of high-profile lesbian feminist activism, acknowledges that passion wanes with age and that sex inevitably requires more time and effort, but nonetheless warns against falling into a false sense of security through which, by confining sex to the past, we forget the pleasures of sexual intimacy.

The opinions and accounts expressed in *Les Invisibles* and *Las ventanas abiertas* key into the ways in which desire among older people have been approached in culture more broadly. As the above discussions reveal, some of the films' interviewees exemplify instances of positive ageing in which getting older does not necessarily foreclose sexual desire. It is because *Les Invisibles* emphasises such positive ageing – in which, as Lynne Segal notes, 'experiences of loneliness, loss, envy, fear or anger' as well as issues of 'frailty, dependence and cognitive deterioration' (Segal 2014: 93) are downplayed – that, according to the responses we collected, it is so warmly received by its audience. Of course, both *Les Invisibles* and *Las ventanas abiertas* confine sexual experience to verbalised accounts. *80 Egunean* could be said to go further in showing (rather than recounting) erotic intimacy between two women, even if this too stops short of actually portraying the sexual encounter. This film was shown at the Cinémarges festival in Bordeaux on 1 May 2011 and is described in that festival's archived synopsis as follows:

> Axun, 70 ans, mariée, mène une vie bien rangée, dans la province de San Sebastian. Elle est appelée par l'hôpital pour prendre soin d'un proche dont elle est la seule famille. Dans la même chambre, un autre patient est veillé par Maité, lesbienne baroudeuse devenue professeure de piano. Elles se sont perdues de vue depuis plus de 50 ans mais elles réalisent qu'enfants, elles étaient les meilleures amies du monde. Egrenées sur 80 jours, les visites quotidiennes à l'hôpital deviennent le prétexte à de troublantes retrouvailles, au cours desquelles d'anciens sentiments resurgissent . . . Après *Ander* de Roberto Caston, le cinéma basque nous

livre un deuxième bijou, avec cette histoire délicate traitant à la fois de l'autonomie des femmes, de la fluctuation des identités, et surtout de l'amour – qui n'a pas d'âge! (Cinémarges 2015)

(Axun [Itziar Aizpuru] is seventy years old, married and leads a structured life, in the region of San Sebastian. The hospital telephones her to come to look after a close one of whom she is the only family member. In the same room, another patient is being looked after by Maité [Mariasun Pagoaga], an adventurous lesbian who has become a piano teacher. They have not seen each other for more than fifty years but they realise that, as children, they were the best friends in the world. Split across eighty days, the daily hospital visits become the pretext for troubling reunions, during which old feelings resurface . . . Following *Ander* by Roberto Caston, Basque cinema gives us a second jewel, with this delicate story that treats, at the same time, women's autonomy, fluctuating identities and above all love – which does not have an age!)

The final words of this review encapsulate the key issue that *80 Egunean* depicts: love and physical intimacy in old age. After kissing Maite during a picnic on the tiny island of Santa Clara off San Sebastián, Axún is ashamed, but she soon succumbs to her feelings and desires when the two women share an intimate moment together in Maite's lounge. In this scene, the camera lingers on Axún and Maite as they embrace and cuddle, hovering closely over their skin, visibly marked by the signs of ageing, before cutting to Axún waking up the following morning, their assumed sexual encounter contained and rendered invisible by an ellipsis. Despite this reunion, the film's coda is less optimistic; after staying by the bedside of her husband Juan Marí (José Ramón Argoita) because of his terminal illness, Axún bumps into Maite outside the hospital, where the two former lovers exchange a few words, before, seemingly, moving on with their day and lives.

We organised a focus group discussion on *80 Egunean* during the Flare festival in London on 17 March 2013. It was held in a basement training room in the British Film Institute. As always, we screened the film and then put our basic set of questions to the group. The group consisted of: Ruby, sixty-six, white, female, born in the USA, retired; Joss, twenty-six, white, genderqueer, British, bicycle mechanic; Carolyn, thirty-eight, white, British-Scottish, female, did not declare occupation; Zadie, no age supplied, black, British, female, dancer and choreographer; Liz, forty-one, white, British-Scottish, female, researcher; Oxana, thirty-two, white, Spanish-Basque, female, photographer. The project's research assistant, Ros, knew Joss and Carolyn, although she had not seen them for some time before the discussion, she had met Zadie once and occasionally bumped into Ruby at gigs. She had never met Oxana, who was a friend of a friend, or Liz. Liz and Oxana knew each other well and were possibly in a relationship. Carolyn barely participated and both she and Zadie had to leave

Figure 3.3 Axun (Itziar Aizpuru) and Maite (Mariasun Pagoaga) on their island picnic in *80 Egunean* (Jon Garaño and Jose Mari Goenaga, 2010). Image © IRUSOIN, S.A.

after twenty minutes because of prior commitments. As a whole (possibly with the exception of Carolyn), the group seemed to appreciate the film. The discussion flowed feely with minimal prompting required from the researchers, which can be seen as a positive sign of the relaxed atmosphere (see Morrison 1998: 214), although we maintained control in a hands-off way by ensuring that we covered the themes contained within our basic list of questions.

The issue of representing sex and sexuality among older people arises twice and is broached for the first time by Ruby, who asks whether the rest of the group thought that Axún and Maite actually 'made it'. However, rather than answer her question, most of the others shift to a discussion of ethics – that is, whether Axún had made the correct choice in staying at her husband's side after he announced his terminal illness. The film's obvious moral dilemma, how an older married heterosexual woman should deal with her romantic attraction to another woman, supersedes the question it raises more implicitly: how far can it go in representing erotic attraction and fulfilment between two older women? Ruby describes the characters as 'very cautious', which is then diametrically opposed by Liz, for whom their actions 'ring true': 'it was exactly how I imagine that kind of thing to progress, if somebody were married'. Joss concurs with Ruby's stance and insists 'I felt like it . . . it would have been more challenging if they'd had like a proper sex scene or something'. Liz interjects, stating that 'I don't think you need a sex scene . . . I mean, maybe that's good because it's good to see older people having sex and being normal like everybody else, of course, but do you need a sex scene?' At this stage, *80 Egunean* is not framed as culturally distinct, its themes and implications thus taken as having relevance to these viewers who reside in a very different environment from that depicted in the film.

This brief exchange reveals some of the issues that representations invoke for viewers who may perceive themselves to be affected by a film, to differing degrees of intensity, thus illustrating Barker's point about the importance of salience for the ways in which we watch films (2016: 153 – see Introduction). As seen, *80 Egunean* presents a sensitive depiction of a romantic encounter between two mature women for whom sex can be fraught with insecurities and anxieties. Yet, it is the oldest and youngest members of the group for whom this is qualified as timid and thus limited – Ruby saying so somewhat tentatively and Joss more forcefully. There may be less at stake for Liz than for Ruby in the ways in which films approach desire among older lesbians; as mentioned, it seemed as if she was in a relationship with Oxana and she was younger than Ruby, whose age is not too distant from that of the protagonists. Moreover, Ruby displays the strength of her personal connection to the themes by referring to the characters as if they were real people. That Joss appears to echo Ruby's frustrations that *80 Egunean* did not go far enough illustrates, of course, that these views are not dependent on a deterministic association between the life experiences of the viewer and those of the characters.

Joss amplifies the extent of their position as 'interested' or 'affected' by the themes by declaring, early on, 'I could empathise with all of those characters and I got really involved with them'. In choosing 'empathise' rather than 'identify' Joss maintains some distance. As Carl Plantinga has written, identification suggests the 'losing of the self in the other, whereby our identity as a separate individual momentarily becomes lost or weakened as we identify with a character on the screen' (Plantinga 1999: 244). He prefers the term engagement, which, he notes, 'is broader and more neutral' and 'allows for empathy and antipathy, sympathy and indifference, and certainly implies no melding of minds or identities' (244). Empathy 'consists of a capacity or disposition to know, feel, and to respond congruently to what another is feeling, and the process of doing so' (245). Joss might choose empathy because of the age gap, perceived national, cultural or linguistic distinctions or because of an ethical respect for the uniqueness of individual experience.

Both Joss and Ruby eventually state that they empathise mostly with Maite, the city-dwelling lesbian in the film's central same-sex romantic coupling, which, in simplistic terms, allows them to affiliate themselves with an urban lesbian identity that resonates across borders. However, as seen, Joss avows an ability to understand and feel connected to all of the perspectives, adding 'even though it felt like . . . like not much was expressed emotionally . . . it felt so emotional'. Affect, then, is the declared trigger of this capacity to empathise, which is then echoed and developed by Liz who pinpoints the heterosexual husband as another character with whom she felt some proximity: 'they're all (.) characters I can easily recognise and empathise with, including the husband, you know, I mean, it's not his fault that it's traditional . . . we live in a world where things change and people want different things and you can't communicate'. Liz's tone is conciliatory and she seems careful not to be seen to affiliate herself too simplistically with any specific community or delineated collective viewpoint.

For Zadie, the film's rather strange approach to race and ethnicity seems to function as a barrier to empathy and also appears to undermine her pleasures in watching the film. She recalls the scene in which two older women make racist comments: 'it was like this weird bit of racism with like no accountability, no supported narrative . . . it just wasn't relevant, didn't make any sense that the film with completely, like white characters, in a completely conservative place, and then to bring up this racist statement, and then it doesn't have any consequences, I was just like, well that's bullshit'. The point Zadie raises is absolutely crucial; while *80 Egunean*'s whole narrative allows audiences to understand reignited lesbian attraction in old age by constructing a whole narrative around it, it leaves this casually racist exchange hanging in the air, as if to say that it does not merit such careful exploration. While perhaps an inadvertent omission or exploited as a marker of narrow provincial morality, the difference in approach nonetheless nods to the predominance of white bodies in LGBTQ visual representations and, more controversially still, the added value attached and ascribed to white people in Western culture, including LGBTQ culture. This chimes with the response to their viewing of *Les Invisibles* at the March 2013 London Lesbian and Gay Film Festival by Rupah, a twenty-seven-year-old British-Indian social worker from London, who commented 'I wonder perhaps if there were a similar doc about older, queer people of colour, would I have identified more?' Here discussants from ethnic minority backgrounds articulate a valid critique about how films approach race and ethnicity, although, in the case of Zadie, much more emphatically. It is interesting that the subject of race or ethnicity is not raised by any of the other respondents. In the case of Rupah and Zadie, race and ethnicity mitigate or temper feelings and expressions of cross-cultural self-recognition and community allegiance based on LGBTQ identities and politics.

In response to Zadie's comment, Oxana simply (perhaps conveniently) states 'I just kind of switched off for a second and I didn't get what they said'. Allegiance here may connect to regional identity, given that Oxana is from the Basque region in Spain depicted in *80 Egunean*. At various intervals, Oxana projects herself as an authority on the local customs and cultures portrayed. She 'confirms' that *80 Egunean* is true to life with regards to its specific cultural context. Of the family relationships between Axún, Juan Marí and their daughter Josune (Ana Gabarain), Oxana observes 'it's like a typical Basque family from the countryside . . . where everything is so traditional . . . there's all these pride issues all the time . . . it's just this pride always kind of (.) kind of head against the wall'. While the discussion as a whole serves as an example of transnational reception, Oxana, though she views it in a transnational context, occasionally forecloses expressions of cross-cultural empathy, sympathy and understanding by the others, by reclaiming the film as a locally distinct product.

Liz engages Zadie and attempts to explain the inclusion of the racist exchange by the two women as a parody of rural mentalities. However, she then likens

80 Egunean to the kind of representations transmitted in Britain thirty years ago. In this part of the discussion, familiar stereotypes about Spanish society are circulated: 'Spain is sort of thirty years behind us in terms of, umm, gender roles . . . it's because it's a Catholic country . . . this could have been Shirley Valentine thirty years ago . . . it's Catholic, it's conservative, it's rural'. Spain is projected as timelessly traditional compared to Britain. Moreover, despite her close associations with Oxana, Liz reduces the Basque region as representative of Spain as a nation. And yet, once again, she changes tack, warning against the kind of observation she makes elsewhere: 'I don't think it's fair for us to say, oh, well that's just because Spain is kind of backwards or because it's Catholic because I think Britain's (.) very similar in lots of ways. I mean not living here in London, but pretty much anywhere else in the UK there's a lot of people that age or older trapped in that sort of (.) traditional set-up'. Revisiting and revising previous stances is commonplace in focus group discussions, as individuals are called upon to respond to the observations of others (see Waldron 2009: 194–5). However, one preconception replaces another, in that it is the British provinces, and no longer Spain, that emerge as symbolising retrograde views in terms of non-normative sexuality among older people. Where Liz's vision of Spain was expressed through a comparison with Britain, her view of morality according to space is affirmed through a comparison of the British capital with its regions.

Lives Driven, and Constrained, by Passion:
L'Inconnu du lac (*El desconocido del lago*; *Stranger by the Lake*) (Alain Giraudie, 2013), *Notre paradis* (*Our Paradise*) (Gaël Morel, 2011), *Eastern Boys* (Robin Campillo, 2013) and *El sexo de los ángeles* (*Le Sexe des anges*; *The Sex of Angels*) (Xavier Villaverde, 2012)

One of the most well known and widely released of the films for which we were able to gather responses was *L'Inconnu du lac* (Alain Giraudie, 2013), and it is also one which uses a small and intimate part of provincial life to dramatise same-sex desire and to amplify certain themes of significance to LGBTQ audiences. As will be explored in Chapter 5, audiences and critics alike have been drawn to the film for its curious mixture of fantastical erotic thriller and slow cinema style, in particular its aestheticisation of the pleasures and banalities of gay cruising in the out-of-the-way outdoors (here the Sainte-Croix lake near the Gorges du Verdon in south-east France). We gathered completed questionnaires following screenings of the film in Bilbao on 25 January (seventeen responses) during the 2014 Zinegoak festival (where the film was shown as part of the festival's ongoing collaboration with the Institut Français, Bilbao), London on 30 March 2014 (eighteen responses) during the BFI's Lesbian and Gay Film Festival, and Manchester on 20 August 2014 (twelve responses) at a Pride Fringe and POUTfest screening of the film at Cornerhouse. At the Bilbao festival one of the respondents wrote that he had selected the film on the basis of its having won a prize at the Seville European Film Festival 2013 ('un festival hetero-general'; 'a hetero-generalist festival') (Salvador, forty-three-year-old male unemployed worker), one because of an apparent liking for French cinema, and three for its subject matter (specifically, cruising), while others were attracted by festival publicity. At the London LLGF, one attended the screening at the recommendation of some French friends, another, Tim, a fifty-five-year-old white male civil servant, described having been attracted to *L'Inconnu du lac* by the impression given to him by the festival publicity of a 'racy' film with 'gay sexual content', and the rest of the respondents put their attendance down to publicity or word of mouth more generally. At Manchester two stated that they had been drawn to the film because of the Pride Fringe framing, and two wrote that they had come explicitly because of an interest in foreign film.

The Zinegoak programme presented *L'Inconnu du lac* (the English text translated closely from Basque and Castilian originals) in this way:

> A crystal-clear lake situated next to a forest, ideal for 'cruising', it's where Franck meets two mysterious strangers: the smug, static Henri ['impasible e ingreido' in the Castilian], with whom he talks daily in what is a friendship/platonic love, and the attractive Michel, with whom he falls in love, ignoring the obvious danger involved in getting close to him. Franck makes a conscious decision to see this dangerous attraction through to the end, in a summer marked by that stranger (Henri, Michel) at the lake. Guiraudie's work with tempo, space, and light is simply perfect. It comes as no surprise that *Cahiers du Cinéma* magazine chose it as the best film of 2013. (Zinegoak 2014: 15)

Figure 3.4 Franck (Pierre Deladonchamps) and Michel (Christophe Paou) in *L'Inconnu du lac* (Alain Giraudie, 2013).

The programme note's division of the stranger of the film's title into two (Henri, Michel) corresponds to the elements of erotic thriller and intimate psychological drama, and maps well on to our respondents' modes of engaging with the film as described in the questionnaires. Twenty-five (out of forty-seven responses overall) say that the solitary Henri (Patrick d'Assumçao) was their favourite character and a further twelve identify the scenes between Franck (Pierre Deladonchamps) and Henri as their preferred ones. In Bilbao, Fernando, a forty-year-old male businessman identifying his ethnicity as 'citizen', makes an interesting assumption about Henri – physically much less in shape than Franck or Michel (Christophe Paou), and in early middle age – in attributing his loneliness to his age: 'me he identificado con la soledad de ciertas personas al llegar a cierta edad' ('I identified with the loneliness that people feel when they get to a certain age'); in fact, Henri's backstory has other possible causes for his reticence and desire to remain seated apart from the other men on the beach – a recently failed, though consummated, heterosexual marriage and a barely started, incoherent process of coming out (as bisexual, it seems) which has led to a form of emotional withdrawal and a defensive self-identification as asexual. Fernando's response, in attributing Henri's loneliness first to his age, is attuned to dominant assumptions about age (as well as body type) in recent gay culture in general and no less so in Spain (Fouz-Hernàndez and Martínez-Expósito 2007: 111–34), despite the notable success there of the less ageist and bodyist, if still potentially exclusivist and normalising, 'bear' scene (Sáez 2003; 2013).

In the Bilbao responses, loneliness is cited in four cases as particularly well portrayed and as linked to anonymous sexual encounters (rather than age); in London, Adam, a thirty-one-year-old white male actor, states that the film was true to life in that it 'commented well on the nature of loneliness and how we try to fill the void in the wrong places' and links this, answering the questions on favourite character and scene, to Henri's kindness, honesty and how 'he sacrificed himself for his friend'. Taking a different, more positive perspective in Manchester, John, a thirty-year-old white British secondary teacher, focuses on Franck and says he identified with him as 'a good guy simultaneously looking for love and meaning to life', suggesting too that this was 'surely identifiable to much of the audience?'. John's response clearly has to do with an aspect of the 'shared emotional connection' underpinning the sense of community constructed in certain Western cultures (McMillan and Chavis 1986: 13, 15) (see Introduction). For John, Franck's pivotal position between two forms of intimacy (and his role, as it were, in two generic forms in one film) makes him an agent in everyday human negotiations of feeling, belonging and identity. Such basic ethical and philosophical issues arising from viewings of the film, and from its narrative trope of open-air cruising, are returned to in Chapter 5.

When the focus switches to the far less everyday encounter between Franck and Michel, the film's sex scenes are mentioned as favourites or convincing and true to life by five respondents in Bilbao (with one, however, judging the treatment too explicit), but only two in London, one of them being the aforementioned Tim who described how this 'racy' film with 'gay sexual content' had appealed to him. In London, three respondents described their surprise at the directness of the sex scenes; in Manchester five expressed the same view, with four using the term 'graphic'. These contrasting responses simply indicate range and variety across different screening contexts, of course, rather than being able to point us to reactions distinctly conditioned by the cultural geographies of these variously multicultural locations. The film as heightened erotic thriller strikes our respondents variously as exciting, engaging or disconcerting; as a drama of quieter human emotion, it is cast by some as poignant and true. Combining these views, in London, Saraiva, a thirty-nine-year-old Portuguese male artist who identifies his ethnicity as 're-mix', asserts that he identified with all the characters because 'I am queer' – suggesting either a pluralistic or a transnational understanding of queer identity (or both), and matched verbatim by a response to the Manchester VIVA Festival showing of *Born Naked*, Phil, a fifty-seven-year-old British male carer, who identifies his ethnicity as English. Also in London, Aldo, a thirty-seven-year-old white Italian male graduate student, qualifies the way the film dealt with its themes as 'realistic, queer, not conventional'.

That suggestive pairing of realistic – in the sense of being true, for Adam and for Saraiva, to queer life – and not conventional connects in our study with reactions to another erotic thriller enhanced with psychological and social realist observation, *Notre paradis* (Gaël Morel, 2011), screened at the 18th Madrid LesGaiCineMad LGBTQ film festival on 2, 3 and 10 November 2012. This film's detailed attention to marginal, precarious, and extreme situations and feelings makes it very much not a conventional version of an otherwise familiar gay narrative premise – the flowering of love between differently aged men in the face of adversity yet in picturesque circumstances. Its challenging way with genre-bending also queers it – lets it defy labels and fixed reactions; helps it blur and distract the desiring gaze of viewers and characters alike – as love story, thriller, sex-work chronicle and tale of lost youth and splendour combined. The festival programme synopsis described the film like this:

> Vassili es un chapero entrado en años con instintos asesinos. Una noche se encuentra con un joven inconsciente en el bosque de Boulogne y se lo lleva a casa. Se hacen amantes y cómplices, convirtiéndose en una pareja que se prostituye robando y matando a sus clientes hasta que no le queda otra opción que huir de París. (LesGaiCineMad 2012: 45)

> (Vassili is a male prostitute who is getting on in years, and with killer instincts. One night he finds a young man unconscious in the Bois de Boulogne and takes him home with him. They become lovers and

Figure 3.5 Vassili (Stéphane Rideau) and Angelo (Dimitri Durdaine) passing under the Pont de la Concorde, Paris, in *Notre paradis* (Gaël Morel, 2011). Image reproduced © Courtesy of Alfama Films Production.

accomplices, working together to rob and to kill their clients until the day comes when they've no other choice than to flee Paris.)

The film, then, shares with *L'Inconnu du lac* (which it predates) the theme of extreme violence as linked to casual sexual encounters and the combination of masculine physical attractiveness with psychotic instability. In as much as Angelo (Dimitri Durdaine, the young man of the synopsis) is the blond and smooth-skinned innocent to Vassili's (Stéphane Rideau) swarthy looks and darker moods, Angelo anticipates the Franck of the later film (although Vassili, unlike Michel, is not set on killing the one he loves). Following Morel's own testimony, Rees-Roberts (2008: 30) has noted that Morel is part of a 'French cinematic tradition of poetic naturalism' admixed with a 'directorial desire for the marginalised populations he chooses to film', and later describes *Notre paradis* as furnishing a 'dystopian vision of gay male sexuality' which is 'brutally disturbing' (2015: 444). A particularly revealing aspect of this Spanish audience's view of this French film and its rich associations is an interest shown in the disruptive potential of lyrically passionate same-sex male desire in a context of a celebration of the marginal and of age difference.

Among thirty-seven questionnaire responses (out of a combined audience of approximately two hundred), thirteen answer that the film is not 'true-to-life'; but among the nine unequivocal 'yes' responses one makes a connection between realism and extreme situations, another links the inner conflicts of the characters to the film's realism, and Jesús, a forty-two-year-old white male Spanish television cameraman, says 'Sí, porque el asesino vive en otra realidad, hay muchos asi' ('Yes, because the killer lives in a different reality – there are a lot like that'). Overall, the respondents point to perspectives on: the construction of both reactionary and progressive forms of erotic bonds between men in a context of generational difference; links between local and transnational collective memory; and resistance to dominant modes of representation through engagement with marginal characters and narrative topics. Seven of those responding indicated that they were in the twenty-to-twenty-nine age range, eight in the thirty-to-thirty-nine age range, eleven in the forty-to-forty-nine and three in the fifty-to-fifty-nine. Six declined or omitted to indicate their age. However, a majority of the responses use the word *niño*, *chico* or *joven* (boy, lad, youngster) in talking about Angelo, suggesting anyway that awareness of the age difference is part of an expressed appreciation of the dynamics of the film across the age range of the respondents. As will be seen shortly, this appreciation is sometimes grounded simply in immediate erotic fantasy and visual pleasure, but José María, a forty-two-year-old white Spanish male researcher, describes Angelo as attractive and his favourite character, 'quizás porque me habría gustado que en mi época de adolescente me hubieran pasado algunas cosas que le pasan a el, como enamorarse y ser correspondido' ('perhaps because when I was an adolescent I'd have liked some of the things that happen to him to have happened to me, like falling in love and being loved back'); and Rubén, a forty-one-year-old white Spanish male engineer, claims tempered proximity, identifying 'ligeramente con la ilusión de proyección de futuro en la relación afectiva homosexual' ('a bit with the dream of a future life together based on a homosexual affective relationship'). These two responses to the film, as well as Morel's affectively charged interest in the poetry of the marginal past (yet insistently present), map on to wider questions of queer temporality in academic circulation since the early 2000s (Edelman 2004; Muñoz 2009; Jones 2013; Yekani et al. 2013), and in most queer lovers' and activists' minds since long before that. On the one hand, the fictional characters Angelo and Vassili prompt José María and Rubén to imagine a place for their own personal experience in a real shared history. On the other hand, Rubén's comment also has utopian romantic fantasy (much encouraged by the film's presentation of marginal exceptionality) as the germ of an engagement with the question of securing a queer future tipped more towards the personal than the political. Both respondents, however, locate in the film some figuration of a queer genealogy to which they subscribe. Both Rubén and, particularly, José María use discursive frames that convey a particular emotional investment in this kind of representation – language that, in José María's case specifically, transmits a certain melancholy with regards to his actual youth when compared with the fictional adolescence depicted.

Other respondents focus more on spontaneity and the labile present than on futurity, pasts that might have been or the prospect of stability. Gonzalo, a thirty-eight-year-old white Spanish male, writes that he identified with the character of Vassili because of his readiness or ability to fall in love with

Angelo ('su capacidad de enamorarse') soon after their first meeting. Similarly, Michel, a forty-four-year-old French male resident in Madrid, describing his ethnicity as 'European', responds to the question on whether he liked the film describing how he appreciated the way it dealt with 'la pasión amorosa, el encubrimiento por Amor' ('passion, truth withheld in the name of Love'). Vicente, a twenty-nine-year-old white Spanish male, wrote that he liked the fact that the film was able to 'asociar la relacion sexual al asesinato por "proteccion"' ('make an association between the sexual relationship and killing in order to protect the "younger man"'). Javier, a fifty-two-year-old Spanish male who declined to indicate his ethnicity, also wrote in relation to identification with the characters that he enjoyed 'la crudeza del film' ('the raw directness of the film'). There would appear to be an engagement here with the edginess of the film's highly direct representations of passionate same-sex male desire; alternatively, bearing on these responses might be a more homely and somewhat un-queer trust in a kind of pre-social, essentialist and humanistic popular belief in the raw power of love (or Love).

In the film, Morel further develops visual and narrative tropes of outsiderdom that he had earlier explored in a cycle of films on teenage masculinity, culminating in *Le Clan* (*Three Dancing Slaves*) (2004) (Rees-Roberts 2008: 28–9). In the same vein, *Notre paradis* described by our Madrid audiences is informed by the dynamics of libertarian same-sex desire between men and by perversely eroticised criminality. Like Araki's *The Living End* (1992) (a link also made in Rees-Roberts 2015), which injected the New Queer Cinema with the radical ideology of the Bad Homosexual – uncompromisingly unavailable to assimilation by comfortable, liberal acceptance into the heteronormative fold – Morel's film is plotted around reckless love, *amour fou*. It also explores an old dramatic trope of doomed love, of a paradise attained only to be lost (the dénouement of the film seeing a luxurious mountain retreat turn into a scene of mayhem and eventual arrest). The film cites a Paris glamorously enhanced by the marginality of the main characters, for example kissing on a Seine river boat passing under the Pont de la Concorde, and posed in intimate conversation on the Passerelle Debilly, with the Eiffel Tower in the centre background. These are the elements, it can be assumed, strongly inducing an audience to bond with a certain Frenchness.

Equally strong, according to the Madrid audience's responses, were the associations and looks of the actors themselves. Specifically, Rubén, a forty-one-year-old white Spanish ITC engineer, writes that he knew 'que eran los actores de *Los juncos salvajes*' ('that they were the actors who were in *Les Roseaux sauvages* [*Wild Reeds*] [André Téchiné, 1994]') as does Enrique (age, nationality and place of residence not given), adding 'y el mismo actor que *Primer verano*' ('and the same actor as in *Presque rien* [*Come Undone*] [Sébastien Lifshitz, 2000]'). Two other respondents make this connection back to *Presque rien*. Five stated that they were attracted to the film simply because they like Rideau physically; and Lucas, a forty-nine-year-old male who identifies his ethnicity as 'Spanish', draws on a more specifically personal prior context of viewing and explains that 'quería verlo dirigido por su compañero en *Los juncos salvajes*' ('I wanted to see him being directed by his companion from *Les Roseaux sauvages*'). Lucas 'wanted' to see Rideau, that is, replay a homoerotic role but also to find out how he might become inserted into a creative genealogy in which Morel the director has carried forward into the process of making the film some of the qualities of troubled intimacy which inhered in the plot of the earlier film and were acted out in his character there, François.

This is an interesting critical move, which synthesises diegesis, performance and directorial engagement in one larger field of responsive association. Lucas follows up, by email (17 November 2012), saying 'Soy absoluto fan de *Los juncos salvajes* . . . y adoro también a Stéphane Rideau' ('I'm a complete fan of *The Wild Reeds* [and] adore Stéphane Rideau'), noting that the film is a cult film among Spanish gay men. Here, like those looking back to *Presque rien*, is a member of the audience who has a clear understanding of the points of reference within French gay cinema for the formation of Spanish gay male tastes. In his follow-up email, Lucas also notes of French LGBTQ films that 'presentan la realidad LGTB de una manera descarnada, sexualmente muy excitante, directa, sin tapujos ni estereotipos, y precisamente poco adornada, lo cual me gusta' ('they present LGBT reality in a raw, sexually very exciting, direct way, without pretence or stereotypes, and, especially, without dressing it all up, which I really like'). Apparently less pleased, Marc, a French national resident in Madrid (age and ethnicity not given), writes that he found the film 'romántica. Literaria-pretenciosa (destino trágico de los gays; Bonnie and Clyde gays . . . Eros y tanatos, con tratamiento burdo)' ('romantic. Novelistic-pretentious – the tragic destiny of gays; gay Bonnie and Clyde . . . Eros and Thanatos, but crudely'). Marc and Michel, who are both French but who watch the film in transnational contexts thus articulate different views, one broadly positive, the other generally negative. Marc's response is particularly enlightening when compared to the other respondents in that it illustrates that the very same qualities that some viewers from abroad can claim to admire about a certain culture and its values are those that others from that culture reject. Via his response, he articulates a certain frustration with the country and culture of his birth, characterising the approach to sexuality in a film from that country, not as direct or realist, as others do, but as pretentious. Interestingly, though, he opts for the very same terms and frames for his analysis that are commonly taught to school students in France in order to equip them with the tools of critical analysis (antitheses such as Eros and Thanatos), which he then merges with more popular cultural and cinematographic references (Bonnie and Clyde).

Also responding to perceived elements of cliché in the film, Santiago, a fifty-six-year-old Spanish male, writes 'que todavía estemos con el gay maldito me parece démodé' ('it seems pretty *démodé* to me that we're still going on about the gay outsider, the tragic, doomed gay'). It is noteworthy that Santiago keys his response to the particularity of French terms of value – the one, in Spanish translation (*maldito*) literary historical – the idea of the special being who is *maudit*, cursed to live as the prophetic outsider – and the other, 'démodé' to do with taste more generally. Both Marc's and Santiago's responses would seem to reject the queer potential in extreme and marginal romance, although Santiago at the same time shows a partial allegiance to a queer discourse that would reject stereotyping around a fixed category of 'gay'.

These responses to the film reveal tensions and contradictions in process. On the one hand, there is a consolidation of a certain form of collective memory that borrows from the foreign past – the way French films have represented rebellious love, for example, or fostered a sense of the value of being open, permeable to the shattering effects of other people's desires or of extreme experience. Other responses show an awareness of the importance to the present – to the political now – of avoiding normalising representations through an insistence on the embrace of transgressive difference. In yet other ways, explicitly or implicitly, these respondents indicate that they place value on the more direct and simple pleasures of seeing images and following stories that carry an audience reasonably far away from normalising representations to link them imaginatively with other times and other, proximate, cultures.

Eastern Boys (Robin Campillo, 2013), which was screened at FIRE!! on 7 July 2014, fictionally portrays different kinds of precariousness – those affecting young undocumented migrants, a rentboy and a blackmailed but smitten older professional man. It portrays its main protagonist, Daniel Arthuis (Olivier Rabourdin), as not only open and permeable to new, extreme and intimidating experiences but actively and bravely courting them in the end. The festival's synopsis describes the film in this way, on its English-version pages:

> Robin Campillo rose to fame in 2004 with his first movie *They Came Back (Les Revenants)* from which he created an extraordinary adaptation for TV. Now, with the same grace and elegance, he presents *Eastern Boys*, where he deftly mixes claustrophobic intrigue with a sensitive love story between Daniel, a respectable businessman and Marek, an Eastern European rent boy. What starts as a clumsy blackmail plot by a street gang operating out of Paris's Gare du Nord, becomes a story of desire, redemption and hope. This fascinating and aesthetic piece about immigration, prostitution rings, and the idealised relationship between client and rent boy, serves as a post-modern Cinderella story of sorts, masterfully playing with plot, cinematography, and an extraordinary soundtrack to reveal the brutal contrast between violence and tenderness. A captivating and intense movie. (FIRE!! 2014)

Though captivating, *Eastern Boys* is unsettling in parts, not so much because of its story of prostitution and the age difference that separates the two protagonists – Daniel is in his middle age, while Marek (whom we later learn is called Rouslan) (Kiril Emelyanov) has just transitioned from adolescence to adulthood – but because of its scenes of attempted extortion and the precariousness that blights the lives of those forced to migrate to other countries. It encapsulates in many ways the rawness and candour often associated with French films, praised in Lucas's response cited above, and their ability to ask probing and sometimes troubling ethical questions, as evidenced in *L'Inconnu du lac* and the reactions it triggered. Although he had arranged for Marek/Rouslan to come to his house for sex for €50, Daniel finds himself opening the door to a different, clearly under-aged boy – part of the gang of young Eastern Europeans whom Marek/Rouslan lives with – who threatens to expose him to the authorities. The gang, led by their narcissistic psychopath leader, aptly named Boss (Daniil Vorobyov), then take over Daniel's flat and steal his possessions. Marek/Rouslan returns, Daniel pays him for sex and later gives him an allowance and keys to the apartment. When Marek/Rouslan tells him of his traumatic experiences in Chechnya and the loss of his family, Daniel refuses to go on having sex with him and gives him his own makeshift room. The film ends after Daniel successfully retrieves Marek/Rouslan's passport and other papers from Boss's locker in an overcrowded budget hotel where the gang, and other migrants, are temporarily resident and, having telephoned the police, causes a raid, although Boss escapes. Somewhat surprisingly, the final scene reveals that Daniel is applying to adopt Marek/Rouslan. Herein lies the 'Cinderella' dimension alluded to in the above synopsis. For Daniel shifts from a lonely older man, paying for sex, to a 'Prince Charming' of sorts, whose intervention frees Marek/Rouslan from his oppressors. Tragically, though, the hotel's other residents, who may also have experienced pasts as traumatic as that of Marek/Rouslan, serve as collateral damage in this 'native-saves-foreigner' narrative.

In dealing with the effects and affect of migration, *Eastern Boys*, which was made in 2012, is highly topical. It is oddly telling then that, of the circa eighty questionnaires distributed at the beginning of the screening at FIRE!!, only seven were returned, with one declining to allow their responses to be used in our publications. Moreover, the two respondents who engage specifically with the theme of 'migration' have themselves emigrated to Spain from elsewhere: Pablo, a twenty-seven-year-old male, from Colombia but living in Barcelona, mixed race and employed; and Antonio, a thirty-nine-year-old male, from Venezuela but living in Barcelona, who describes his ethnic identity as Latin and works as a masseur and journalist. In answer to the question asking whether he liked the film, Pablo replies 'molt, el tema migratori. L'evolució de la relació' ('a lot, the migration issue. The way the relationship develops') and, when thinking about how it deals with its themes, categorises it as a social as well as a gay film: 'no només toca una tematica gay, sino social, els personatges son molt reals' ('it's not just about gay themes, but also social ones, the characters are very real'). Pablo identifies his favourite scene as the moment when Daniel tells Marek/Rouslan that he no longer wants to sleep with him, precisely the point at which he – Daniel – becomes a more consensually good citizen. For Antonio, taking a contrasting approach, the adoption storyline is both disappointing and implausible – 'no entendí por que intenta adoptar al chico y no casarse con él'; 'me hubiera gustado que se casaran' ('I did not understand why he tries to adopt the boy and not marry him'; 'I would have liked them to get married'). Antonio responds from a position of self-implication, stating explicitly that he identifies with Marek/Rouslan 'porque he sido prostituto' ('because I've been a prostitute'). His evaluation of the film appears unconstrained by external pressures and unease around generational dissonance and power relations in same-sex relationships. Familiarity with the film's story, issues and characters is also implied in his answer to the question asking whether it was 'true-to-life'; he writes that groups of Eastern European boys are 'una cruda realidad en Europa' ('a brutal reality in Europe'), although the nature of his personal encounter with such groups and his actual opinions about them are not specified.

Antonio's investment in the passion narrative, emphasised by his implied disappointment in the shifting nature of Daniel and Marek/Roulan's relationship, is echoed by Roberto, a fifty-seven-year-old white Spanish retired male who lives in Barcelona. He claims to have liked the theme of love driving actions ('actuar por amor'). Such a romanticised interpretation is then extended when he writes that his favourite character is Daniel, with whom he 'perhaps' identifies because of his age. Roberto claims to admire Daniel's 'actitud, primero ante la adversidad y luego su comportamiento por amor' ('attitude, firstly in the face of adversity and later his behaviour in relation to love'). Manuel, a forty-seven-year-old Spanish male psychologist who identifies himself as Caucasian who lives in Barcelona, echoes Roberto's emotional investment in the film. When writing about whether he liked *Eastern Boys*, he immediately replies 'm'atreu el tema del xapero i les emocions que es despleguen al darrere d'una transacció econòmica' ('the theme of prostitution and the emotions underlying a purely economic transaction attract me'). Manuel projects himself as someone who prefers an emotional engagement with the outside world when justifying his choice of Daniel as his favourite character: 's'implica a la vida amb les seves emocions' ('he involves himself in life through his emotions'). Interestingly, though, given his age, nationality, ethnicity and professional status, and in contrast to Roberto, he claims to identify with Marek/Rouslan, although he specifies the universal need and desire to feel loved and secure as the reason for his sense of closeness to the character: 'per la necessitat de sentir-me acollit, contingut per algú que t'estimi i et desitgi' ('through the need to feel welcomed in, and held safe by someone who loves and desires you'). As in some of the responses to *Notre paradis*, then, shared values are portrayed as arising from universal themes such as love and passion rather than necessarily from any affiliation to LGBTQ community or politics.

Another respondent, however, assumes a more distanced, critical engagement with the film. Artur, who is the same age as Manuel, and is a Catalan administration official who lives in Barcelona, describes the romantic and filial relationship between Daniel and Marek/Rouslan as 'worrying' ('m'ha inquietat'), difficult to accept, unrealistic ('poc versemblant'), extreme and daring. He nuances his response to the question on identification by writing 'no realment, però em puc posar en la pell d'algú que viu la crisis de la mitjana edat' ('not really, but I can imagine myself in the place of someone who is going though a middle-age crisis'). Artur is the only one of the participants consulted to have adopted such a position, which suggests that these viewers, though few, covet the making of the self ready and available to new encounters, relationships and subjectivities. Of course, for some, this is contained within the realm of fantasy, which cinema affords and facilitates, furnishing them with a means, as in previous responses to other films, of momentary escape from the restrictions that govern their everyday lives. Others, though, claim that such openness serves a more structural function in how they negotiate their existence and relationships, as implied, principally, by Antonio.

The lure of an unanticipated passionate encounter is central to Villaverde's *El sexo de los ángeles*, although this encounter is less concerned with geopolitical issues such as migration and prostitution. It does, though, include a strongly bisexual component and, in this, differs from most of our films. *El sexo de los ángeles* was screened at the Chéries-Chéris festival on 6 October 2012 and at Des images aux mots in Toulouse on 8 February 2013. It was advertised in the Chéries-Chéris programme with the following synopsis:

Quelles sont les limites d'un couple ? Qu'est-ce qui se passe quand la passion se confronte à la raison? Comment être fidèle et ne pas tourner le dos au désir? Carla et Bruno pensent qu'ils ont toutes les réponses à ces questions, jusqu'à ce que Rai, un homme, séduisant et mystérieux, adepte de danse et d'arts martiaux, et qui vit selon ses propres règles, apparaît dans leur vie. Le coup de foudre entre les deux hommes va ébranler les convictions du couple. Dans cette histoire d'amour et d'amitié, les limites vibrent au rythme du break et du funk pour offrir une vision provocante et excitante des relations amoureuses. (Chéries-Chéris 2012)

(What are the limits of coupledom? What happens when your desires and will to do the right thing clash? How do you stay faithful without turning your back on desire? Carla and Bruno think that they've got all the answers, until the appearance of the seductive and mysterious Rai, a dancer and martial arts expert who lives life on his own terms. Love-at-first-sight between the two men turns out to be a challenge to Carla and Bruno's convictions as a couple. In this story of love and friendship, rules shift much like the rhythms of break dance and funk to offer a provocative and exciting picture of romantic relationships.)

It is notable that this text deploys elements of the dichotomous representation of French and Spanish characteristics as discussed in Chapter 1, with Carla, particularly (Astrid Bergès-Frisbey), as reason, Rai (Álvaro Cervantes) and Bruno (Llorenç González) as passion and Rai in particular as seduction. Despite its location in Barcelona, an air of Frenchness hangs over *El sexo de los ángeles*. The father of the protagonist Carla is French, and is characterised by Carla and her boyfriend Bruno as dogmatic, judgemental, remote and chauvinistic, thus casting him as a symbol for the patriarchal French culture against which so many French rebels (fictional and real) have railed. Carla's physicality and sartorial style could also be seen as a gallicisation, with her waif-like figure, long brown hair and pale, almost diaphanous skin. Her friend Marta (Sonia Méndez) sports a T-shirt emblazoned with the names of the cool French pop stars Françoise Hardy and Katerine. This professional setting in the offices of a magazine, combined with the party-going set that revolves around it, evokes Stéphane Giusti's coming-out comedy *Pourquoi pas moi?*, also set in Barcelona as mentioned in Chapter 1, while the *ménage-à-trois* plotline, itself a staple of Gallic comedies, momentarily recalls the gritty, urban musical *Les Chansons d'amour* (*Canciones de amor*; *Love Songs*) (Christophe Honoré, 2007) (shown at FIRE!!, July 2012, but yielding only three responses and none of these giving consent to quotation). Shot in winter, Barcelona takes on an air of Paris at times, cast in a palette of greys and beige, and despite the occasional view of landmarks such as the Colón tower and Barceloneta.

However, apart from a passing mention of *Jules et Jim* (François Truffaut, 1962), none of the twenty-four respondents who returned questionnaires remarked upon any such French connections. By contrast, five stated that they had selected *El sexo de los ángeles* because it is Spanish, with another comparing it to the portrayal of passion that defines the films of Pedro Almodóvar. The expectation of an encounter with a 'foreign' LGBTQ culture through film might have led these viewers to overlook the similarities with their own culture on display. Yet, the absence of allusions to such resemblances more likely points to the fact that they are more concerned with visual pleasure than with identifying cultural connections which to them might seem irrelevant. Contrary to Lucas above, for whom cult appreciation of *Les Roseaux sauvages* is invoked in his response to *Notre paradis*, displaying transnational knowledge of queer film is also not a primary concern of these viewers. Given that all bar one watched the film at the Chéries-Chéris screening, this suggests a departure from the more traditionally cinephiliac reception practices cultivated by the Paris festival in its early years and could reflect the impact of attempts by the organisers to broaden its appeal beyond specialists and activists by bringing in an audience whose motivations are concerned with visual pleasure and even erotic stimulation (see Chapter 2). Certainly, some among the audience that filled the large Salle 500 (named after its capacity) in the Forum des Images seemed preoccupied with the immediate pleasures offered by this revisiting of the familiar narrative trope of a straight male (Bruno) being seduced by his queer admirer Rai. Unsurprisingly, Bruno and Rai are played by two physically striking actors (in classical terms) and their normative masculinity is by no means compromised by their sexual connection. Some viewers appeared to have bought into the erotic appeal of both actors and storyline through their focus on looks. One, who did not give a name, but who is a thirty-four-year-old mixed-race French accountant who lives in Paris, describes Bruno as 'le plus mignon' ('the cutest') while Jérôme, a fifty-eight-year-old white male news editor from Paris, describes Rai as 'trop beau, libre et séduisant' ('too handsome, free and seductive').

Yet, it would be inaccurate to reduce all the responses, and the representations on which they are based, to the film's potential to titillate. In fact, some respondents objected to the casting of good-looking actors and generally dismissed the film as absurd and unrealistic. Others shifted their attentions to more affective and philosophical concerns, notably its exploration of romantic relationships, fidelity and commitment, as outlined in the above notes. One, who again omitted to give a name, but who is twenty-five, French and lives in Paris, wrote that they felt a personal connection with 'les questions que se pose le couple quant à la place de la fidélité' ('the questions the couple ask themselves about the role of faithfulness'), questions, they are quick to affirm, that are universal.

The film's inclusion of bisexuality is a feature that received explicit praise or expressions of self-recognition by five of the twenty-four questionnaires returned (one at Des images aux mots and twenty-three at Chéries-Chéris). Louis, a fifty-three-year-old white bank worker, writes that he enjoyed the themes of 'bisexualité, ouverture d'esprit, beauté des acteurs' ('bisexuality, open-mindedness, the beauty of the actors'). Daphne, the forty-year-old French female volunteer with WWOOF (Worldwide Opportunities on Organic Farms) International, cited at the start of this chapter, writes, 'je ne connaissais pas le sujet. Agréablement surprise. Il montre la décontraction qu'ont les Espagnols vis à vis de l'homosexualité, [la] bisexualité et l'ouverture d'esprit que n'ont pas les Français' ('I didn't know what it was about. Pleasantly surprised. It shows how relaxed the Spanish are about homosexuality, bisexuality and the open-mindedness that the French lack'). Hicham, a twenty-nine-year-old French-Moroccan bank cashier who lives in Paris, places bisexuality among his reasons for selecting *El sexo de los ángeles*, which include 'fidélité . . . la raison et la tentation quand on [est] en couple' ('fidelity . . . doing the right thing and temptation when you are in a couple'). He conveys a degree of intense emotional connection, acclaiming the film with an emphatic 'BRAVO!' in capitals and awarding it a maximum score of five out of five. He writes of the 'beautiful' storyline, praises Rai for allowing his feelings to flourish and buys into the 'le bonheur à trois' ('happiness in three-way relationships'), something that he claims he has also lived through. Hence, while Daphne's response constructs the type of open and inclusive sexual and romantic relations portrayed in *El sexo de los ángeles* as something that pertains to another culture, and she thus illustrates the arguments in Chapter 1 that Spain and Spanishness can be depicted as an antidote to the perceived constraints of French moral attitudes, Hicham depicts them as familiar, closer to home. Others also make assertions of a direct correlation between the events depicted in the film and their lived realities, although here the implied emphasis is on the discovery of homosexuality. Rémi, a thirty-six-year-old mixed-race French-Malian student from Paris, states succinctly in answer to whether he thought the film was true-to-life 'situations connues' ('experienced situations') and names Bruno as his favourite character because he has to face up to his homosexual desires. Similarly, writing about whether he felt that he identified with any characters, Jérôme states, again with concision, that he has experienced 'un peu la même histoire' ('the same thing to a degree').

Other respondents describe the free, unconstrained set-up they view on screen as corresponding to their personal conceptualisations of romantic and erotic relationships, to which some claim to aspire. A twenty-eight-year-old Mexican who did not give a name, occupation or gender (though using the masculine forms in writing), but who defined their ethnicity as Latin American, wrote 'je pense qu'il existe plus de situations qu'on ne peut imaginer' ('I think that there are more situations than people can imagine'). They state, somewhat wistfully, in writing about whether the film is true-to-life 'oui, car c'est une situation à laquelle, en tant que bisexuel, j'adorerais être confronté' ('yes, because it's a situation that, as a bisexual, I would love to face'). Like Hicham, they appear keen to endorse *El sexo de los ángeles*, writing that it approached its subject 'avec suffisament de légèreté pour que ce soit juste sans être ridicule et tomber dans la caricature' ('with enough lightness for it to be believable and not ridiculous and avoiding caricatures'). All of these viewers' articulations of these experiences and aspirations allows them to make specific identifications with bisexual identities, thus nuancing and refining their place within the LGBT (and Q) communities targeted by the festivals. Hicham, Jérôme, Rémi and the Mexican respondent affiliate themselves with a construction of social identity and a sense of community that is defined by a less rigid and homogenised understanding of sexual desire and subjectivity than encapsulated by the labels 'lesbian' or 'gay'. Such identifications are facilitated here by a Spanish film watched at a French LGBT film festival, which, at least in this screening, avoids the charge of tokenism in its inclusion of the 'B' in its festival title. As Geneviève, a twenty-seven-year-old Caucasian film policy officer from Bordeaux, remarks, 'le polymorphisme et la bisexualité [sont] encore peu abordés habituellement' ('polymorphism and bisexuality [are] usually still rarely broached').

Another respondent, who also failed to give a name and, this time, an age, but who is a female Caucasian student, remarked 'j'attends que quelque chose d'aussi forte et riche m'arrive – rencontrer de telles personnes' ('I'm waiting to experience something similarly strong and rich – to meet such people'). This is extended in her response to the question asking whether she watches the same film multiple times, to which she replies 'oui . . . pour toutes les chaleurs, tous ces moments, sentiments me prennent pour être basculée' ('yes . . . for all this heat, all these moments, feelings that seize and shake me up'). The impression of a person held – or rather who holds themselves – in suspense for a life driven by passion is thus conveyed here and the yearning that can be discerned in this response might well come from a similar place to the 'passion' and 'readiness to fall in love' that Michel and Gonzalo claim to admire in Vassili in *Notre paradis*. This female viewer gives the impression that films offer escape into a world that they have not yet realised, but to which they aspire, or even that its representation is enough to allow her to live her fantasies vicariously via fictional characters. Once again, such responses illustrate the utility of LGBT (and Q) film festivals in offering opportunities to encounter stories about lived sexuality from elsewhere, in this case Spain. Where French films were typified by Lucas, earlier, as raw, direct, devoid of stereotypes and stripped back, this Spanish film affords this viewer and the others cited above a perspective on sexuality that appears to comply with their actual sense of social self or the person that they aspire to be even if – unlike Daphne quoted above – they do not qualify this openness with Spanishness in particular. In this, then, these viewers echo the emotional connection experienced by the unnamed American respondent in her reaction to *Les Invisibles*, for whom that film mobilised a candid discourse on love and sexuality, and they construct themselves as unconstrained in terms of how they love, live and desire.

Concluding Remarks

Investment, care, surprise (in the sense of an epiphany), pleasure, aspiration, (self-)recognition, implication and projection, and direct identification are the most recurring modes of engagement of the viewers cited above in their responses to the films discussed in this chapter. They all claim varying degrees of closeness to the subjects, characters and people viewed on screen, which can be expected given the universal resonances of the themes depicted: ageing, desire, romance, self-acceptance and freedom. While such proximity also emerges in the data collected in response to the films on trans issues, examined in the next chapter, as will be seen, the perspective adopted by the majority tends to be more distanced and negotiated.

Note

1. Email of 14 November 2012: '¿y crees que el cine gai tiene una responsabilidad de mostrar imágenes positivas de la homosexualidad?' ('and do you think gay films have a responsibility to show positive images of homosexuality?'). The question deliberately masks conventional critical caveats concerning the incompatibility of positive images arguments with a queer, rather than gay, take on film (Rich 2013a: 3–37).

4. TRANS ISSUES

C'est une forme de militantisme féministe, anticapitaliste qui remet en cause le genre et, euh, j'ai l'impression que c'est des choses qu'on peut voir ici aussi à Lyon (.) . . . J'ai pas trouvé ça exotique en fait.
(it's a kind of feminist, anti-capitalist militancy that questions gender and, um, I feel that these are the kinds of things we can see here in Lyon (.) I didn't find it exotic in fact.) (Alex, thirty-seven-year-old white French genderqueer project manager, during group discussion about *Guerriller@s*)

[És] important coneixer la nostra història.
(It's important to know our history.) (Oriol a twenty-six-year-old trans male in questionnaire responses to *Bambi* at FIRE!! 2013)

'No me siento chico, pues, no puedo empatisar en grado sumo con él, porque no he sentido eso, pero entiendo que tiene que ser una solución muy complicada, porque no parece que tienes que ser siempre lo que te marca ya de nacimiento. (I don't feel as if I'm a boy, so I cannot empathise at the highest level with him, because I've not experienced it, but I understand that it must be a very complicated solution, because it seems that you have to always be what you were defined as at birth.) (Marta Isabel, twenty-four-year-old Spanish white European female lesbian undergraduate student during group discussion about *Tomboy*)

These comments illustrate the range of reactions among our participants to the corpus films about transsexual, transgender and intersex identities. Their modes of engagement vary from affirmations of identification to expressions of sympathy and non-specialist understanding, via empathy and recognition, that transmit a sense of shared values around gender and, in the first case, class-based politics. Each position depends, of course, on the identity and lived experience of the individual respondent and is formed, as always, within the knowledge that they are participating in academic research. Beyond Oriol's comment, which provides further evidence of how people who consider themselves to be affected by a film's subject transmit a sense of community affiliation, Alex demonstrates how those from outside that community draw on themes that have salience for them, that coincide with their own understanding of their social identities and self-positioning with regards to ideas of bourgeois and heteronormative culture and the 'mainstream', while Marta Isabel adopts a more distanced stance.

The particularly diverse range of positions presented in this chapter is partly a product of one of the major challenges of our project: reaching out and appealing to those we felt were most addressed by our films – in this case trans-, intersex- and genderqueer-identifying viewers. While we have succeeded in recruiting some who identify in these ways, as Oriol and Alex show, the majority of those who responded to these films identified themselves in cisgender terms. This has consequences for some of the data produced, since, particularly in the focus group discussions, participants embark on philosophical – and to a lesser extent political – debates about the broader implications of the films for gender identity as a whole. This said, many respondents locate, in these stories of determination and affirmation of the self, accounts that they allege resonate with their own journeys towards acceptance and emancipation.

These subjects are approached through five documentaries, two of them focused on a single figure – *Bambi* (Sébastien Lifshitz, 2013) and *Ocaña, retrat intermitent* (Ventura Pons, 1978) – and three on collective and activist experience, as well as the naturalistic melodrama *Tomboy* (Céline Sciamma, 2011). As in the previous chapter, different formats inflect the data. The chapter draws on philosophical and theoretical texts with regards to trans and intersex identity politics, as well as political texts and activism. It opens with a contextual overview of trans political activism as it relates to each country and region, and the place of trans films in LGBTQ festivals.

Trans Politics, and the Place of Trans Identity in LGBTQ Film Festivals, in Spain and France

Nearly twenty years after the formation in Spain of the Asociación Transexual Español (later Asociación Española de Transexuales: AET-Transexualia), and with the gradual emergence of city and regional trans groups across the country, in 2006 a white paper for a new gender identity law was introduced after long discussions with AET-Transexualia and related groups (Ramos Cantó 2007; Junta Directiva AET-Transexualia 2007). Once passed, Ley3/2007 was the most progressive law in Europe at the time because it allowed trans people to change their gender identity on official documentation without having undergone surgery. This caused much discussion amongst trans communities, with some arguing that it was not enough, and that the underlying and persistent problem lay, rather, in the continued pathologisation of trans identities and the state's interference in how individuals choose to define themselves.

In France, twenty-seven years after the rejection of a bill (no. 260) proposed by the radical left-wing senator Henri Caillavet on 9 April 1982 to allow trans people to change their civil status irrespective of whether they had undergone reassignment surgery or not (Foerster 2012: 156–7), and fifty-four years after the creation of the first support group for transsexuals (AMAHO) by concentration camp survivor Marie-André Schwindenhammer, the Health Minister Roselyne Bachelot-Narquin announced on 16 May 2009 that transsexuality would no longer be considered a psychiatric disorder (Espineira 2015: 109). France was heralded as the first country in the world to remove transsexuality from the list of psychiatric disorders (111), although this has been dismissed as a purely administrative move to reclassify transsexuality for the purposes of social security payments (as 'affection de longue durée' or 'long-term condition') (Bourcier 2011: 192, n. 44). Bachelot's announcement raised concerns, among some, that their treatment costs would no longer be reimbursed (Espineira 2015: 111). The legal and medical situation is in flux at the time of writing, with a new bill being drafted for consideration by the French parliament. However, it remains the case that changes to civil status are considered by public prosecutors only when proof of physical and physiological transformations have been provided (see Silberfeld 2015), external validation by medical professionals is still a requirement for access to treatment and self-diagnosis continues to be denied trans people (Bourcier 2011: 192, n. 44; Espineira 2015: 112). These issues, and the continuing struggle to shed dichotomous representations of transitioning (through before-and-after, same-and-different narratives), subtend the films discussed in this section and inflect audience responses, as will be seen.

The first trans collective to form in Catalunya, following the murder of a trans woman in the Parc de la Ciutadella, was the Col.lectiu de Transsexuals de Catalunya in 1992. In 2000 the FTM contingent of the collective formed the Grup de Transsexuals Masculins de Barcelona, of which one of the founders was Moïsès Martínez, the subject of Cecilia Barriga's 2003 documentary *El camino de Moïsès* (*Le Chemin de Moïsès*; *Moïsés's Journey*), and author of a key piece on trans identity in the seminal collection by the Grupo de Trabajo Queer (Martínez 2005). Out of the Grup de Transsexuals Masculins de Barcelona, a splinter group, Guerrilla Travolaka, was formed by trans activists who had been in Paris at the October 2006 annual Existrans protest march (for trans people and those who support them: Espineira et al. 2012: 176) and had been impressed by the stance of the radical Groupe Activiste Trans (GAT) (2002–6) (Espineira et al. 2012: 176).

The GAT was formed outside of pre-existing social and political groups and unions (Espineira et al. 2012: 65), and harnessed the radical practices of Act-Up Paris. It was constituted of four members and intended to be a transient movement that sought to raise the consciousness of trans- and intersex-identifying people about trans politics. Its slogan, formulated in 2006, was 'Parce que, TRANS, la France vous préfère mortEs: RESISTEZ à l'hétéro-norme sociale' ('Because, as TRANS, France would prefer you to be dead: RESIST social heteronormativity' (Foerster 2012: 197) and it embarked on 'zaps', publicly denouncing, where possible in spectacular ways, the main proponents of transphobic discourses and ideologies (Foerster 2012: 195–7). Guerrilla Travolaka's own slogan echoes the stance of the GAT – 'Ni homes, ni dones. Ni disfòrics, ni transtornats, ni transsexuals. Només som … [d]issidents de l'heteropatriarcat' ('neither men nor women. Neither dysphoric, disturbed, nor transsexual. We are just … [d]issentors from heteropatriarchy') (Guerrilla Travolaka 2009); like the 'zaps' of the GAT, their actions included a protest on the doorstep of the psychiatry unit of the Hospital Clínic, the largest trans treatment centre in Barcelona, as well as outdoor performances.[1]

At the festivals we attended, programming showed an uneven and gradual integration of films of, by and for trans people. The festival Des images aux mots (Toulouse) has labelled itself LGBT since its beginning in 2007, while Ecrans Mixtes (Lyon) labels itself a queer and LGBT festival, as mentioned. Chéries-Chéris rebranded itself as 'gay, lesbien, bi trans et ++++' (although the 2007 and 2008 Paris festivals also included the tagline 'films de tous les genres') and has managed to give space for trans films via various sections – 'Transversales' (2006) and 'Intersexe-intergenre' (2007) – and selections (for example, trans and FTM films in 2010), special screenings (in association with Existrans) and series of shorts. The Spanish documentaries *El camino de Moïsès* and *Fake Orgasm* (Jo Sol, 2010) have both featured in the programmes (in 2006 and 2010 respectively). Paris's film festival specifically geared to the trans community – Festival IdentiT – was short-lived, lasting only two years (possibly as a result of the Chéries-Chéris organisers' efforts to be inclusive and cater for a broad spectrum of identity-based communities and taste groups). In 2013, Ecrans Mixtes was given, as seen, the caption 'Sweet Transvestite' and arguably catered more for gay male and queer tastes than trans viewers. Zinegoak (Bilbao) has since its inception in 2004 called itself 'gay/lesbo/trans' and has had regular screenings (eight, for example, in the 2015 programme) of films labelled as having a trans theme. In Madrid, LesGaiCineMad has included 'y transexual' in its official festival name since 2009 and screened between six and twelve films with a trans theme between 2009 and 2014, in which year it introduced a dedicated session TransDocuMad. FIRE!! (Barcelona) does not include any trans tag in its festival title or traditionally have significant trans programming, but in 2009 ran a special strand on transsexuality in Asia, showed *Romeos* (Sabine Bernardi, 2011) in the Official Section 2011 and ran a five-item Trans Screen strand in 2014, including *Bambi*. FICGLB (also Barcelona) similarly lacks a trans tag, although it introduced a prize in 2013 for LGTIB documentaries (which is yet to go to a trans-themed film). It has shown the short *Mathi(eu)* (Corlie Prosper, 2011) and *Fille ou garçon, mon sexe n'est pas mon genre* (*Girl or Boy, My Sex Is Not My Gender*) (Valérie Mitteaux, 2011). More significant in this regard for Barcelona was the organi-sation by Guerrilla Travolaka, alongside other trans groups in Barcelona, of the first Spanish trans and intersex film festival, MosTra'ns, in June 2009 (as mentioned in Chapter 2), with fourteen films over five evenings – six Spanish and one French: *L'Ordre des mots*.

L'Ordre des mots (Binding Word) (Cynthia Arra and Mélissa Arra, 2007), Guerriller@s (W@rriors) (Montse Pujantell, 2012) and Fille ou garçon, mon sexe n'est pas mon genre (Girl or Boy, My Sex Is Not My Gender) (Valérie Mitteaux, 2011): Negotiating Transsexuality and Intersex

Many of the political contestations outlined above emerge in three varyingly political trans and trans-intersex documentaries that feature in our corpus, *L'Ordre des mots*, *Guerriller@s* and *Fille ou garçon*. The responses these films receive, from two focus groups and various questionnaires, differ according to the affiliations and subject positions projected by the viewers, prescreening awareness of the film's issues and declared predisposition to its content. As will be seen, non-specialist viewers of *L'Ordre des mots* either resist its politics or take up and think through the philosophical issues and questions it raises, a group of self-constructed political activists acclaim the openness, flexibility and pacifism of *Guerriller@s* and some of the questionnaire respondents judge *Fille ou garçon* according to their occupations as therapists and counsellors (and as teachers and students).

The documentary *L'Ordre des mots* targets the pathologisation of trans people and identities, and features some of the aforementioned GAT members, as well as the activist Maud-Yeuse Thomas. The English language pages of the film's website describe it this way:

> The film aims to give Trans' people whose quest for gender identity is fettered by established norms a chance to voice their tribulation. Their means of resistance consist of searching for tools of knowledge, for corporealities, sexualities and alternative identities to those of the conventional schemas. Far from the usual treatment of Trans issues, this film, through the choice of its portrait subjects – all contemporary actors [in the sense of those taking part] and precursors of the Trans' and Intersex movement in France – addresses the gender identity issues head-on by questioning our often unchallenged societal norms and analysing the nature of the oppression and repression faced by the Trans' and Intersex community. (L'Ordre des mots 2015)

The film refuses to allow doctors, family members or anyone else to talk about trans identity, giving the space only to trans and intersex people themselves (Rees-Roberts 2008: 73). It combines autobiographical accounts of trans and intersex trajectories with political and philosophical reflections on trans and intersex identity, and recurrently questions binary gender structures, medical

Figure 4.1 Official poster for the documentary *L'Ordre des mots* (with Maud-Yeuse Thomas, Tom Reucher, Vincent Avrons, Vincent He-Say, Carine Boeuf and Vincent Guillot) (Cynthia Arra and Mélissa Arra, 2007), design by Vincent He-Say. Image © Courtesy of Cynthia Arra and Mélissa Arra.

expertise and the recourse to surgery in 'treating' intersex children. It provides honest, direct and uncensored accounts of the hardships its subjects have faced (73), and demonstrates the material consequences of the requirement of external diagnosis for trans lives (that is refusal of treatment for some purely on the grounds of a medical professional's opinion and long delays – sometimes lasting many years – before being allowed to undergo surgery). It ends with footage of the direct actions by the GAT, most notably depicting their zap against the clinical psychiatrist Patricia Mercader, who argues in her 2000 book *L'Illusion transexuelle* (*The Transsexual Illusion*) that transsexuality is a pathological condition that should be cured, a syndrome rather than a subjectivity. Activists storm the stage at a seminar entitled 'Le Clinicien et la demande transexuelle' (The Clinician and the Transsexual Demand) held at the Sainte-Anne hospital in June 2004 and refuse to allow Mercader to speak, amidst booing, hissing and even heckling from Mercader's colleagues. *L'Ordre des mots* documents the consciousness-raising of trans people with regards to trans politics sought by the GAT group.

L'Ordre des mots has a website offering past and future viewers a host of related resources facilitating and encouraging an immersive engagement with the film. This engagement can be experienced across many platforms (on Internet, mobile phones as well as in cinema auditoria or at home on DVD), thereby revealing how a political documentary attempts to exploit the potential of convergence and overflow, enabling a 'fluid, flexible' encounter that exceeds the 'proscribed time slot and single medium' (Brooker and Jermyn 2003: 323).

Talking about *L'Ordre des mots* in the context of the 2013 FIRE!!, members of a small focus group – Emma, a twenty-nine-year-old Puerto Rican student, David, a thirty-nine-year-old self-identifying 'citizen of the world' and film critic, and Cliff, a fifty-three-year-old self-identifying gay male of American nationality who works in patient liaison – were drawn to this footage. Emma was the girlfriend of one of Ros's friends and both Ros and Darren had met her the evening before the discussion. This group was recruited alongside the festival, at which *Bambi* was screened. In attendance at that screening were trans people, some activists, including Miquel Missé who features in *Guerriller@s* (discussed below), and the film's main subject responded to questions from the audience and festival organisers at the end. Given the presence of trans viewers in the audience and the prominence afforded to trans issues in that year's festival, we sought to invite some trans-identifying respondents to the discussion that we organised in the Casal Lambda on 15 July 2013. However, that hot afternoon only three people attended, none of whom was trans; two more arrived and then promptly left before the screening. Consequently, this small audience was not composed of viewers who would necessarily be drawn to a documentary that sets out a radical perspective on trans and intersex issues, and none claimed to be addressed specifically by the film. Of all of our discussions, this therefore threatened to be the most contrived, and promised, initially, to be of limited use. However, non-specialist viewers and those who do not claim to be affected personally by subjects represented in films are notoriously difficult to access. The viewing positions adopted by the participants in this group, then, are illuminating with regards to what unsuspecting audiences do with films that they are unlikely to encounter or seek out beyond their participation in the study.

Analysis of the discussion reveals a split in the group, with David adopting a broadly oppositional position (Morley 1980; Bobo 2003) and Emma and Cliff conveying varying degrees of sympathy and openness with regards to the film's issues and politics. Yet, David is careful to qualify his scepticism as arising from his lack of awareness of trans and intersex politics (he uses the term 'sentirse vinculado' – feel connected):

> estoy hablando siempre desde el punto de vista cinematográfico (.) no entro en el tema de la transexualidad porque, bueno, he venido aquí como crítico, ¿no?, más que nada por la película.

(it's the cinematographic point of view that I'm talking from (.) I'm not going into the transsexuality issue because, well, I'm here as a critic, you see, more for the film itself than anything else.)

From this particular position, David notes that the aforementioned footage lacks an external perspective and that the viewer hears neither what the pro-testers say to the panel of experts nor what the views are of those 'supuestos expertos, esos psiquiatras' ('supposed experts, those psychiatrists') who are also 'los que supuestamente son los malos' ('the supposed baddies'). For David, 'aquí la cosa [se pone] un poco maniquea' ('things [get] somewhat manichean here'), which he repeatedly characterises as a flaw. Of the whole film he states 'yo pienso que un documental, el mérito que debe tener es al espectador [se] le permita sacar sus propias conclusiones. Y aquí no te da margen. Aquí te lo dice todo, absolutamente' ('I think that what is good about documentaries is that they allow the spectator to make their own conclusions. And here, you are not given any margin. Here, they tell you absolutely everything'). Interestingly, David omits reference to the members of the seminar audience in the film who angrily object to the GAT's presence. Although he applies the frames of analy-sis commonly seen in film criticism – an attention to structure and balance – emerging from his response is a tangible sense that *L'Ordre des mots* had frustrated him (evidenced in his use of the adjective 'supuestos' and its variant 'supuestamente'). His application of a discourse of aesthetic criticism is, possi-bly, a way of putting his instant affective reaction (a kind of visceral recoil) and the emotions and feelings that ensued (see Turnbull 2008: 184–5) into words that he is able to countenance, a process through which he dismisses the film as a poor example of its genre. David's objection, that alternative points of view are not incorporated in *L'Ordre des mots*, is countered by Cliff, for whom 'la sicología y los médicos van retrasados' ('psychology and the medical world are out of date'), and he argues that what should have happened in the conference was to invite the protesters in to be there 'compartiendo sus vidas un poco' ('sharing their experience a bit'). Cliff, then, projects a greater awareness of the political issues that led to the activists' direct action and to the creation of the film. Indeed, Bourcier has made a similar critique about the conference's sister seminar 'Les Troubles de l'identité sexuelle' ('Sexual Identity Trouble') (Bourcier 2005: 54). Specialist or activist and non-specialist or non-activist objections align here, even if the tone of Cliff's comment is rather more concil-iatory than Bourcier or the documentary.

Emma takes up the film's more philosophical questioning of gendering and transmits some awareness of what is at stake by evoking wider concerns about the role of medical professionals in determining gender identity. She refers back to the film's treatment of reassignment surgery on young children, picking up on the idea of complexity, and how the subjects of the film (and those protesting at GAT) are saying that medical discourse needs to recognise that it is wrong to assign the child 'niño' or 'niña' ('girl' or 'boy'), '[y] que el mundo es mucho más complejo' ('[and] that the world is a lot more complicated than that'). Cliff makes a similar point and, again, displays some understanding of the political debates around transsexuality by raising the importance of self-definition or self-diagnosis: 'no tenemos que ser hombre o mujer, con hormonas o sin hormonas, o lo que sea' ('we don't need to be a man or a woman, with hormones or without hormones, or whatever') and that 'cada uno . . . podemos definirnos como nos da la gana casi' ('each one of us . . . we can define ourselves more or less as we wish'). Although Emma comes from Puerto Rico and Cliff is from the USA, and both live in Barcelona, neither one identifies the specific and local political and social contexts to which *L'Ordre des mots* refers as a hindrance to their ability to draw resonances and recognition from its discourse on gender identity. They shift their attention to what Pidduck describes as the film's inclusion of the 'transnational discourses that tend to frame transgender experience with recourse to humanist gender identity' (Pidduck 2011: 15).

All three discussants register the 'effects' of the film, and, when asked if anything surprised them, Emma and David note one of the interviewee's recollections of being a four-year-old struggling with her assigned male identity. Again, David expresses his objections by describing how he had been struck by the 'unpleasantness' of this aspect of the documentary, drawing a contrastive comparison with the Argentinian film *XXY* (Lucía Puenzo, 2007), which he depicts as a more sensitive treatment of the issue. Earlier in the discussion, when the group is asked whether they often watched documentaries, he draws attention to 'unos primeros planes así muy agresivos' and 'sensacionalismo . . . no sólo por lo que hablaban sino por las imágenes, el tratarlos a ellos como una especie de héroes' ('some very, well, aggressive close ups' and 'sensationalism . . . not only in the way they spoke but in the images, treating them as kind of heroes'). Paradoxically, while *L'Ordre des mots* is unapologetic, its overall tone and mood are philosophical and reflective rather than aggressive, and its use of – what may be termed – graphic shots is minimal; indeed, the strippedback style – fixed cameras and long takes showing its subjects talking in semi-obscurity, voiceovers set against stills of parts or all of the subjects' faces – might be said to offset the charge of sensationalism. That David contends the film's treatment of its subjects as 'heroes' reinforces the point above that his oppositional response appears to derive from his sense of being preached to. And yet, somewhat contradictorily given his strong reservations, he nonetheless claims to have liked *L'Ordre des mots* since it had informed him about 'un tema que no conocía mucho' ('an issue I didn't know much about') and he attempts, albeit in vague terms, to relate aspects to himself: 'aunque yo no sea trans, yo sí puedo sentirme rechazado según las circunstancias' ('even though I'm not trans myself I can feel rejected, too, in certain circumstances') – which could be a comment about his life experience in general or relate more imminently to how he feels as the group's sceptic. David's reiterations of where he is not, in terms of gender identity, seem to show how what he interprets as a polarised presentation on screen can engender the adoption – perhaps for the duration of the exchange, no more than that – of similarly polarised subject positions.

David's comments differ from those of Emma, which are keyed into more abstract issues of philosophical choice and identity, a reading perhaps informed by her status as a postgraduate student. In a paraphrase from Maud-Yeuse Thomas in the film, she states 'cambio mi soledad por . . . por un género' ('I'm exchanging my loneliness for . . . for a gender') and, again reworking Thomas's words, adds that 'nunca puedes cancelar lo que fuiste, y lo que fuiste va siempre acumulando' ('you can't cancel out what you once were, and what you were keeps accumulating more'). She affirms an interest in 'la relación que hay entre lo biológico y el discurso' ('the relationship that there is between the biological and discourse'). A comparison of this discussion, then, reveals one set of interpretations which has a markedly post-structuralist frame of reference, and which keys into the philosophical comments of an activist on screen, and another, David's, whose stance is more old-school and aesthetically orientated, as well, possibly, as being adopted for the occasion; in fact, he talks of feeling overwhelmed by the philosophical discourses transmitted by *L'Ordre des mots*.

However, David denies, when asked, that the film's occasional philosophical tone is anything that can be qualified in cultural terms as pertaining to a specifically French approach to social and political issues. He lists a series of fictional films, including *Les Témoins* and *Drôle de Félix* (Olivier Ducastel and Jacques Martineau, 2000), as examples of 'good' French films because they are more closely attached to their subjects and characters (unlike the films of Pedro Almodóvar, which, he alleges, are far removed from his own sense of self and identity). Perhaps it was the fact that *L'Ordre des mots* is French, then, that drew David to the screening and to anticipate that it was his film knowledge that would be called upon (as seen, he says that he had come to the event as a critic). As in some of the responses to *Les Invisibles*, French 'gay' fictional cinema is something that he appears to seek out both because he alleges it to be of a distinct aesthetic quality and because it is described as getting closer to 'real' or 'actual' human experience, something that ironically *L'Ordre des mots* might also be said to do, but this 'humanity', David claims, is obscured by its philosophical and radical political modes of address.

Where the militant activism of *L'Ordre des mots* elicits consternation or is interpreted as a reflection on gender issues more broadly, the attitudes portrayed in *Guerriller@s* (Montse Pujantell, 2012) are praised by the attenders at the focus group held in Lyon on 10 March 2013 for their perceived breadth and inclusiveness, tolerance and humanity. *Guerriller@s* covers similar terrain to *L'Ordre des mots*: it challenges external diagnosis and tackles the psychiatrisation and pathologisation of trans people. Its mood is lighter, less sombre, its approach less introspective, although it includes images of bodies before, during and after surgery. Political rather than insurgent, then, *Guerriller@s*, according to the 2011 Cineffable festival programme, English version:

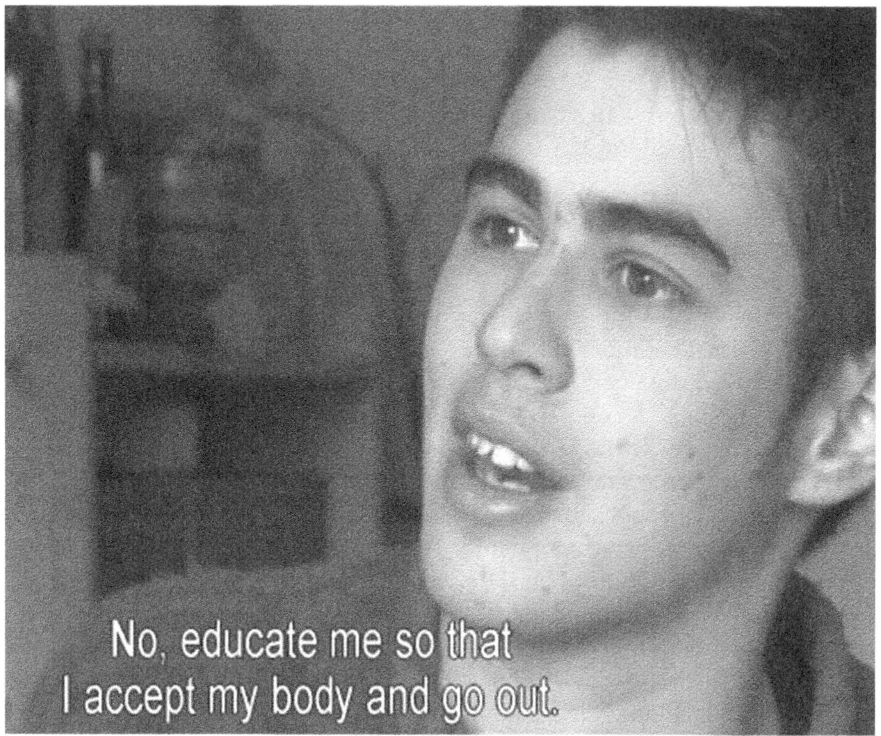

Figure 4.2 Miquel Missé in interview in *Guerriller@s* (Montse Pujantell, 2012). Image reproduced with kind permission of Montse Pujantell.

is a documentary that reflects upon sexual identity, an approach to gender development and its 'control strategies', based on a heterogeneous group of activists who stand for the transsexual and transgender community. It has been selected and awarded in various festivals. (Cineffable 2011)

One of these trans activists is Miquel Missé, who speaks of taking part in the aforementioned 2006 Existrans protest in Paris, of how it proved pivotal to an understanding of their own identity and of how it inspired their 2009 campaign Stop Trans Pathologization. *Guerriller@s* bridges activism and theory, with references by interlocutors to Judith Butler, but also to Foucault as well as to the trans-Atlantic and bilingual lesbian theorist Monique Wittig (whose *Les Guérillères* of 1969 might have been in Pujantell's mind). *Guerriller@s* was screened at LGBTQ film festivals in Paris, Tours and Nantes and can be said to have influenced French trans documentary, particularly *Fille ou garçon* (discussed below).

The focus group discussion was assembled to coincide with the 2013 Ecrans Mixtes festival in Lyon and was held at La Luttine, a space for social groups in the city centre. Five participants attended: Barbara, a twenty-five-year-old white American female, occupation not provided; Cyprien, a thirty-three-year-old white French male, occupation not provided; Maxime, a twenty-seven-year-old white French, 'male/genderqueer/faggot', works in dance; Alex, the genderqueer project manager mentioned at the start of this chapter; Camille, a twenty-nine-year-old white French carpenter, 'genderfucker'. All live in Lyon and are all Ros's friends or acquaintances. Barbara and Cyprien are a couple, as are Alex and Camille, while Maxime lives with Barbara.

While all of the members of the group explicitly or implicitly project their political awareness or involvement in political activism, the degree of connection to and knowledge of trans politics and concerns displayed varies. Despite their familiarity with political contestation, albeit in relation to divergent though related issues (feminism, queer politics, anti-capitalism), they warmly welcome what they characterise as the non-aggressive, pacifist stance of *Guerriller@s*. For instance, Barbara, Alex and Camille all claim to admire Missé's tolerance and pacifism with regards to those who continue to discriminate against trans people. Barbara talks of being 'moved' by their story and adds 'il a éclairé beaucoup de choses . . . qui ont traîné dans ma tête' ('he shed light on many things . . . that were going around in my mind'). Alex agrees and extols their way of 'ne pas se définir comme un homme, ne pas se définir comme une femme, ne pas sentir la nécessité de recourir à la chirurgie, euh, les questions qui se posent sur les hormones' ('not identifying as a man, not identifying as a woman, not feeling the need to have surgery, um, those questions that are raised about hormones'). For Camille, Missé is commendable in maintaining good relations with neighbours and they are 'vachement tolérants à l'ignorance des gens' and because he values 'le fait que les gens reconnaissent de s'être trompés et lui présentent leurs excuses quand ils ont pas, euh, compris son identité' ('really tolerant about the ignorance of people'; 'people admitting that they were wrong and apologising to him when they haven't, um, understood his identity'). According to Camille, this conciliatory attitude stems from the fact that the interviewees are at ease with themselves which allows them to have 'un discours qui est hyper incluant, qui est amoureux, qui est généreux' ('a hyper-inclusive discourse, that is full of love, that is generous'). These three viewers read *Guerriller@s* as gentle and conciliatory despite its shots of body transformations, which recur more frequently than in *L'Ordre des mots*, and which David interpreted as sensationalist and aggressive. This difference might speak particularly to the impact of a dynamic and light overall mood compared to a more morose one for engagement among some viewers.

In addition to its perceived lightness, dynamism and conciliatory tone, the group also stated that they appreciated the diversity of opinions presented in *Guerriller@s*, although diversity here does not extend to the inclusion of external views about transsexual identity that David posits as lacking from *L'Ordre des mots*. Rather, they acclaim the film's flexibility with regards to whom it considers as experts, including trans activists, an artist and a philosopher. Barbara comments, for instance, that 'quand tu traînes dans un certain milieu, tu vois plutôt les, euh, les perspectives et les politiques radicales, et c'était génial d'avoir une . . . gamme dans le film' ('when you hang out in a certain group, you see mainly, um, radical political perspectives and it was great to have a broad range [of perspectives] in the film'). Maxime, though, appreciates the film's incorporation of more political feminist and queer viewpoints alongside these less militant perspectives. He notes that 'les mouvements féministes sont pas très queer' and that 'les mouvements trans . . . peuvent être assez rapidement isolés du féminisme et de, et du mouvement LGBT' ('feminist movements are not very queer'; 'trans movements very quickly can be disconnected from feminism and from, from the LGBT movement'). Here, Maxime is projecting a familiarity with the issues. His comments align with broader debates on how trans identity and experience sit in relation to both queer and feminist discourses, debates that reach well beyond France. While Jay Prosser, for example, recognises that queer theory – and particularly Judith Butler – have made discussions of transsexuality possible, he nonetheless criticises the ways in which it presents transition as discursive rather than exploring the 'bodiliness of gendered crossings' (Prosser 1998: 6). For Prosser, 'in transsexual accounts transition does not shift the subject away from the embodiment of sexual difference but more fully into it' (6). Films such as *Guerriller@s* and *L'Ordre des mots* allow a similar repositioning of trans issues from the realm of the abstract to that of the embodied materiality of trans and intersex existence, even if *Guerriller@s* still flirts with queer sensibilities (upbeat mood, separation of scenes with shots of toy dolls and lipstick, and occasional insistence on gender fluidity).

Maxime also implies awareness that, as Stryker has argued, the 'T' (in LGBT) can be 'reduced to merely another (easily detached) genre of sexual identity rather than perceived, like race or class, as something that cuts across existing sexualities' (Stryker 2004: 215). Critique of the incorporation of trans concerns within queer activism in France can be muted among activists and intellectuals, where the radical power of queer politics can be defended as a potentially fruitful position from which to challenge French republican assimilationism, as seen. This said, while 'le queer a su être ce mouvement culturel qui a produit une circulation et fait co-advenir la culture trans' (Espineira et al. 2013: 15) ('queer was able to be this cultural movement that created a dynamic and also made trans culture come into being'), it is also noted that 'la population trans se pense souvent comme étant "coincée" entre plusieurs fronts: soit la pathologisation et l'aspect juridique trop fixes, soit une queerisation trop vague' (16) ('the trans population often considers itself as being "stuck" between several points: either fixed pathologisation and legal aspects, or a queerisation that is too vague').

However, while all the respondents implicitly and explicitly, and to varying degrees, convey their connections to and involvement in various forms of activism, that activism is not specified as trans-related. Of course, this reflects the diversity mobilised in the film, in which trans issues are related to feminism and the normative gender binary is explained as perpetuating capitalism, sentiments with which these respondents can and do agree. Yet, although Maxime, Alex and Camille self-describe as 'male genderqueer-faggot', 'genderqueer' and 'genderfucker' respectively, they tend to adopt positions of solidarity, empathy and understanding, rather than implicating themselves within a trans community.

The political awareness displayed by these respondents and the views articulated by Emma and Cliff coincide in some cases, particularly with regards to the more general questioning about how people are gendered by society. This distances us from the territory of the specifics of material trans existence and experience, and into what some may see as the more vague realm of queer debates, but, as mentioned, it is also a discourse mobilised within *Guerriller@s*. When asked about whether there were any points of view expressed in *Guerriller@s* that they preferred to others, Maxime focuses on the philosopher Miriam Solá, because she questions fixed notions of sexual orientation and argues that people should not reduce their sexual desires to binary gender structures. This, according to Maxime, allows us to consider the role of fetishes and character types in attraction, desire and seduction, which Maxime claims to find particularly interesting. Maxime's singling out of the philosopher could be because her comments have a practical resonance with what Maxime experiences in the everyday (as a participant in queer cultural and political scenes, both in France and beyond – including attendance at a Queeruption event in Manchester), which differs from Emma, who extols the philosophical discourse of *L'Ordre des mots* for its abstract qualities.

Given their verbal recognition and awareness of some of the issues presented and discourses mobilised in *Guerriller@s*, it is perhaps not surprising that the fact that this film is Catalan-Spanish does not impact on their expressed ability to engage with it, according to their responses. Their sensitivities and sense of solidarity cut across not only different interest and political groups (anti-capitalist, feminist, queer and so on) but also national and cultural boundaries. Hence, it is the theme of activism that Alex highlights as the element that makes *Guerriller@s* seem familiar, not exotic, as their response cited at the opening of this chapter illustrates. At the end of the discussion, all the respondents state that it would be worthwhile showing *Guerriller@s* to a broader audience, which might include school children, although Cyprien is more cautious, advocating screening it only to people who might already be sensitised to its subject. In fact, although Cyprien conveys understanding of the issues portrayed in *Guerriller@s*, by contrast to Alex he nonetheless characterises it as intrinsically different from what he implies are typical French approaches to its themes. He identifies the film's aforementioned ability to bring together people from different backgrounds and milieux (including not only the philosopher, the sociologist and an artist but also the 'punk' activist) as the reason for this distinction: 'c'est des gens qu'on ne voit pas dans des milieux sur la sexualité ou sur les genres en France' ('these are people that you don't see in gender and sexuality circles in France'). Here, the subject position of a viewer of *Guerriller@s* may recall the activists' stance in *L'Ordre des mots*, but, where they contested their exclusion from public debates on trans and intersex issues in France, Cyprien advocates greater inclusivity and extols a degree of balance in which no particular perspective is treated as having precedence over another. A Catalan–Spanish documentary is appreciated by a French activist-viewer as offering a more open appraisal of the issues than he would expect to witness in France.

Maxime also notes important differences between the ways in which France and Spain approach trans concerns. Again, Maxime projects his knowledge of trans politics by invoking the material hurdles to reassignment in France:

> en France il y a quand même . . . plus de difficultés qu'en Espagne . . . le changement d'état civil, et l'accès aux . . . traitements hormonaux et les chirurgies sont quand même un peu compliqués, et demandent des . . . parcours médicaux un peu longs (.) et difficiles.

> (there are actually . . . more difficulties in France than in Spain . . . changing civil status, access to hormonal treatments and surgery are actually a little complicated, and require . . . long and difficult medical processes.)

Maxime adds 'en France, il y a cette nécessité d'être (.) opéré, stérilisé' ('you're required to be (.) operated, sterilised in France'). Maxime thus questions France's approach to trans issues despite the laudatory declarations by government ministers that transsexuality has been declassified as a pathology, an approach seen in Bourcier cited above and illustrated in the criticisms by the OUTrans movement, which also defines itself as a feminist movement and argued in 2009 (like Bourcier two years later) that France's claims to 'de-psychiatrise' trans people were a medico-administrative convenience that left trans people still considered as sick and subjected to a psychiatric evaluation to validate their will to transition (Espineira 2015: 150).

Maxime's comments, and those of Cyprien, speak to how citizens approach their own, and other, nations and cultures. For them, it seems, Spain symbolises greater openness with regards to trans and gender issues more broadly than France, which is still implied as being held back by its apparent need to see any social issue through a specialist lens, where specialist means medical professionals and academics as opposed to those with material experience of those issues. This chimes with the longstanding perception, outlined in Chapter 1, that Spain represents a more relaxed stance towards or is more accepting of difference than France (a view expressed in Daphne's reading of *El sexo des los ángeles* that opened Chapter 3). And yet, David's declared preference for French films because they are more 'real', 'human' and get closer to their subjects than the films of Almodóvar (in the *L'Ordre des mots* discussion) confirms how perceptions of national and cultural difference as they are portrayed in cinema change according to the film or filmmaker under discussion and the perspective or agenda of the individual viewer. Maxime and Cyprien in particular share a critical perspective with regards to their home nation and articulate a common opinion that things are better elsewhere, thereby echoing Marc and Daphne's criticism of France as seen in Chapter 3.

Like *Guerriller@s*, *Fille ou garçon*, which, as mentioned, may have been influenced by it, is less politicised, perhaps owing to its being produced (like *El camino de Moisés*) for mainstream TV, albeit by the European culture channel ARTE, with its reputation for making more nuanced films. According to the 2012 BFI London Lesbian and Gay Film Festival reviewer, the film:

> follows the lives of four trans men, Kaleb, Lynnee, Rocco, and Miguel, and takes the audience into their worlds and what being trans means to them. Kaleb chooses non-binary gender as a response to a system that forces gender upon them. Lynnee, who also identifies as non-binary but prefers male pronouns, has opted out of hormone replacement due to the impact on his liver. Rocco has fully transitioned and lives in New York with his girlfriend. And Miguel muses on what being male is. (Basford 2012)

Whilst trans men in this film are free to define their own gender, there is a visual insistence on before-and-after logic (through still photographs), as well as on getting views from the outside (interviewing friends, family and partners) which risks sidelining trans people's self-definition. These possible problems notwithstanding, some members of the audience at the FICGLB Festival screenings of the film on 25 and 26 October 2012 considered it to be clear or straightforward (four responses out of eleven) and, according to Maite, a thirty-one-year-old white female Spanish therapist, respectful, and, according to Carola, a thirty-four-year-old white female Spanish professional counsellor, useful from a sex-educational point of view. Respondents conveyed their openness to the subtleties of the sexual politics underpinning the film and its reception: Carola commented that she appreciated the representation of different modes of being trans and – from a professional point of view – the attention to non-normative and non coito-centric sexuality, and related the film to times in her own life when she had rethought her sexuality, whereas Maite noted the denial of labels and categories. Such comments project some awareness of the specificities of trans existences, which recalls Maxime's observations above, although here it is arguably not involvement in activism or the assumption of alternative lifestyles that may have informed this understanding but their occupations. Another viewer, Sofia, a twenty-three-year-old female student who offered no further details about herself, implies a concern with gender politics and an alignment with feminist critique by noting the anti-sexist and questioning approach to the social privileges of masculinity. Taking a more critical stance than all three, though, Monica, a thirty-two-year-old white female Spanish university teacher, writes of having been surprised by 'algunos testimonios que me han parecido bastante binarios para ser trans' ('some of the accounts which seemed to me too binary to be trans'). As with *Guerriller@s*, this issues-based documentary from 'abroad' invites politically informed reactions from some of its viewers (roughly half of those who filled in the questionnaire), thereby allowing these respondents who do not identify as trans the means through which they can convey a degree of understanding.

Bambi (Sébastien Lifshitz, 2013) and *Ocaña, retrat intermitent* (*Ocaña, an Intermittent Portrait*) (Ventura Pons, 1978): Histories of Trans Lives and Struggles

If *Fille ou garçon* is a film in which, arguably, 'we don't see very much of how each individual lives their lives' (Basford 2012), *Bambi* and *Ocaña* are very much focused on one individual each. These individuals are defined, in the films at least, by their determination, resolve and apparent authenticity, personality traits that viewers particularly admire, according to our data. In the main, such admiration is articulated by people who define themselves in cisgender terms, thus revealing how non-trans-identifying viewers of films about trans people and, in the case of *Ocaña*, those who avoid gender identifications, draw out those aspects that they claim resonate with their own experiences, particularly in coming to terms with their sexuality. Once again, in some of these cases, respondents relate to their own lived reality either the feeling of alienation and marginalisation or the quest for self-expression and self-determination of the trans, non-gendered or genderqueer subjects portrayed and recounted on screen. The data thus show that, while there are of course legitimate questions about the visibility of trans identity and existence within LGBTQ politics and cultural representations (including film festivals), and about conflations of gender with sexuality when talking about trans concerns, their stories of emancipation key into the kind of shared experience and broad sense of community facilitated by festivals and some special screenings of LGBTQ films. That Bambi and Ocaña are endowed with similar qualities, but hail from two different countries and are encountered by audiences from 'abroad', shows that, in the reception of these two films at least, such courage and individuality are not necessarily attached to imagined or discursively differentiated cultural spaces, although Ocaña prompts some critical reflection on Frenchness for some respondents.

The subject of *Bambi*, Marie-Pierre Pruvot, had been destined to be included in *Les Invisibles*, but Lifshitz was so taken by her story that he decided to devote a medium-length documentary to her. Screenings of the film at FIRE!! on 7 and 13 July 2013, as part of the 'Pantalla Trans' ('Trans Screen') section, were accompanied by this programme note and synopsis:

> Marie-Pierre Pruvot is a figurehead in the French transsexual community. Born a boy in Algeria, she moved to Paris to be who she really is,

and there began a long and prominent career in the well-known cabaret Carrousel. She adopted the name Bambi, by which she is still known in public. She forms part of that first generation of transsexual women who, in the fifties, travelled to Casablanca to be operated on. She is a mythical figure in the history of transsexuality, and this marvellous documentary pays her a splendid homage at 77 years of age. With a subtle collage of archive images, songs, recent interviews, Super 8 scenes shot by herself throughout her years at Carrousel and other recent recordings from the places of her childhood, this valuable documentary is a brilliant account of her transformation into a radiant woman, of her friendship with the famous transsexual artist Coccinelle, and of how she ended up being a teacher and a writer. (FIRE!! 2013b)

The style of *Bambi* both resembles and exceeds that of *Les Invisibles*. As in the other documentary, *Bambi* traces an arc from repression to emancipation, although it keeps its most surprising elements for its final minutes: Bambi's long-lasting relationship with a woman, Ute, and her twenty-six years' service as a teacher of literature in secondary schools near Cherbourg. Footage from

Figure 4.3 Poster for *Bambi* (Sébastien Lifshitz, 2013), featuring Marie-Pierre Pruvot (Bambi). Image © Courtesy of *Un Monde Meilleur*.

the past and personal photographs intertwine with film of Bambi today. Moreover, as the above reviewer notes, *Bambi* amplifies its sense of auto-biographical agency, not only in effacing any reference to its filmmakers, giving the impression that Bambi speaks for herself, but also in stamping her signature on the film: at various points, we shift from direct address to the camera to use of her voice to narrate the sequences we see, some of which she filmed herself. *Bambi* is a world away from *L'Ordre des mots*. Not only does it present the trajectory of one transsexual in narrative form, and in so doing it articulates aspects of the history of transvestites and transsexuals in Paris in the 1950s, but it also celebrates the glamorous allure of that trans scene. Its musical score, including two of Bambi's own song covers and two by the famous transsexual Coccinelle, complements its broad appeal as a retrospective of a 'golden age' in which two famous Parisian review cabarets dominated nocturnal life: *Madame Arthur* and *Le Carrousel de Paris*. In the 1950s and 1960s, Paris was perceived as the world capital of transgender cabaret culture (Foerster 2012: 100). By 1954, transvestite performers were being replaced by transsexuals, partly because the Paris police chief, Léonard, had banned transvestite performances in public from 1 February 1949 (Foerster 2012: 106). Some, including Coccinelle and later Bambi, travelled to Casablanca to undergo a vaginoplasty performed by the renowned surgeon Georges Burou. *Bambi* prefers irony to militancy; at one point, a virulent anti-trans discourse is heard in voiceover, but the image-track depicts the nocturnal world in which Bambi and her peers found solace, expression and self-determination. Bambi and her friends emerge as pioneers who paved the way for later trans activism, of the kind we see in *L'Ordre des mots*. As Bambi recalls, the police were heavy-handed and their lives were far from comfortable and secure, but they nonetheless could access hormones over the counter and transsexuality had yet to be pathologised.

Viewers expressed appreciation for the film's transparency, simplicity and naturalness, with one, Abel, a thirty-six-year-old Catalan male journalist who did not describe his ethnicity, attributing its sincerity to its protagonist. Diego, a forty-eight-year-old white male Spanish worker, writes that he thought the film very true 'a la seva realitat. Ella ha construït la seva realitat' ('to her own reality. She has made her own reality'), but also notes, when prompted by the question on identification, that it resonated with moments in his own life when the way he perceived himself ('la meva realitat interior') had clashed with the way others had seen him. Here, Diego is making an implicit reference to the first section of *Bambi*, in which its subject recounts her childhood when she was named Jean-Pierre, and the actions, particularly of Bambi's mother, to prevent Bambi from transgressing Bambi's ascribed gender. Arcadi, a twenty-six-year-old white Catalan male worker, goes further and makes a direct connection with Bambi: 'la construcció del meu jo és força semblant a la viscuda per la protagonista' ('the way my own sense of myself is constructed is very similar to the way the protagonist experienced it') and Fran, a thirty-eight-year-old white Spanish male film critic, refers to the resonances between Bambi and the viewer, though he avoids subjective self-implication, noting that the film underlines 'la necessitat de descobrir-se ara mateix' ('the present need to find oneself'). Amina, a forty-year-old Catalan female worker who does 'not believe in any ethnic group', takes a slightly less upbeat approach and shifts the focus from self-awareness to alienation from the self, saying that she identified with the sense of 'sentir-te un extrany de tu mateix a vegades' ('feeling that you are a stranger to yourself at times').

Looking away from the individual to the collective, Oriol's comment, cited at the beginning of this chapter, that it is important to know 'our' history, articulates transnational community allegiance through his use of the first person plural possessive form, which recalls Sarah's reading in Chapter 3 of *Les Invisibles* as addressing a community in which she implicates herself. The entity hailed as prompting that sense of cross-cultural community affinity is a shared history that, though specific, in terms of importance is heralded as resonating universally. This echoes the reactions to the film and Bambi herself at FIRE!!, with various members of the audience, from Bambi's generation and younger, claiming it as an archive of the historical development of the (global) trans community. Such comments recall Steve's observations about *Les Invisibles*, which illustrate the significance for some of recording and representing those lives and experiences that are '"hidden from history"' (Perks and Thomson 2006, viiii, citing the title of Rowbotham 1973). Both Oriol and Arcadi write that they enjoyed the use of archive footage in the question asking what they liked about the style of the film. Lucy, a twenty-seven-year-old female student of Venezuelan nationality who did not describe her ethnicity, writes that the archive images add to the authenticity and that she liked seeing 'el mon trans en aquells anys' ('the trans world of those [past] years'), while also noting that what is narrated seems 'similar a ara' ('similar to now'). Once again, this history is not localised, but is broadened out as a collective history ('el mon trans'). For Ignassi, a thirty-one-year-old white Spanish male teacher, who makes a link between the individual and the collective, it is the struggle ('lluita') that resonates across borders, a sentiment echoed by Iván, a twenty-seven-year-old male voluntary worker, who notes simply that 'hi ha molt feina a fer' ('there's still a lot of work to do').

The above viewers, then, articulate political positions through their positive appraisals of the film's content and style, using it either to affirm transnational allegiance and convey a sense of cross-cultural community affiliation, as mentioned, or as a reminder of outstanding battles to be won. However, another viewer makes a somewhat divergent political point, though one that ultimately conveys a similar investment in increasing public awareness of trans issues. Dolors, a fifty-seven-year-old white Spanish female health worker who works with trans people, highlights the separation between Bambi's idealised existence and the lives of other trans people: 'no totes les persones tenen una realitat que els permet decidir la seva vida' ('not everyone's everyday experience allows them to decide how to live'). Dolors establishes a distinction between the individual, and 'special', life recounted in the film, glamorised and treated cinematographically (she states) and that of trans people less able to determine their own identities and life paths (and with whom, we might assume, she comes into contact in her occupation). Dolors's critique contrasts with Oriol's enthusiasm and suggests that the history *Bambi* presents is still a privileged one, styled to appeal to certain 'dominant' tastes, while other pasts remain silent or hidden from view. Fran and Amina, on the other hand, appear to buy into the film's idealism in their observations about the distinction between representations and 'reality'. When asked whether they felt *Bambi* was true to life, they ask what is meant by reality. Here they evoke Brenner's lack of interest in seemingly objective constructions of 'truth' in response to *Les Invisibles*, which, as seen, shows their emotional investment in *Les Invisibles*, and they elide the more cynical and realistic view articulated by Tom in reaction to that film that actual experience can often be embellished when recalled from memory.

For Jemima, a seventeen-year-old white British female student, watching at Cornerhouse (Manchester) when it was screened as part of a film season entitled 'French Connection' on 4 December 2013, what made the film 'more touching and REAL' (her emphasis) was the fact of its being a 'personal account' and 'an honest outpouring of the soul'. The overlap at this venue of an LGBTQ audience (five out of nine respondents saying they regularly attended LGBTQ film festivals) with a cinephile one, as well as the film's screening as part of the cinema's commitment to programming non-English language film, produced less specific responses than in the case of the Barcelona audience to the question asking whether they were able to identify with any of the people or situations in the documentary. Richard, a forty-two-year-old white British male writer from London, said that he attended the screening because of its 'original subject matter' and, like Diego and Arcadi, claimed to identify with aspects, remembering 'feeling different as a child and being punished by family for this'. Again, experiences of feeling 'other' seemingly because of sexuality are related to the experience of gender nonconformity in children as recounted by Bambi. William, a seventy-four-year-old white male retired teacher, though, claimed a more distanced position, writing that he did 'not personally [identify]', but added 'I have trans friends' and described enjoying this 'story of a wonderful woman going through self-discovery'. That the majority (seven: two identifying as male, five as female) claim to have felt no identification might reflect the mixed status of the audience and the non-LGBTQ-specific contexts in which the film was encountered.

While Oriol and Lucy, in Barcelona, had highlighted the history portrayed in *Bambi* as that of trans people, Kenneth, an eighty-five-year-old white British male retired professional, who spontaneously self-identifies as 'homosexual not gay', reveals the importance of the cabaret clubs of the 1950s and 1960s as part of a broader 'homosexual' history. He writes in response to the question asking why he chose the film, 'Algiers (oh, that music!); France/Paris;

show-biz; sexuality – all of my favourite things!' When asked whether he enjoyed *Bambi* he cites 'memories of Paris and "Madame Arthurs". Backstage scenes'. On the one hand, the past is related to geographical space ('Algiers, France, Paris') while, on the other, that same space is framed as resonating beyond borders, a past defined, as Kenneth states, by 'show-biz, sexuality' and in which he implies that he was an active participant (the 'memories', he suggests, are his). Kenneth's nostalgic recollections of this history illustrate the cross-border dimensions of participation in a culture and community that attracted not only trans people and their heterosexual audiences but also, in his term, homosexuals. *Bambi* serves as a brief interlude in the era before Stonewall and the UK Sexual Offences Act (1967) that prompts fond memories for those fortunate enough to dispose of the means to travel abroad to escape local repression. Much like some inhabitants of the south-west of France mentioned in Chapter 1, for whom Barcelona can be their LGBTQ hub, Paris served a similar function for those living outside of France during the 1950s and 1960s. Paris is, thus, at once exotic other (as is Algiers) but also a site of familiarity and recognition – in fact, a site that provided a greater sense of self-recognition than perhaps Manchester (where he watches the film) does in the present. This reveals how such hubs change according to geography, local politics and period, although this does not always mean that the city itself is a liberal space recognised and accepted by its inhabitants; it was those who owned the Parisian trans cabarets (Marcel Oudjman / Monsieur Marcel in the case of the *Carrousel*) and the fascination of the public for the 'perverse' or 'exotic' that created a market for trans shows, as well as the defiance and creativity of the trans community that kept the scene going despite clampdowns by the police (Foerster 2012: 103–6). This is also an era of limited awareness of the specific issues affecting trans people and the difficult lives they led; as an undated show programme notes (c. 1960s, guesses the curator), 'things really get gay . . . both on stage and backstage, where the boys who will be girls like to relax and let their wigs down between shows' (Doyle 2015).

Another historical moment is represented in the Catalan-Spanish biographical documentary *Ocaña, retrat intermitent*, made three years after Franco's death in 1975. Unlike *Bambi*, *Ocaña* is contemporary to the historical period in which it is set. *Ocaña* was famously both a socio-cultural milestone for Spain's transition to democracy and 'una de las muestras más tempranas de placer visual explícitamente queer del cine español' (Fouz-Hernández 2013: 133–4) ('one of the earliest displays of explicitly queer visual pleasure in Spanish cinema'). *Ocaña* was made not only in the transition period between Franco's dictatorship and democracy, symbolised by the *movida*, but also before globalisation had developed in Spain. As a result, it offers a glimpse of a highly individual and localised culture, and one that coincides with and plays upon some of the stereotypes of Spanishness outlined in Chapter 1.

Ocaña was Pons's first feature and he has since acquired renown as a queer filmmaker. Winner of the 2015 Acadèmia del Cinema Català Gaudí prize (the Premi Gaudí d'Honor Miquel Porter), Pons is not only the most prolific and one of the most internationally renowned directors, in Catalan cinema (Acadèmia del Cinema 2015) but also well known for his role in 'la visibilització del col·lectiu LGTB' (Acadèmia del Cinema 2015) ('enhancing the visibility of the LGBT community'). Popularly in Spain and Catalunya among gay audiences he is a high-profile presence (Fouz Hernández 2013; Perriam 2013a: 76–9). Guest appearances at screenings of his third documentary *Ignaci M.* (2014), a portrait of the HIV-positive museum conservation expert Ignaci Millet, at LesGaiCineMad and the Barcelona International Gay & Lesbian Film Festival (October 2013) and at the closing gala of Zinegoak, Bilbao (January 2014), have enhanced this. The film has since shown at the Désir désirs festival, Tours, February 2014, the Different! L'Autre cinéma espagnol festival, Paris, June 2014, at Cinespaña, Toulouse, October 2014, and back in Catalunya on the television channel TV3 on 18 November. *Ocaña* was shown at the Ecrans Mixtes festival in Lyon on 10 March 2013 and the screening was followed by a question and answer session with its director. The festival's brochure presents the film like this:

> 'Je ne suis pas un travesti, j'aime simplement m'habiller en femme' explique le peintre barcelonais Ocaña dans ce documentaire qui lui est consacré. Artiste prolifique et figure singulière, fantasque et provocatrice de l'Espagne post-franquiste et pré-Movida, Ocaña fait preuve dans ces années 70 d'une liberté et d'une audace réjouissantes . . . *Ocaña* est un documentaire qui frappe notamment par la force de son sujet à un moment charnière de l'histoire de l'Espagne . . . Le récit parfois douloureux, de l'existence du peintre dans un pays ultra-catholique alterne avec ses exhibitions dans la rue, ses performances, ses déclarations à l'emporte-pièce, ses concerts . . . Document historique autant que manifeste politique et identitaire, *Ocaña* est un jalon important du cheminement du cinéma espagnol vers la liberté. (Ecrans Mixtes 2013)

('I am not a transvestite. I simply like dressing as a woman', explains the Barcelona artist Ocaña in this documentary devoted to him. A prolific artist and singular figure, who is both whimsical and provocative and who came from post-Francoist and pre-Movida Spain, Ocaña displays cheerful freedom and audacity in 1970s Spain . . . *Ocaña* is a documentary that strikes the viewer especially because of the strength of its subject during a key moment of Spanish history . . . The sometimes painful story of the artist's existence in an ultra-Catholic country alternates with his showing off in the streets, his performances, his rash declarations, his concerts . . . A historic document as much as a political and identity manifesto, *Ocaña* is an important milestone on the road towards freedom in Spanish cinema.)

Figure 4.4 José Pérez Ocaña, 'Ocaña', accompanied (left) by the artist 'Camilo' as they appear in *Ocaña, retrat intermitent* (Ventura Pons, 1978). Image reproduced with kind permission of Els Films de la Rambla S.A.

Unlike *Bambi*, Ocaña does not identify as a trans woman, nor does he wish to transition, he refuses to be considered as a transvestite, as the above review confirms, and he rejects labels such as 'gay'. And yet, his cross-dressing has a social and political impact, given that he does it in public spaces, although, in the footage we see, his performances elicit appreciation from the locals rather than disdain. Ocaña self-describes variously as a bohemian, an anarchist and a marginal, he identifies with pimps and prostitutes and takes a prominent part in the insurgent demonstrations against Franco's 'Ley sobre peligrosidad y rehabilitación social' (Law on Social Danger and Rehabilitation) which, since 5 August 1970, building on previous legislation, had penalised 'antisocial' activities, including homosexuality, prostitution and pimping, stepping up police raids and individual arrests, further pathologising gay men and sentencing them to time in rehabilitation centres (Huard 2014: 100–5; Pérez-Sánchez 2007: 24–33). He might thus be perceived as a queer figure in its most political sense, someone who seeks to subvert, who attracts and is attracted to the margins, whose sexuality is not normative, but who also rejects fixed labels (Fernández 2007; Mira 2013: 60–3).

On the one hand, the film illustrates some of the concerns that trans issues become obscured within queer movements and cultural representation. In the figure of Ocaña, gender transgression is a form of creative expression, even if that expression is part of broader political efforts to align with and promote so-called 'marginal' identities. One of our respondents, Luc, a twenty-one-year-old white French male student, appears to endorse this confining of transvestite display to public performance, describing how he enjoyed 'le fait de montrer que son travestissement fait partie d'un spectacle' ('the fact that his transvestism is part of a show'). However, on the other hand, Ocaña also illustrates that transgender performance, when functioning as a manifestation of queerness, has opened a space for discussions of trans issues in contemporary culture. Ocaña may thus be seen as a pioneer, much like Bambi, who has contributed to greater awareness of gender nonconformity and, possibly, recognition of trans people.

The screening of *Ocaña* was poorly attended, with only twelve viewers in the auditorium at the advertised start time – the presence of Pons seemingly not having an impact on the popularity of the event, although we later discovered that only two people attended another screening that same evening. The festival programmer delayed the beginning for approximately twenty minutes to allow more people to arrive and, in the end, about forty people attended. The question and answer session gave people the time to fill in our questionnaire: we received thirteen completed questionnaires, a relatively high response rate.

According to Luc, art and an attraction for 'Spanish culture' brought him to the screening: 'j'aime beaucoup l'art et j'aime connaître la vie des artistes et j'aime la culture espagnole' ('I love art and I love knowing about the lives of artists and I love Spanish culture'). Luc circumvents suggestions of identification or empathy with Ocaña on the grounds of sexuality or gender, stating only that the artist's spontaneous and disordered recollections gave rise to feelings of self-similarity. Elsewhere, Michelle, a thirty-nine-year-old white female French library worker who lives in St Etienne, expresses a similar view, emphasising the specificity of the contexts in which Ocaña lived and of his individual identity when asked whether she identified with any aspects: 'encore faut-il avoir vécu dans la Barcelone post-Franquiste!' ('you have to have lived in post-Franco Barcelona'). However, Antoine, a thirty-two-year-old white male French nurse, is more ambivalent. While he states that he chose the film 'pour son sujet, l'époque dans laquelle il se déroule, le personnage' ('for its subject, the era in which it unfolds, the character'), and, in considering whether the film was true to life, notes 'à la réalité des années 70 en Espagne, oui' ('to the reality in Spain of the 1970s, yes'), he also writes that he could identify with Ocaña 'par rapport à la découverte de son homosexualité, au vécu dans l'environnement familial' ('because of the discovery of his homosexuality, his lived experience within the family environment'). The familiar story of self-discovery in terms of sexuality is thus once again highlighted as a shared experience that allows French viewers to relate to a Catalan–Spanish documentary.

Another respondent, who refrained from giving a name, but who is a fifty-six-year-old white Irish female film programmer living in Lyon, stated that she chose the film because 'c'est un classique, [un] film important' ('it's a classic,

[an] important film'). She does not clarify why she attaches such importance to *Ocaña*, but she claims to connect with Ocaña 'de manière empathique' ('in an empathic way'), thus displaying her 'capacity' and 'disposition' for congruent feelings (Plantinga 1999: 244), while also articulating an ethical care to recognise the distinctiveness of Ocaña's identity and experiences when compared to their own. For another participant, who also does not provide a name, but who states that they are twenty-six, white Franco-German and an accountant, the oppressiveness of normative dress codes is highlighted as the factor that causes a cross-cultural sense of self-recognition. Despite Ocaña's peculiarly Spanish existence and Andalusian persona and the fact that the audience encounters him with a temporal interval of thirty-five years, these viewers from 'abroad' nonetheless find points of common values and understanding.

The qualities that the respondents claim to admire most is Ocaña's spontaneity and tenacity in expressing himself in the way he chooses. Answering the question about what they thought of the film's approach to its subject matter, Luc acclaims the fact that 'ça laisse place à la théatricalité de Ocaña de s'exprimer' ('it leaves space for Ocaña to express his theatricality'). Michelle states 'le fait de lui laisser la parole, de l'accompagner dans ses rencontres en font un moment de liberté réussi' ('allowing him to speak, accompanying him in his meetings [with others] create a very good portrayal of freedom'). Ocaña is characterised, then, as having agency and authorship, with the director being mentioned only once (by Michelle, who wrote that hearing Pons speak after the film was one of the reasons why she decided to come to the screening). As with *Les Invisibles*, *L'Ordre des mots*, *Guerriller@s*, *Fille ou garçon* and *Bambi*, the respondents convey their appreciation of (the impression of) direct access to the subjects; in fact, some of the *Ocaña* respondents dismiss questions around whether the film is 'true-to-life' and, again, like Brenner in relation to *Les Invisibles*, express a preference for a more individualised, negotiated and contingent understanding of truth as being related to the subject's own perceptions and experiences.

For three participants, Ocaña's perceived courage and self-determination are identified as triggering introspective comparisons of themselves with the artist. Benjamin and Flora, who filled in the questionnaire together, who are eighty, French and retired, and describe their ethnicity as 'gaulois, hélas' ('Gallic, sadly'), state that while they did not identify with Ocaña 'on se sent un peu coincé après avoir vu un personnage si LIBRE' ('you feel a bit uptight after having seen such a FREE character' – their emphasis). Similarly, Gérard, a sixty-five-year-old white French retired telecoms maintenance engineer, shows a hint of regret when he asks rhetorically 'qui n'a pas rêvé un jour de vivre au moins une fois cette liberté!' ('who has not dreamed one day about living that freedom at least once!'). The appeal of a more visceral life structured by passion and freedom of choice or the pleasure in being able to experience that life vicariously, in the present, through subjects on screen, implied by some of the respondents to *Notre paradis* and *El sexo de los ángeles* arises once again in these responses. In the case of the reception of *Ocaña*, though, a paradox emerges in that people watching this film in Lyon in 2013, at a time when freedoms possibly unimaginable to Spanish queers in the late 1970s appear to have been achieved, use a Spanish film from that period as an example of the liberty that, they suggest, they did not seize. Although the reviewer describes Spain as an 'ultra-Catholic country', it is France in 2013 that is characterised as retrograde by these viewers when compared to the film within which that supposed ultra-Catholicism weighs heavy.

These comments return us to the tensions between the 'here' and 'there' that underlie perceptions of the differences between domestic and foreign cultures. As noted in Chapter 1, in dominant Western discourses the Orient represented what the West was deemed to be lacking (Ahmed 2006: 114). This can also be said of Spain in these and other responses; viewed from 'here' (France) everything 'there' (Spain) seems better, but the precise qualities that are understood as being so much better 'there' are less clear. Maxime, in his response to *Guerriller@s*, suggests that reassignment is easier in Spain than in France, but he tells us little about the specifics and shifts his focus to the limitations of France, apart from a vague claim that changing civil status for trans people is easier in Spain (in fact, Spain receives only three direct references throughout the whole discussion). While, in some cases, the 'there' in the response – that is, Spanish or French culture – is endowed with specific qualities and characterised as prompting feelings of particular recognition and connection (as in Kenneth above), in others it serves as a springboard for articulating frustrations about 'here'. 'There' is thus a hazy place in cultural terms in such observations, 'known' only to a degree (and doubtlessly informed by stereotypes of the kind outlined in Chapter 1) and constructed superficially, via association or sweeping statements. According to our data, France is the country that is most often the object of expressions of dissatisfaction by its own nationals; David's comment about Almodóvar targets a personality rather than a nationality, even if that individual is often hailed as a symbol of that nationality. While Benjamin and Flora's description of their ethnicity as 'Gallic, sadly' conveys investment in the home culture – they would not mention it in that way if it did not matter to them – when combined with their other comments mentioned above it sets France up as conservative and repressive.

A Fictional Trans Narrative: Tomboy (Céline Sciamma, 2011)

So far, all of the films mentioned that examine trans issues have been documentaries, which might be perceived as a privileged genre for the exploration of marginal concerns and which has become crucial for avant-garde and countercultural filmmaking in recent years. However, fictional films have also approached trans identities in recent times, including Pedro Almodóvar's *La piel que habito* (2011) and *Une nouvelle amie* (François Ozon, 2014) – both discussed in Chapter 5 – and *Tomboy*. *Tomboy* did not feature in the programming of the festivals that we covered in this project, although it was advertised on the FIRE!! site when it was screened at the French Institute, Barcelona, on 16 April 2013 and had been shown at that festival in 2011 (and five further Spanish festivals between then and 2014). The site does not provide a synopsis, but the Spanish online RadioGay publishes the following overview:

> Laure tiene 10 años y es transgénero. Después de una mudanza llega a un nuevo barrio donde, debido a su aspecto y al corte de pelo que lleva, en un primer momento es confundida por un niño. El verano se convertirá en un gran parque infantil donde Laure se convierte en Michael, un niño como cualquier otro. Todos los niños lo acogen como a un muchacho más e incluso una niña del grupo, Lisa, se enamora de él. Laure se aprovecha de su nueva identidad para divertirse con su nueva vida, pero el final del verano y la vuelta al colegio revelarán su inquietante secreto. (Staff RadioGay 2014)

> (Laure is ten years old and is transgender. After moving house, she arrives in a new area where, because of her looks and her short hair, she is instantly confused for a boy. The summer becomes a large children's playground where Laure converts herself to Michaël, a boy like any other. All of the children welcome him as another boy, including the girl of the group, Lisa, who falls in love with him. Laure takes advantage of her new identity and has fun with her life, but the end of the summer and the return to school will see her troubling secret revealed.)

Tomboy is thus a fictional feature with a consistent attempt within this at the style of *cinéma verité*, although with an admixture of family melodrama and building to the narreme of the shocking moment of revelation (Michaël being revealed as Laure to his/her neighbours). We decided to include *Tomboy* because of the pertinence of its subject to our project and because of the polemic it caused when *Tomboy* was screened as part of a 'School and Cinema' programme for pupils between the ages of eight and eleven in France. One mother from Niort reportedly wrote to the local newspaper (*Le Courrier de l'Ouest*) on 9 December 2013 complaining that it was dangerous to allow nine-year-old children to think that they can change their sex without any harm (quoted in Fabre 2013). Another regional newspaper, *La Nouvelle République*, noted that the movement that had demonstrated against the introduction of same-sex marriage in France, and so virulently and in such large numbers, was beginning to mobilise once again. The Christian organisation Citizengo, known for campaigning against LGBTQ rights, organised a petition on 28 November and by 20 December 15,360 people had signed demanding that the film be removed from the curriculum (quoted in Fabre 2013). Citizengo is based in Madrid, which interestingly illustrates that the transnational flow of the production and reception of LCBTQ films is matched by a similar cross-Pyrenean flow of protest against LGBTQ rights. Of course, that representations of non-normative gender in a child should provoke such apparent outrage is hardly surprising; as queer theorists have noted, the child is a privileged figure, vested with the perpetuation of heteronormative values and logic (Sedgwick 1991: 18–27; Edelman 2004: 1–31). *Tomboy* portrays childhood development along the lines of what Kathryn Bond Stockton (2009: 11) calls 'sideways growth', which refers to the 'versions of children that both histories and childhood studies have under recognised, oddly conceptualised, or not even seen' (17) because 'we are in a time that does not officially recognise children as growing sideways instead of up' (16). The parents, seemingly outraged that their children had to watch *Tomboy,* adopt positions against such alternative accounts of horizontal child development.

Tomboy was shown to a focus group in Salamanca in April 2014. The group of six (four women two men) was recruited locally and all live in the city and all have a high level of education or are still studying: Pedro, a thirty-six-year-old white Spanish hotel administration manager; Andrea, a nineteen-year-old white Spanish female undergraduate student; Leonora, in her mid-thirties, a white heterosexual Argentinian research assistant; Marta Isabel, in her early twenties, a white European Spanish lesbian second-year undergraduate student; María José, in her mid-thirties, a white Spanish lesbian FE teacher; Sergio, in his early thirties, a white European gay Spanish biotechnician. Salamanca is a major university city in the centre-north of Spain, without its own LGBT festival but with a strong, politically alternative youth culture and a university-based LGBT group.

The session took place in a study room of the city's municipal library, a historic monument of major public and touristic interest, the Casa de las Conchas. The interest of the head librarian and her team in generously opening up this space to the group, as well as the building's high profile, gave the session a particularly open feel while the distance from cinemas and festival alike had a similar democratic effect. The Salamanca group generally adopts an objective perspective with regards to the trans issues portrayed in *Tomboy.* This might well be informed by the combination of high level of education, the auspicious surroundings of a historical monument and library, and the fact that they are participating in a research event facilitated by a professor from a foreign university. The point here is not that *Tomboy* failed to move them on an emotional level – 'audience responses are always *emotionally-charged understandings* and *educated emotions* . . . there is no way of separating out the cognitive and the emotional responses, regarding these as separately shaped or driven' (Barker 2006: 29; his emphasis) – but critical interpretations of the film's issues and implications are precisely what this group emphasises. Of course, the Lyon and Barcelona (and indeed London and Manchester) group discussants also express critical evaluations, but affect and emotion, self-implication in the film's subject, story and issues, and the impulse to affirm solidarity with its perceived politics are all also very much in evidence. In short, a strong sense of empathy (or, in the case of David, antipathy) frequently arises, whereas this is much less in evidence in the Salamanca group, in which, where a member does convey an emotional response, this is explained or conveyed as sympathy. For instance, Marta Isabel qualifies *Tomboy* as 'una historia muy tierna' ('a very sweet story'), which, while implying that she was moved to a degree, still holds the film at a distance. Consequently, cross-cultural affirmations of transnational affinity and solidarity are relatively absent, even if the fact that *Tomboy* is from France does not appear to have had an impact. The group takes its issues as being automatically pertinent to the reality of the country in which they encounter the film, even if, they suggest, it is less relevant to their own individual reality.

In accordance with this objective perspective, issues around whether *Tomboy* can be viewed as realistic came into the discussion early on, in advance of the direct question on this aspect. María José describes *Tomboy*'s approach to its subject as one of the things she liked, but she also questions whether this treatment is realistic. She qualifies it as 'un poco alejado quizás del, eh, como yo interpreto la realidad. Um, um, y casi que me parece, um, un tratamiento idealizado' ('a bit far from what, ah, from my idea of reality. Um, um, and I'd almost say it seems like, um, an idealised treatment'), thereby conveying scepticism similar to Dolors in her reading of *Bambi*. María José does, however, attribute realism to the depiction of the mother when thinking about possible identification with characters, describing her as 'muy cercana a la realidad, o sea me parece una, una reacción común de una señora de su generación ante el shock de, de descubrir . . .' ('very close to reality, I mean it seems like, like a common reaction coming from a woman of her generation to the shock of finding out . . .'). Also alert to the structuring devices of the film and their impact for an impression of realism, Pedro suggests that certain conversations, with the adults, are not dramatised or shown 'a lo mejor quizás lo han hecho así para que tu te imagines en el contexto social en que vivimos cual sería esa conversación' ('so perhaps they did it that way so that you could put yourself in this social context and imagine what such a conversation might be like').

Tomboy is notable for combining the issues of transgender and adolescent sexuality (whereas, as we have seen, a more usual combination in LGBTQ film from Spain and France is that of adolescent sexuality and homosexuality). The group approaches this, once again, through a critical lens, with Laure/ Michaël evaluated according to her/his narrative and political function. María José notes how the focalisation through the younger characters encourages an unprejudiced openness to alternative viewpoints and gives a refreshing clarity to the story: 'me parece una forma de, no disponer al espectador (.) y de hacerle comprender visiones diferentes' ('it seems a way of, not influencing the spectator (.) and making them understand different viewpoints'). Though she is also a viewer, she refers to the spectator as if they constituted an entity completely separate from her. For Leonora, the focalisation via a child character serves to soften the potential blow of the film's subject matter; she suggests that 'se

Figure 4.5 Laure/Michäel (Zoé Héran) in *Tomboy* (Céline Sciamma, 2011).
Image © Courtesy of Pyramide Distribution.

suavizan un poco las cosas' ('things become a bit easier'), with the perspective offering 'una visión ... con pocos prejuicios, inocente' ('a vision with few prejudices attached, innocent'). Laure/Michaël is described as a bridge between normative and non-normative gender identities, providing a point of access to transgender experiences and concerns, which contrasts with theoretical critiques of the figure of the Child as the ultimate gatekeeper of the continuation of heteronormativity.

The group's preoccupation with the philosophical and political implications of *Tomboy* traverses the exchanges. In response to the question asking about favourite scenes, Andrea expresses a preference for moments when Laure/Michaël 'se siente cómoda, bueno él, como él se siente cómodo con el cuerpo masculino no con el cuerpo femenino' ('feels, well, he, comfortable with a male body and not a female one'), which prompts Marta Isabel to agree and add that here 'no es sólo el ámbito social' ('it's not just the social context'). For both, then, feelings about one's body are as constitutive (or more) of a sense of identity as is socialisation, thus portraying an attention to the importance of embodiment for trans subjectivity. In the discussion about the friends with whom Laure as Michaël plays football, and about Lisa with whom Laure/Michaël has a kissing friendship, the borderlines between semi-conscious transphobia and homophobia and thoughtless playfulness are explored. Pedro takes this indeterminacy a step further, drawing attention to how Laure/Michaël, in this stage of development:

no sabe si realmente, eh, está, está expresando un deseo por cambiar de sexo, para atraer a otras personas, o simplemente porque tiene una crisis de identidad, y no sabe que realmente podría querer a alguien del mismo sexo sin necesidad de cambiar de sexo.

(doesn't really know, eh?, or is, if s/he is expressing a desire to change sex, to attract other people or simply because s/he has an identity crisis, and doesn't know that really s/he could feel attracted to someone of the same sex without changing sex.).

Near the end of the discussion he reformulates these ideas, developing them into the statement 'que allí está la frontera entre ser gay o lesbiana y heterosexual') ('so that's where the borderline is between being gay, lesbian and heterosexual'). Elsewhere, Leonora questions whether Laure's behaviour is 'simplemente porque esté confundida acerca de qué género tiene, o simplemente porque quiere hacer cosas que no están permitidas (.) como transgresión, ¿no?' ('simply due to being confused about what gender she has, or simply because she wants to do things that aren't allowed (.) sort of like transgression'). These attempts at explaining Laure/Michaël's situation within the frames of sexuality and childhood rebellion, rather than trans identification, conjure concerns in society more broadly about diagnosing trans children when they are young and about offering gender realignment treatment at an early age (see Waldron 2013). In fact, in this area of seeking reasons for Laure's situation, the group conveys a certain conservatism not reflected in the film itself, which focuses on the material realities in the present of Laure/Michaël's gender dilemma.

It is here that we get a rare glimpse of a more empathic connection between viewer and film in the discussion. Pedro, much like some of the respondents in the *Bambi* and *Ocaña* questionnaires, relates Laure/Michaël's gender nonconformity to his early discovery of his homosexuality: 'cuando yo era pequeño yo me gustaba vestir de niña en casa y hacer gimnasia rítmica . . . yo soy gay, y no, no me gusta vestir de mujer, quiero decir por eso, creo que es un momento también de duda, que no sabes qué estás haciendo y porqué lo haces, pero te gusta lo que haces' ('When I was little, I liked dressing up as a girl at home and doing rhythmic gymnastics . . . I'm gay, and I don't, don't like dressing up as woman, I want to say that's why I believe that it is also a moment of doubt, that you don't know what you're doing and why you're doing it, but you like what you're doing'). For Pedro, then, identification with his gender opposite is a passing phase, which allows him to affirm and confirm his present compliance with normative gender identities and which at the same time contains trans identity as child's play.

Marta Isabel conveys greater alertness to more permanent experiences of bodily dissonance. She notes that 'tiene que ser muy complicado no sentirte a gusto contigo mismo' ('it must be very complicated not feeling at ease with yourself'). However, while she conveys understanding, she nonetheless distinguishes between her own position and the protagonist's situation, stating that she never identified as a boy, as seen in her response quoted at the opening of this chapter. Like Pedro, it can be said that Marta Isabel projects her normative gender compliance here, although she focuses on the absence of feelings of transsex identification rather than her performance of her own gender identity. Hers is a sophisticated position that amplifies the impression she creates of herself as someone who reflects upon the political implications of the issues. She recalls Joss's responses in relation to *80 Egunean*; Marta Isabel underlines the difference between empathy 'en grado sumo' ('at the highest level' – a proximity with the protagonist, if not actually standing in their shoes) and understanding (an ability to comprehend but from a distance). She implies a sensibility about the ethical implications of empathy as a cisgender woman with a trans subject.

Like Emma in response to *L'Ordre des mots*, Sergio broadens the themes of *Tomboy* out (in a less abstract way) by considering the links between biology and how gender identity is viewed and confirmed externally. He turns attentions to the scene in which Laure/Michaël creates a phallus from modelling clay, stuffs it into her/his speedo trunks and admires her/himself in the bathroom mirror. For Sergio:

> yo creo que el momento de, de la plastilina, de intentar a hacer un pene con la plastilina, creo que refleja totalmente cual es el problema: que se vuelve como algo físico es simplemente por tener, eh, algo distinto, mm, cambia totalmente la visión de, de la otra persona.

> (I think that the modelling clay moment, of trying to create a penis from modelling clay, I think that it reflects totally what the problem is: it becomes a physical thing simply to have, um, something different, mm, it totally changes the vision of the, the other person.)

He adds 'ese pedazo de carne marca la diferencia. Tal vez no sea un 0.5% de todo tu tiempo de vida, algo así, que realmente haga que todo sea diferente, que todo gire en torno de eso, mm' ('that piece of flesh marks the difference. Maybe for only 0.5 per cent of your time, something like that; but for it to make everything so different and for everything to revolve around that, well . . .'). Sergio's extrapolation seems simultaneously to show awareness of the restrictive inadequacy of genital-centric, binary thinking about sex and gender and to use it in order to frame a response to the film. Though his position with regards to gender and trans issues is not explicitly clear, he nonetheless raises the absurdity that underlies biologically deterministic interpretations of gender identity and the privilege accorded to men by virtue of biology.

The more philosophical tenor of the discussion develops further in an exchange between Pedro and Marta Isabel, in which both attempt to identify the motives for Laure/Michaël's gender nonconformity. What, in her discussion of the trans body, Salamon (2010: 1) frames as the productive epistemological uncertainty underlying transgender and transsexual experience and its perception appears to complicate their dialogue. This debate hinges on whether Laure's external self-construction as Michaël is due to an essential identification as a biological male or whether it is in fact the only means for her of expressing her same-sex desires. At first, Marta Isabel struggles to say where she stands in relation to popular perceptions that gender dissonance is a marker of homosexuality, but then notes that, while 'socialmente se considera como transexuales son gays llevados al extremo o al máximo' ('it's socially assumed that transexuals are gays pushed to an extreme, or to the limit'), there are 'transexuales homosexuales o bisexuales, etcétera, etcétera' ('transexuals who are homosexual or bisexual etc., etc.'). Pedro asks, then, whether Marta Isabel understands that 'la chica era lesbiana o que quería ser transexual?' ('the girl was lesbian or wanted to be transexual?'), to which Marta Isabel replies 'yo creo que se siente, sea, yo pensaba que se siente chico' ('I think s/he feels, or, well, I thought that s/he feels s/he is a boy'), clarifying subsequently, 'explico, entonces a él, sí que lo veo (.) transexual desde, desde el principio' ('let me explain, so, yes, I see him (.) as transexual from the start'). This fascinating, zig-zag exchange, conflating transsex and transgender, moves rapidly from awareness of the significance of the felt sense of the body and its dissonance with the physical body (as explored, for example, by Salamon 2010: 13–68), through a form of deterministic socialisation (the gay pushed to an extreme; the lesbian perhaps inclined by peer pressure to be a boy), and through a contrary idea of self-determination (wanting to be transsexual), back to the idea that the film's narrative presents Laure as transsexual (rather than transgender) 'from the start'. Despite the fact that their comments prompt reflections about trans issues that are also invoked in scholarly work on trans identity and existence, the material, embodied trans person disappears in such justifications of her/his existence as governed by same-sex desires, transsex identification from birth or childhood impudence.

Concluding Remarks

Where the responses to the films in Chapter 3 come from viewers who, generally, portray themselves as having a stake in the specific subjects depicted, the reactions outlined above come principally from those who position themselves as external to the trans and intersex stories they encounter. There are, though, some instances of affirmations of proximity and recognition: Oriol's talk of 'our' history, Kenneth's memories of a past 'homosexual' scene and the recurrent association of trans emancipation with experiences of self and collective acceptance. Here, we see a projection of the kind of shared values and history that contribute to a sense of community, even if the nature of that community and the precise place of the viewer within it are not specified. That the particularities pertaining to the national culture and contexts portrayed in the films receive relatively limited mention by respondents to the films discussed in this chapter attests to the transnational relevance and salience of their broader discourses on gender identity, even if, as mentioned, it reveals limited insight into precisely how a foreign culture is perceived as differing from a domestic one. Such differences can be more of a preoccupation for critics than for audiences, perhaps; and the relationship between critical and audience readings of films is the focus of the next chapter.

136

NOTE

1. We are indebted to Dr Ros Murray, research associate on the project of which this book forms part, for her input to the historical material on trans issues in Catalunya presented in these pages.

5. AUDIENCES AND CRITICS: DIALOGUE AND DISAGREEMENT

Where Chapters 3 and 4 interpreted audience responses collected at festivals, and often to relatively low-profile films, this chapter turns to a slightly different space. The focus now is on queer fictional films and directors who have attracted critical attention from established and professional reviewers in France and Spain. We survey the reception of two of the most controversial and talked about French queer films in recent times – 2013 Palme d'Or winner *La Vie d'Adèle* (Abdellatif Khechiche, 2012) at Cannes and the Queer Palm winner of the same year *L'Inconnu du lac* (Alain Guiraudie, 2013) – and consider how the reactions of mainly LGBTQ viewers and online critics diverge from and converge with received critical evaluation. We adopt a similar contrastive and comparative approach in an analysis of the images and reputations of mainstream directors whose work mobilises queer aesthetics, affect, sensibilities and tastes but who, to differing degrees, have achieved canonical status in both countries: André Téchiné, François Ozon and Pedro Almodóvar. Queer films such as *La Vie d'Adèle* and *L'Inconnu du lac* have become, as Rosalind Galt and Karl Schoonover write, 'major players in contemporary world cinema' (2014), while Almodóvar, to take one of the directors in question, partly thanks to his enthusiastic reception among some revered French critics writing for highbrow film magazines, has become a key global figure, whose audience share, in France as elsewhere, can rival and even surpass that of Hollywood and domestic blockbusters. The discussion of Almodóvar leads into a study of the responses, again comparing reviews by established and professional critics with occasional or amateur LGBTQ critics, to *La piel que habito* (2011) – released under its original Spanish title in France – and *Los amantes pasajeros* (as *Les amants pasagers*) (2013), the two films he released during the time-period of our project.

The chapter engages with forms of cinephilia and politically or socially informed film reception. It attempts to show how the finely detailed and often immediate responses by mainly LGBTQ audiences in questionnaires and in discussions (in blogs and forums) nuance the equally finely detailed but close technical analyses of academic and high journalistic writing. Perhaps the most notable impacts of this 'aggregated opinion' come out of the simultaneously dialogic and sometimes antagonistic relationships between the old and the new cinephilias, between cinephile discourse and on-the-ground-responses not necessarily tethered to film history and received systems of taste, and between non-LGBTQ aligned and LGBTQ-aligned critical perspectives (as confirmed in the response or inferred from the place of consumption, the choice of viewing or the site of the production of commentary).

Looking at how high-profile directors and auteurs, and the critical packaging of films, contribute to the creation of an imaginary for French and Spanish LGBTQ film-goers and film-watchers enables fresh theorisations of the construction and emergence of critical discourses. By making active responses – audiences – the point of articulation, the chapter offers fresh theorisations of the construction and emergence of critical discourses.

Queer Critics and the Canon: Old and New Cinephilias

As Buse et al. (2007: 4–7), Mira (2005: 5–10), Pujol Ozonas (2011) and Triana Toribio (2014) have established, the complex film culture that has been formed in Spain by the politics and economics of the post-Franco era up to the time of writing is one which in its dominant critical discourses combines auteurist, film historical and canonical values, and it has done so in a persistently patriarchal frame of reference (Arranz et al. 2010; Martin-Márquez 1999; Pujol Ozonas 2011: 37–40). Cerdán and Fernández Labayen (2013) give a chronologically nuanced account of the effects of aspects of this evolving value system on the reception of Pedro Almodóvar's films to 2002, for example. This account turns on the 'fragmentary and contradictory construction of a national canon' (Cerdán and Fernández Labayen 2013: 130–1) and 'a schematic [critical] vision' based on high/low dichotomies (148); and Almodóvar, indeed, has become iconic of what might be termed the battle over values, having resigned in early 2005 his membership of the government-linked Academia de las Artes y las Ciencias Cinematográficas (AACC – the Madrid-based institution controlling the annual Goya film awards), and ostentatiously maintaining his distance (and that of his brother's production company) from it until 2010. His increasing international fame in the 1990s led to elitist critical perplexity, or 'embarrassment' (Triana Toribio 2003: 158), in Spain, while abroad his 'auteurist prestige and hence his canonicity' grew (Smith in D'Lugo and Smith 2012: 111). Almodóvar, as a cog in the cultural and industrial machinery of queer transnationalism, will be returned to in the latter part of this chapter in a discussion of French elite, popular critical and LGBTQ responses to his films.

Auteurist imperatives have informed the enduringly hierarchical values associated with dominant film discourses in France. The French 'regulatory framework', introduced in the 1950s and which features the famous *avances sur recettes* (advances based on prospective receipts and which 'only goes to projects that arguably could not be financed without public funding' (Creton and Jäckel 2004: 11)), has served as a much envied model for national cinemas globally and has been a fundamental force in ensuring the elevation of the auteur-director as the ultimate figure of pre-eminence in filmmaking (see Austin 1996: 13). It was pivotal in bringing about French cinema's most influential 'movement' or, rather, 'moment' (Hayward 2000: 145), the *nouvelle vague*, which has served as a blueprint for independent and creative cinema worldwide (Catalunya included: see Chapter 1), but which has been famously criticised for privileging a 'masculine, singular' view of the world (Sellier 2005: 6). In fact, although France has a relatively high number of women filmmakers and is home to one of the longest running women's film festivals at Créteil, which shows only films made by women, gender is often 'disclaimed' by these women as a motivating force and 'critical engagement with feminism and feminist film theory' is rare (Tarr and Rollet 2001: 1). Anxiety about being pigeonholed and, as a consequence, constrained within 'minority cinema' may also inform the resistance to labels by Almodóvar and Ozon themselves, as will be seen.

Almodóvar and Ozon, alongside Ventura Pons and André Téchiné, are among those directors whose recent work inhabits both LGBTQ niche and mainstream and who, to varying degrees, elude the gatekeepers of the French, Spanish and British critical systems. However, as is becoming increasingly recognised, such critical systems are less and less closed, just as such distinctions between niche and mainstream are becoming more and more blurred (Jenkins 2007). In particular, the processes of digital innovation and development, or 'disruption' (Iordanova and Cunningham 2012), have led not only to easier dissemination and reception of 'peripheral', 'alternative' and 'niche' content (Iordanova 2012: 6–7) but to new modes of discussion and sharing views on films (21–2). The rise of 'internet-enabled cinephiles' can rival official channels of recommendation, authority and critique (22; also Behlil 2005). This new cinephilia is one where the comments and opinions of fans can build into a body of critique more visible and prolific than scholarly and professionalised film criticism (Leberg 2011; de Valck 2010). The impacts of the 'decentralisation of critical comment and recommendation' and of 'aggregated opinion' (Gubbins 2012: 74–5) make their mark on the LGBTQ audiences and films with which this book is concerned as much as on the generality of films and audiences. Indeed, these impacts may well be amplified in some cases by the specific ways in which the cultural-political emphases of LGBTQ filmmaking and the priorities and preferences of LGBTQ audiences in France and Spain stand aside from conventional critical discourses on film as well as from standard cinephilia whether in print or online. France, of course, is considered to be the birthplace of cinephile culture (Elsaesser 2005: 27–9); and the Internet has facilitated a 'consecration of amateur culture' (Jullier and Leveratto

2014: 144), which had been 'obvious for years', to enter the public sphere, and which, for some, has allowed for a 'break with the elitist definition of cinephilia', even if it does not incur a rejection of the 'technical superiority of professionals' (144). Yet, not all French viewers are initiated in classic forms of appreciation, of course, and, in France as elsewhere, as we have seen, the 'life situations and engagements' (Barker 2014: 189) of the kind we have been exploring in this book can and often do supersede aesthetic concerns in the attribution of quality, importance or impact of any particular film or director. These issues can be explored as we turn now to the reception in Spain of *La Vie d'Adèle* and *L'Inconnu du lac*, as well as some of the responses we collected at their screenings in London and Manchester.

CONTRASTED RESPONSES:
LA VIE D'ADÈLE (*LA VIDA DE ADÈLE*; *BLUE IS THE WARMEST COLOUR*)
(ABDELLATIF KHECHICHE, 2013) AND *L'INCONNU DU LAC* (*EL DESCONOCIDO DEL LAGO*; *STRANGER BY THE LAKE*) (ALAIN GUIRAUDIE, 2013)

The combination of universalising, normalising and old-style cinephile gestures of value attribution that are to be found in professional critical writing on *La Vie d'Adèle* in professional Spanish film journalism – as explored below – set these writings apart from many of the discussions and opinions online, although some of these too, indeed, have recourse to one or more of those other discursive gestures. Going against the grain of the professional critical acclaim of the perceived authenticity of the film's representation of love between women, Emma (2014) comments, in the non-LGBTQ-specific blog CGnauta, that if lesbian films have to be like this then she would rather none were made at all: '[m]ucho decir que visibilizan y normalizan pero parece que nadie ve que en realidad estamos en lo de siempre' ('there's a lot said about how they give visibility to and normalise lesbianism but it seems nobody sees that really we're stuck with the same old thing'). Sex between women becomes an 'objet[o] de morbo masculino' ('an object of prurient male desire') (Emma 2014). She continues, '[l]as propias lesbianas somos tan críticas con esta película precisamente porque nos vemos reducidas a una fantasía absurda de un hombre heterosexual' ('we lesbians ourselves are so critical of this film precisely because in it we see ourselves reduced to a heterosexual man's absurd fantasy'), subject to the same old treatment ('lo de siempre') (Emma 2014). Just over twelve months later, these objections are substantially complemented by a list posted in the same blog of thirteen reasons why 'tantas lesbianas estamos en contra de esta película' ('why so many of us lesbians are against this film'). This includes the observation that 'toma por idiota al espectador queriendo venderle una supuesta gran historia de amor que no es más que vulgar pornografía' ('it takes the spectator for a fool, selling them a supposedly great love story when it's nothing more than common porn') (Contra La Vida de Adele 2014) and is also cited in Respvblica Restitvta, Time Out Barcelona and

Figure 5.1 Front cover of *Caimán Cuadernos de Cine* June 2013.
Image reproduced with kind permission of Carlos F. Heredero, Managing Editor,
Caimán Cuadernos de Cine.

the blogs Crónicas de Valhalla and Kinefilia – along with Emma's comments and phrasing, now attributed to 'Paula'.

Turning now to professionally published comment, love, rather than objections by 'tantas lesbianas' ('so many of us lesbians'), is in the sights of the middlebrow *Cinemanía*'s coverage, which highlights the terms 'amor' and 'tormento y . . . éxtasis' ('love' and 'torment and . . . ecstasy') – the latter only ostensibly referring to the troubles undergone in the making of the film – and situates the film within a phototextual montage of 'Lesbianismo en el cine' ('Lesbianism on Film'). This consists of ten English-language films, the Swedish *Fucking Åmål* (*Descubriendo el amor*; *Show Me Love*) (Lukas Moodysson, 1998) and the French *Les Biches* (*Las ciervas*) (Claude Chabrol, 1968), with only one woman director amongst the examples, Patty Jenkins, for *Monster* (*Monster – Basada en una historia real*) (2003) (Cinemanía 2013: 90–5). Less context-blind and more politically aware, writing in *Caimán Cuadernos de Cine* (originally a Spanish-language version of the prestigious French *Cahiers du Cinéma*), the male critic Ángel Quintana Morraja nonetheless concludes a piece carefully structured around the film's links to Pierre de Marivaux,

Maurice Pialat and Jean-Luc Godard's *Eloge de l'amour* (*Elogio del amor*; *In Praise of Love*, 2001) (Quintana Morraja 2013: 7). Perhaps less carefully thought out is the evasive comment: 'el amor entre dos mujeres estalla aquí con absoluta normalidad' ('here love between two women bursts out with absolute normality') (8). The claim here is that this 'normality', this normal love, makes a clearer political statement than any at the time being debated in the French parliament (around same-sex marriage) – 'es preciso poder amar libremente a quien te atrae' ('one must be free to love whoever one is attracted to'), he concludes (8). Similarly (and attentive in this case to the literary intertexts of the films), Beatriz Martínez writes in the prestigious *Dirigido por* magazine of the film's interest in getting inside the soul ('alma') of its protagonist (Martínez 2013), of its interest in the search for identity and of how it moves around

> los contornos del alegato feminista y la reivindicación homosexual para erigirse, sobre todo y ante todo, como una gran historia de amor.

> (the edges of feminist debates and homosexual [rights] to stand out, above all and before anything else, as a great love story.)

These are, in fact, positions taken up by some LGBTQ audience members and commentators. In Manchester, at a Pride/POUTfest screening on 25 August at Cornerhouse, Louise, a twenty-seven-year-old white female student, writes that she felt that the film was true to life because it 'reflected the mysteriousness and unplanned nature of finding love' and that it was 'realistic in terms of how it feels to be in love'. Helen, a thirty-six-year-old white teaching assistant, at the same screening, describes finding 'true emotion' in the post-separation café meeting scene between the protagonists and trueness to life in the 'emotions and feelings of coming of age', adding, 'been through [it] myself'. Helen claims to relate to Adéle 'so much emotionally', while Leilah, a nineteen-year-old student who identifies ethnically as 'human', writes that she relates to Emma 'a little bit'. In the pan-Hispanic blog site Hay una lesbiana en mi sopa (There's a Lesbian in My Soup), Pautent whose own blog is mainly in Catalan, and can be assumed to be resident in Spain, sees it as 'maravillosa, conmovedora, AMOR en mayúsculas' (Pautent 2013) ('marvellous, moving, LOVE in capital letters'); and Yuki (who says she attended the preview, and might be assumed to mean, then, in Europe) characterises the film as 'poético, subjetivo (te sientes como Adèle en todo momento, en su piel)' (Yuki 2013) ('poetic, subjective – you feel like Adèle right the way through, under her skin'). At Manchester Cornerhouse, Helen and Paula, a fifty-six-year-old white British retired head teacher, write of their appreciation for, respectively, 'the closeness of the camera to the actors' (when asked about what was liked about style) and '[v]ery intense head shots requiring emotion' (when asked about the acting).

The professional essays' impressive attention to questions of form, however, tend to make such moments of closeness and intensity a supplement to other more classically cinephile considerations. These lead away from attention to the effects of the dramatisation of personal dilemmas and feelings on screen towards technique, skill, and wider aesthetic achievement – the camera's love affair with the actor generally, multiple levels of effect and the supremacy of gesturality (Martínez 2013). For another professional critic, there is perfect mise en scène, physicality rendered abstract, the refinement of a method that is particular to Kechiche, a look ('mirada') and technique which leads to 'una especie de plenitud del poder del cine frente a las emociones' ('a kind of apotheosis of the power of cinema to address emotions') (Quintana Morraja 2013: 7–8). This is echoed, in the same issue of *Caimán Cuadernos de Cine*, by Carlos F. Heredero, a renowned film historian, critic and film school professor, who sees the film as epitomising 'el cine, o al menos un determinado tipo de cine' ('cinema itself, or at least a particular type of cinema') in its ability to convey visually 'intensidad y autenticidad' in relation to emotion (Heredero 2013). Quintana Morraja alights, too, on its attention to the importance of smaller moments as what makes it exceptional, rather than any political debates (on homosexuality) or scandalised reactions (to the sex scenes) it might prompt (Quintana Morraja 2013: 7); but Imma Merino, looking at the film and its issues half 'en tanto que autora' (as a writer) and half 'en tanto lesbiana' (as a lesbian) does focus on the sex scenes and on political debates (in this case around pornography) (Merino 2013: 12). With only a few exceptions, Merino identifies the scenes of 'sexo supuestamente lésbico' ('supposedly lesbian sex') as 'brutal y quirúrigo' ('brutal and surgical'), laughable and, to LGBTQ audience members at the Cannes screening that she is documenting, ridiculous precisely because unbelievable (12). She views the film's (explicit and scripted) exaltation of the female orgasm as, quite simply, 'peligroso' ('dangerous') (12), coming closer to blog participant Emma's response, as above, or the disappointment of another online commentator (whose use of Spanish marks her as European rather than Latin American), that the character Emma 'en realidad . . . no es una lesbiana, han puesto a una tía para que haga el papel de un hombre' (beapbeap 2013) ('is not really a lesbian . . . they've put a woman in there to play a man's role').

The references to Godard and Pialat by the critics cited above show that they share with some of the non-professional commentators and audience members a general perception of France as a key source of intelligent films on homosexuality (see David's general evaluation of this, for example, in the focus group discussion of *L'Ordre des mots* in Chapter 4). Shared too is a sense that showing '[e]l otro lado de la frontera' ('the other side of the border') is a signature of 'cine impecable' ('impeccable filmmaking'), a category into which Kechiche fits, alongside *Intouchables* (*Intocables*; *The Intouchables*) (Olivier Nakache and Eric Toledano, 2011) and *Dans la maison* (*En la casa*; *In the House*) (François Ozon, 2012), in the view of one regional arts magazine, the *Revista Atticus* (Cuadrado 2014: 116).

Spanish responses to the second mainstream LGBTQ French film of 2013, though a less commercially exceptional one – *L'Inconnu du lac* (also discussed in Chapter 3) – show points of similarity between the two constituencies of commentators in the appreciation of aesthetics (the look and mood of the film) and substantial divergence in the prioritisation of thematic elements. Eighteen audience members at the 25 January 2014 screening of the film during Bilbao's Zinegoak festival returned questionnaires (out of ninety distributed). One, Salvador (mentioned in Chapter 3), having chosen the film on the basis of its having won a prize at the Seville European Film Festival 2013, one (wishing to remain unquoted) because of a liking for French cinema, three for its subject matter (specifically, cruising), and others attracted by festival publicity. The realistic portrayal of cruising is noted (under the truth to life question) by Salvador and five other respondents, and by one respondent under the question heading of style, with Salvador and two of these others also citing the portrayal of cruising as something they felt they identified with in the film; while another, Fernando (a forty-four-year-old white male translator, resident in San Francisco), answering the same question (about identification with characters or events) says that it reminded him of 'escenas de ligoteo en zonas parecidas' ('pick-up scenes in similar areas') and thus interestingly conflating identification with personal memory – a perspective not seen in the professional critics who, as will be seen, adopt more abstract positions, with the exception of Fernando Solla writing in the Cine Divergente website (an extensive amateur site with a focus on non-mainstream film and festivals) who notes 'la soledad a la que nos enfrentamos muchos de nosotros' ('the loneliness that many of us face') (Solla 2014), where the 'nosotros' ('us') in question might perhaps be read as gay men, given Solla's interest elsewhere on this site in Ozon and Ralf Köenig.

Thinking about the way the film dealt with its themes, three of those in Bilbao who mention cruising under the truth-to-life question heading come back to it, with one, Juan Manuel, a forty-two-year-old white Caucasian male nurse, approving of the way it showed 'los caracteres de las diferentes personas que te puedas encontrar haciendo cruising' ('the characters of the different sorts of people you might encounter when out cruising') but noting that the film seems to 'crear miedo a hacer cruising más que [a] no ponerse preservativo al hacer sexo ('create fear around cruising over and above [the fear of] not using a condom when having sex'). While for Salvador '[e]l tema del cruising me da morbo' ('the cruising thing turns me on'), for Juan Manuel there is a connection with precaution and sexual health – with personal-political realities. In these Bilbao responses, loneliness was cited in four cases as particularly well portrayed and as linked to anonymous sexual encounters; in London, at a screening of the film for the 30 March 2014 BFI's Flare, Adam, the thirty-one-year-old white male actor whose response was also considered in Chapter 3, felt that the film was true to life in that it 'commented well on the nature of loneliness and how we try to fill the void in the wrong places' and linked this, answering the questions on favourite character and scene, to the kindness and honesty of Henri (some reactions to whom we have already seen in Chapter 3) and how 'he sacrificed himself for his friend'.

Eighteen audience members returned questionnaires on this occasion (of seventy-five distributed), with one, Tim, fifty-five-year-old white male civil servant, writing that he was attracted by the impression given to him by the festival publicity of a 'racy' film with 'gay sexual content' (as we saw in Chapter 3), one by the recommendation of some French friends and the rest of the respondents by publicity or word of mouth more generally. Two stated that they found the portrayal of cruising true to life, one not so (answering about the way it deals with its themes), and three identified cruising with their own direct experiences. Saraiva, the thirty-nine-year-old male Portuguese artist, self-identifying as ethnically 're-mix', identifies with the characters and events because 'I am queer'. Saraiva (some of whose responses we discussed in Chapter 3) criticised the film for being limited by its focus on cruising (answering the question about the way it deals with its themes): 'Gay life can't be resumed as a cruising spot'. In answering on whether there were any surprises in the film for him, he also implies that it might have been more responsible in its treatment: 'spotting and fucking bareback is not a good indication for the young gay/queer people. AIDS is a reality so is other STDs'. At a Manchester Pride/POUTfest screening of the film at Cornerhouse, Manchester, on 20 August 2014, while two of the eleven audience members who returned questionnaires (out of fifty distributed) stated that they had been drawn to *L'Inconnu du lac* because of the Pride Fringe framing, two wrote that had come explicitly because of an interest in foreign film. Only one, Matt, a twenty-eight-year-old white male web administrator, identified cruising as part of what might make the film true to life ('gays like cruising') or as being something to identify with ('gay men being interested in just sex'), and he also notes that the style of the film – the repetitions, the 'setting and routine' – made it 'feel familiar and comfortable'.

Whereas awareness of the sexual health-and-wellbeing politics of HIV/AIDS and of cruising seem to underpin some of our audience responses, professional critical responses to *L'Inconnu du lac* in Spain construct instead zones of familiarity out of traditionally cinephile materials such as the recognition of intertexts, auteurist technical markers or high cultural references. Carlos Losilla – a prominent and long-established film critic (and lecturer in film at the Universitat Pompeu Fabra in Barcelona) – brings the Kechiche and the Giraudie films together in a piece in *Caimán Cuadernos de Cine* (Losilla 2014). Moreover, in its main title – 'Los límites del deseo, el deseo sin límites' ('The Limits of Desire and Desire Without Limits') – the essay loosely connects with two queer art films, *La ley del deseo* (*La Loi du désir*; *Law of Desire*) (Pedro Almodóvar, 1987) and the Mexican literary adaptation *El lugar sin límites* (*The Place Without Limits*) (Arturo Ripstein, 1978). Losilla's comparison is itself very high cultural: in Kechiche's film the perfectly filmed love story follows 'un orden convencional' sticking to the dominant bourgeois order of things (Losilla 2014: 18), while in Giraudie's all is problematisation, disorder, hidden danger and unexpectedness:

> Podría decirse que Kechiche ha hecho una película de inspiración human-ista y renacentista, mientras que Giraudie vuelve a los terrenos seculares y a formas de representación más propias del Medioevo. (19)

> (It could be said that Kechiche has made a Humanist- and Renaissance-inspired film, while Giraudie's goes back to secular themes and represen-tational forms more associated with the Middle Ages.)

Having taken this striking comparative leap, this critic then returns to a more pragmatic line, in a couple of shortcuts. Adèle and Emma's story shows that 'las parejas homosexuales pueden conocerse, amarse, separarse y aprender de la experiencia, como todas las demás' (19) ('same-sex couples get to meet, love, separate and learn from the experience, like everyone else'), whereas the men in *L'Inconnu du lac* are unintelligible to one another, intimacy is impossible, because 'todo es un laberinto' (19) ('it's all a maze').

In the same magazine, three months later, there is a more sober response to *L'Inconnu du lac* based on intertextual reference (again), auteurist credentials and genre. The film – a kind of purified culmination in its treatment of place of Giraudie's highly Occitan-specific work to date (Iglesias 2014: 33) – has to it 'un naturalismo extremo que evoca a Eric Rohmer y Jean Renoir' (33) ('an extreme naturalism which recalls Rohmer and Renoir'), mixed with elements of film noir (32) – whereas for some audience members, it will be recalled, the naturalism points, rather, to their own real experiences. For Iglesias, the killer Michel is a male version of the femme fatale (33) (the author, Eulàlia Iglesias, is a lecturer in audiovisual media at the Universitat Rovira i Virgili), rather than, for one of our online commentators, somewhere between 'un cachas rompec-orazones' ('a heart-breaking hunk') and a Freddie Mercury lookalike (Killer Queen, 2014). In *Dirigido por*, the emphasis is again on distinctive directorial marks, recognisability and achievements of form and style – soundscape, tech-niques of alignment and constrained point of view, and the visual and narra-tive ambiguity of the final shot, for example (Casas 2014). In clear contrast to the perspectives taken up by most audience members and online commenta-tors, cruising, and homosexuality itself, are taken by this long-established critic (Quim Casas also teaches Scriptwriting at the Universitat Pompeu Fabra) as just a backdrop to 'cuestiones tan simples pero edificantes como la amistad, el deseo y la confianza' (21) ('questions as simple but also edifying as friendship, desire and trust'). This, nonetheless, chimes with Adam's London response, above – on the more humanist ethical issues there is overlap between the distinct forms of commentary and these different critical constituencies.

Appreciation of the film's aesthetic qualities is not, however, shared by six of the Bilbao respondents, with the film's length, slowness and 'aridity' (Miguel, a forty-year-old male businessman self-identifying his ethnicity as 'citizen') seen as detrimental to the experience of watching; in Manchester no respondents objected to the film's pace, however, with slowness for two respondents being tolerable and compensated by other factors, and one respondent (who did not give consent for direct quotation) positively liking the slowness and commenting on it at some length. In London, Thomas, a thirty-one-year-old white male actor, felt that 'overall [it] added to the tension' and Sonia, a thirty-five-year-old white female French national market researcher, a part-time postgraduate student and a regular attender at the festival, liked the style because it was 'slow-paced and sexy'. Only two respondents said outright that they did not like the style, one a frequent festival attender, one a first-timer. In the blog Planeta Murciano, one commentator links the style to the film's Frenchness, with implicit approval, as making it one of 'Cuatro pelis maricas (que deberías ver)' ('four queer films – that you ought to see'): 'Por supues, el film es muuuy francés; con sus paisajes, su desarrollo pausado, sus atardeceres, sus barridos de cámara por los personajes' (mm 2013) ('Course, the film's veeerrry French; with its landscapes, slow development, sunsets, and the camera panning across the characters' features').

This perception of extremely typical Frenchness in style by an online commentator maps on to the Spanish professional critics' interest in matters aesthetic and it recapitulates some of the statements by those responding to the Spanish festival screenings, in earlier chapters, about what they value in French LGBTQ film. It also, in its way, carries forward the long popular and institutional process of imagining France from Spain, as discussed in Chapter 1.

Queer Auteurs: Téchiné, Ozon and Almodóvar

André Téchiné is an emphatically transnational figure in the sense of embodying and producing French images of desire and personhood that are transmitted to and taken up in Spain, by queer and general cinephile audiences both. He has had substantial general recognition in Spain since the release there of *Les Voleurs* (*Los ladrones*; *Thieves*) (1996) and the French–Spanish co-production *Alice et Martin* (1998) – with the Spanish Carmen Maura as Jeanine. These non-LGBTQ themed films had 68,518 and 69,004 box office admissions respectively in Spain in the period up to 2014. Vertigo films have released these and four other titles, including *Les Témoins* (discussed in Chapter 3); and they have figured regularly in the catalogues of LGBTQ retail outlets as well as the mainstream Amazon, Spain, and FNAC, Spain. As we have already seen in Chapter 1, familiarity with *Les Roseaux sauvages* is also a key starting point for certain audience responses to other French gay films.

This film in particular has a high profile among Spanish viewers, and has registered a respectable 82,000 box office ticket sales in Spanish territory. One commentator posting to a Téchiné thread on the LGBTQ-specific dosmanzanas blog on 11 January 2009 is reminded, by the arrival on the shelves of

Figueres-based Pride Films's re-release of *Les Roseaux sauvages* in December 2008, of having seen it on Televisión Española's channel 2 twelve years previously (he remembers rightly: transmission was at 11.30 p.m. on 21 April 1997) and subsequently buying the film on VHS at the mainstream department store El Corte Inglés (skyzos 2009). 'We' (the 'público homosexual') are still fascinated, this commentator claims, by that film's freshness and power to elicit identification with the troubled, young protagonist François (Gaël Morel) (skyzos 2009). In talking about identification, skyzos is picking up on the lead comment (Rodríguez 2009) in the thread which focuses not only on 'el conflicto de [la] homosexualidad [de François] recién descubierta' ('the conflict felt by [the character] François on recently discovering his homosexuality') but also 'el dolor de sus primeros deseos homoeróticos insatisfechos' ('the pain caused by his first unrequited homoerotic desires'); Rodríguez also focuses on the visual and sensual appeal of the film, noting that it is 'una invitación al gozo cinéfilo' ('an invitation to cinephile pleasures') and bridging thus the worlds of LGBTQ and cinephile response.

Established criticism in Spain also focuses on the technical mastery, seriousness and visual beauty of Téchiné's films, with José María Caparrós Lera, writing for the Catholic conservative publishers RIALP, discussing *Les Roseaux sauvages* in terms of its almost impressionistic brilliance in conveying natural landscape, and Téchiné's combination across his oeuvre of 'Historia y demostración' ('the telling and the showing of History') (Caparrós Lera 1999: 198). The visual pleasures of the film (ambiguously dubbed 'minoritario y premiado'; 'minority-interest and prize-winning': 198) do not, however, include the young male body or 'las relaciones bisexuales entre los protagonistas' ('the bisexual relations between the protagonists') or 'los actos explícitos' ('explicit acts'), whose portrayal this critic suggests might be described as 'excesivo e ilegítimo' ('excessive and illegitimate'), involving as they do, he says, such young actors (198) (although in neither France nor Spain, at seventeen and twenty respectively, would they have been under the age of consent). Elsewhere, in the liberal left *El País*, *Loin* (*Lejos*; *Far*) (2001) is valued for its combination of exquisite intimate portrait, intelligence, and historical awareness, and for its Tangiers-located creation of a 'contrapunto entre el documento urbano y la ficción amorosa' ('counterpoint between urban documentation and romantic fiction') (Fernández-Santos 2002).

In review articles, *Les Témoins* itself is praised, in the newspaper *El País* for its classic novelistic qualities (Costa 2007), and in the cinephile blog kane3 for the signs it shows of auteurist continuity and – again focusing on the dramatisation of place-specific issues – for the way it presents 'un microcosmos quebradizo' ('a fragile microcosm') (Méndez 2007). For another experienced on-line critic-commentator, the value of the film lies squarely in Téchiné's skill as a director of actors who 'deja que sus actores buceen en las profundidades de sus personajes' ('lets his actors go deep into their characters') and in the richness of 'matices y texturas' ('nuance and texture'), concluding that

'*Los testigos* podría estar firmada por François Ozon, sin ir más lejos. Cine de mirada adulta y formas nuevas que, por fortuna, se niega a morir' (Vidal 2013) ('*The Witnesses* might easily have borne François Ozon's signature, to go no further. This is the kind of cinema with a mature outlook and innovative form, which luckily, refuses to die out'); enduring auteurist qualities, then, are once more to the fore. Another, writing in the dosmanzanas site (and, it is to be deduced from this commentator's many postings that they have substantial film-watching experience) values the film's 'escenas de frágil belleza [que] se suceden casi sin respiro, como si Téchiné buscara la tragedia con ansia' (elputojacktwist 2007) ('scenes of fragile beauty that follow on from one another almost without pause for breath, as if Téchiné were eager to seek out tragedy'). This evaluation prompts a response from nemo (2007), who also uses the term 'belleza' ('beauty') alongside 'naturalidad' and 'espontaneidad' ('naturalness', 'spontaneity'). Like skyzos commenting on *Les Roseaux sauvages*, nemo admires the way that *Les Témoins* invites identification with the characters and 'con su palpitante humanidad' (nemo 2007) ('with their pulsating humanity').

We found it striking how this particular queer auteur attracts similar opinions among both amateur LGBTQ commentators and professional critics in Spain; the traction of notions of the humane and the psychologically true to life which were manifest in the reactions we saw mobilised in professional criticism of *La Vie d'Adèle* and *L'Inconnu du lac* is also evident here. Reactions to the films of François Ozon in Spain and those of Pedro Almodóvar in France, however, show less convergence between the different constituencies.

François Ozon has held the attention of the Spanish professional critics, with a modest but significant twelve Spanish academic articles (Dialnet search 17 April 2015) and regular cultural coverage in the daily and non-academic periodical press. *Fotogramas*, as a case in point, has thirty-five items specific to the director or to individual films (online search of the magazine's digital edition, 15 August 2015), and the major newspapers follow this pattern in their coverage, with the tag 'François Ozon' for the digitally archived print edition of *El País* showing thirty-three entries (online search, 16 April 2015) including substantial pieces by the prestige critics Vicente Molina Foix and Carlos Boyero. Molina Foix (himself a one-time gay filmmaker) claims Ozon for 'un *nosotros* cultural y sexualmente desparramado' ('us – we who are culturally and sexually dispersed'), a community of cinephiles (it seems) who are given meaning and coherence by the fictionalised memories furnished us by European cinema – cinema *tout court* ('el cine europeo. El cine') (Molina Foix 2001). Less grandly, but just as pertinently, Ozon has also been a consistent presence as an item of popular LGBTQ consumption. All the feature films from *Sitcom* (1998) to *Le Refuge* (*Mi refugio*; *Hideaway*) (2009) figure as on sale from at least one LGBTQ-targeted retail outlet in Spain, *Gouttes d'eau sur pierres brûlantes* (*Gotas que caen sobre rocas calientes*; *Water Drops on Burning Rocks*) (2000) was screened at Zinentiendo (Zaragoza) in 2006 and *Le Refuge* at FIRE!! in 2010; and opportunities to download pirate copies, up to and including *Jeune et Jolie* (*Joven y bonita*; *Young and Beautiful*) (2013), are plentifully advertised in Spanish online (Google search, 17 April 2015).

The San Sebastián Concha de Oro prize for *Dans la maison* and its loose adaptation of the Spanish dramatist Juan Mayorga's play *El chico de la última fila* (*The Boy in the Back Row*) added a further cultural link between the two countries, although its lack of an obviously LGBTQ theme, despite a queer aesthetic, give it little presence in online discussions in LGBTQ forums, and its cost put it beyond the reach of any festivals polled as part of the project. While Ozon's ironic and equivocal way with queer themes, characters and representations leads to his being discussed by one online commentator as, in *Potiche* (*Potiche*; *Mujeres al poder*) (2010), oddly reactionary (Argüelles 2011; in a review linked to coverage of FIRE!! 2010), at the same time the website chueca.com is easily able to list 'the most gay things' about Ozon films of the period 1999 to 2005 (Ozon himself being the most gay thing about them). In 2014 *Une nouvelle amie* (2014) won the Basque LGBTI association GEHITU's Premio Sebastiane for the best LGBT-themed film in any section of the San Sebastián festival, further consolidating the director's standing with the Spanish film establishment. At another level, Ozon has a reputation in Spain journalistically as 'el "Almodóvar" francés' (Filmin 2015) ('the French Almodóvar'). The film critic Rafael Vidal Sanz in the News and Reports section of the website of the Madrid- and Barcelona-based online provider 400 Films nuances the 'French Almodóvar' epithet by linking it not only to a distinctive mix of styles in Ozon's earlier production but specifically to the presence of homosexual characters 'a los que filma en una exaltación de su sexualidad y de su cuerpo' (Vidal Sanz 2013) ('filmed in a way that exalts their sexuality and their bodies'). Such characters 'no sigue[n] la pauta de las parejas heterosexuales' ('don't follow the mode of behaviour of the heterosexual couple') and this is 'una forma de resistencia' ('a form of resistance'). From a different perspective, the conservative newspaper *ABC*'s 2014 San Sebastián Festival coverage of *Une nouvelle amie* uses a variant of the Almodóvar formula to point up the perceived failings of the film's narrative, as 'un conglomerado de diez o doce películas de Almodóvar, pero sin timbre ni sello' ('a conglomeration of a dozen or so Almodóvar films, but without his distinctive stamp and seal') (Rodríguez Marchante 2014).

Although it was released when the audience research for this project had been completed, it is worth pausing on this film since it is an important and high-profile incursion into trans subjectivity, as discussed in the previous chapter, and an adaptation as is *La piel que habito* (discussed below). Indeed, *Une nouvelle amie* contains allusions to Almodóvar through its depictions of hospital rooms, morgues, dead bodies and implied necrophilia. When Laura (Isild Le Besco) falls ill and dies, her best friend Claire (Anaïs Demoustier) reaches out to comfort Laura's husband, David (Romain Duris), and discovers that he leads a secret life of transvestism which becomes a feature of his everyday existence. His persona, Virginia, is the cause of an increasing closeness to Claire, and the film recalls the French-Canadian director Xavier Dolan's *Laurence Anyways* (2012), in that it subsumes its trans narrative within a story about a heterosexual relationship, although Dolan's film is far more hard-hitting. *Une nouvelle amie* emphasises the fluidity of desire (it is suggested that Claire is attracted to Laura and she starts to be aroused by David when he is in Virginia mode), and this allows it to be co-opted within a more general reflection on sexuality. Some Spanish online responses illustrate this. One writes, for instance, that 'es una película atrevida y arriesgada, hecha con elegancia y maestría, que nos demuestra que el amor es libre, sin fronteras, cuando ambas partes sienten y consienten' (rosagua 2015) ('it is a bold and risky film, made with elegance and mastery, which shows us that love is free, without borders, where both parties feel and consent'). Another comments on the bravery of the characters, 'el atrevimiento', 'la osadía de desprenderse de sus miedos' ('[their] daring in shedding all their fears' of what neighbours, friends and family might say and how they might judge them (Lourdes L 2015). For another blogger, who may well be French given their publishing name, Antoine Roquentin, and that their blog is about French cinema, 'el realizador francés propone un pensamiento reflexivo sobre la noción del Género' ('the French director offers a reflection on the notion of gender') and notes similarities with Céline Sciamma's *Tomboy* because both, in the opinion of this writer, show that 'nuestra identidad es ante todo el resultado de una construcción social basada en las normas adquiridas durante nuestra niñez y que se construye a lo largo de nuestra vida a través de la mirada de los otros y de los grupos sociales que frecuentamos' (Roquentin 2015) ('our identity is primarily the result of a social construction based on the rules learned during our childhood and it builds throughout our life through the eyes of others and social groups we frequent'). Like Emma and Cliff in response to *L'Ordre des mots* and, to a lesser degree, some of the Lyon focus group respondents in their comments on *Guerriller@s*, trans issues are broadened out as a commentary on the contingency and constructedness of gender, although here more than in those documentaries, such a reading appears to be facilitated by the approach, focus and form of *Une nouvelle amie*.

Pedro Almodóvar's significance for French audiences includes and extends beyond his contribution to LGBTQ cultures (Seguin 2013: 432–52). Well-established and highly renowned French critics have been pivotal in enabling this seemingly insolent and anarchic Spanish director's received ascension to the venerated status of film auteur (Seguin 2013: 432). Such esteem and popular success (Attali 2013) have ensured that his new films are given general release, thus absolving him from having to rely on LGBTQ distribution channels to have his work seen (according to available data, none has been screened at the French festivals visited for this study). The *Cahiers du cinéma* critic Frédéric Strauss's publication of a series of interviews (1986), written in French and translated into Spanish and English, is a clear marker of Almodóvar's graduation to the pantheon of auteur filmmakers. With a few exceptions, since the late 1980s, each new Almodóvar film has been greeted with considerable coverage in *Cahiers* by Strauss and other equally revered colleagues, including Jean-Michel Frodon, Serge Toubiana and Jean-Marc Lalanne, and he was invited, alongside other celebrated filmmakers, actors, artists and luminaries, to contribute to the journal's seven-hundredth edition (May 2014). His adoption by the French critical elite was confirmed in 2006 by the season-long exhibition devoted to his cinema at the prestigious Cinémathèque Française, which ran from 5 April to 31 July. He features recurrently at the Cannes Film Festival and served as a member of the jury for the Official Selection in 1992. Among other prizes at Cannes, he was awarded the César award for Best European Union Film for *Hable con ella* (*Parle avec elle*; *Talk to Her*) (2002), Best Foreign Film for both *Todo sobre mi madre* (*Tout sur ma mère*; *All About My Mother*) (1999) and *Tacones lejanos* (1991) and received an Honorary César for the entirety of his work in 1999.

Almodóvar is the object of sustained interest in the general press: searches under his name (conducted on 15 April 2015) reveal 667 entries in *Le Monde*'s digital edition (with thirty-five appearances in the titles of articles) and 452 in *Le Figaro*'s digital edition, while the online cultural magazine *Les Inrocks* has created special pages on its site for the filmmaker, with twenty-seven items. He has also been the subject of a number of academic and journalistic books in France. These range from the partially subjective (Méjean 2011) to the more objectively critical (in particular Obadia 2002, but also Sotinel 2007 and Seguin 2009).

Like Ozon, Almodóvar is reticent about making public declarations about his sexuality (Davies 2007: 14–15 and Perriam 2013a: 52) and, while some French journalists are quick to categorise him as gay (Rajchman 2013), LGBTQ online viewers are more cautious. In his 'subjective' look at thirty years of gay culture in cinema, the blogger Jean-Yves, for instance, lists Almodóvar as part of a generation of homoerotic (rather than gay) directors who portrayed gay people as happy and triumphant (2005). None of the entries under the thread 'Pedro Almodóvar cinéaste espagnol' on za-gay.org, a Francophone site catering to LGBTQ adolescents, makes any assumption about his sexuality (za-gay 2013), while a Francophone Wikipedia discussion forum entitled 'Pedro Almodóvar' elicits confusion from Moonray (2007) about listing LGBTQ as one of the page's external links. Silanoc (2007), the author of the original entry and poster of this link, retorts that, although they have no information concerning his sexual orientation, homosexuality, transvestism and 'transsexualism' are portrayed positively in his films, adding that 'si Almodóvar n'est pas "homo" son oeuvre est marquée par des problématiques LGBT' ('if Almodóvar is not gay, his work is marked by LGBT issues'. Similar care not to categorise the director's sexuality can be found in academic studies of the LGBTQ aspects of his work, including in Didier Roth-Bettoni's *L'Homosexualité au cinéma*, in which he states that homosexuality informs the visual, referential, thematic and political world of this director whom he classifies as 'le plus novateur et décapant de la péninsule' ('the most innovative and caustic director from the [Iberian] peninsula') (Roth-Bettoni 2007: 511). Roth-Bettoni enthusiastically upholds Almodóvar – 'l'un des réalisateurs les plus éblouissants du monde' ('one of the world's most dazzling directors') – as having created the conditions in which Spain was able to ratify same-sex marriage in 2005, which he puts down to his 'vision décomplexée de toutes les différences' ('uncomplicated vision of all differences') (510).

Almodóvar's importance for LGBTQ culture in France can be seen in his online LGBTQ reception. The twelve entries to the forum on za-gay.org are generally highly appreciative, with his technical and creative talents acclaimed as much as – and in some cases more than – his contribution to LGBTQ culture. *La mala educación* (2004), *La piel que habito* and *Todo sobre mi madre* receive the most enthusiasm, while *Los abrazos rotos* (*Etreintes brisées*; *Broken Embraces*) (2009) *Hable con ella* and *Los amantes pasajeros* are met with general indifference. One contributor lauds Almodóvar as 'just perfect', adding that they could 'go on about' his genius for hours and qualifying his cinema as revolutionary (Anonyme1 2013). Another enthuses about:

> sa façon de filmer, de raconter les histoires crûment, le retour à l'époque de la libération du fascisme espagnol, les personnages qui reviennent plus ou moins toujours (on est gay ou on ne l'est pas, et personnellement, si un personnage est gay dans l'histoire, je m'y intéresse encore plus!). (undesmots 2013)

> (his approach to filming, to telling stories in a crude way, the return to the era of liberation from Spanish fascism, characters that return more-or-less always (one is gay or one isn't, and personally, if a character is gay in a story, I'm even more interested!).

Style and themes combine, then, in this avid viewer's glowing appraisal of Almodóvar, with the comment on gay characters confirming the obvious importance of this particular textual feature for his popularity among some Francophone LGBTQ-identifying audiences. Negative criticisms on the page are limited, with even the one sceptic recognising his status as a key player.

Though hardly exhaustive, these comments provide a snapshot of what Almodóvar continues to mean for (here) young Francophone LGBTQ audiences. Moreover, they illustrate the extent to which so-called 'old' forms of film appreciation (Rodríguez Ortega 2013: 535) are invoked in 'new' social networking practices; the originator of the za-gay thread states that they were drawn to Almodóvar because they wanted to practise their Spanish as part of their revision for the Baccalauréat, but are now going through his filmography (Anonyme1 2013), and others remark that they are following suit. This purpose of creating communities around LGBTQ identifications and shared experiences, and exchanging appreciation of Almodóvar's films, thus echoes some of the functions served by LGBTQ festivals, as described in Chapter 2 and illustrated in Chapters 3 and 4, though such reception practices here are effected digitally. This potential in Almodóvar's films (of creating a sense of community) is often overlooked in elite appraisals of his work.

QUEER FRENCH ALMODÓVAR:
LA PIEL QUE HABITO (*THE SKIN I LIVE IN*) (2011) AND *LOS AMANTES PASAJEROS* (*LES AMANTS PASSAGERS*; *I'M SO EXCITED!*) (2013)

The reception of individual Almodóvar films among the contributors to LGBTQ forums, as well as other LGBTQ bloggers and viewers, is predictably more directly emotional and visceral than the criticism in the French general and specialised film press. Where Almodóvar's adaptation of the French crime writer Thierry Jonquet's story of revenge, *Mygale* (1984), in *La piel que habito* divides critics and triggers a competition, among some, of who-can-spot-the-most-film-references (Hitchcock, Buñuel, Franju and so on), online LGBTQ viewers focus their attentions on the film's capacity to entertain. This, it seems, drives its mainly positive reception among these viewers and possibly motivates the listing of *La piel que habito* as one of only five Almodóvar films being sold as DVDs by Les Mots à la bouche, the online store of Paris's longstanding and famous bookshop catering to gay men and lesbians (the others are *La ley del deseo*, *La mala educación*, *Volver* and *Los amantes pasajeros*). Hence, the unnamed contributor on the za-gay.org site explored above appraises *La piel que habito* as having a surprising twist and showing its main actor, Antonio Banderas, as more menacing than in any other film that they had seen in which he starred (Anonyme1 2013). Another, also cited above, comments that they found it 'dérangeant mais compréhensible' ('disturbing but understandable'), adding 'on sent que les personnages sont des personnes proches de la réalité, les sentiments et le temps donné à l'histoire ressortent [comme] de l'encre sur du papier. On arrive à se plonger dans l'histoire!' (undesmots 2013) ('you feel that the characters are people who are close to reality, emotions and the time devoted to the story come alive like ink on paper. You can immerse yourself in the story'). Where proximity and emotion can serve as appendices to technical merit in high journalistic reviews, as seen in the discussion of the critical responses to *La Vie d'Adèle* above, here it is reversed, with the attention to form through a reference to pace functioning as an addendum to this viewer's account of their connection to *La piel que habito*. However, for one professional critic, whose view is not isolated, such emotional proximity is more elusive: Eric Neuhoff, writing for *Le Figaro*, dismisses the film as 'froid, lisse, artificiel' (Neuhoff 2011) ('cold, slick, artificial').

Affective connection to the story of the kind expressed by the above online viewer is also articulated by some of the five respondents who returned questionnaires at a screening at Manchester's Cornerhouse on 4 February 2013 as part of the 'Spanish and Latin America Film in the 21st Century' season of talks and screenings. Jessica, a twenty-four-year-old white Australian actor/performer, writes that she found the film 'unique, unlike anything I'd seen before. [It] made me feel uncomfortable, but that's a good thing!', thus invoking the familiar appeal of Almodóvar's cinema as eliciting pleasure in the perverse (for more on this, see Waldron and Murray 2014: 12). She later states that she was surprised by the ways in which 'relationships developed' and 'the depth of insanity', and conveys an intensified sense of proximity to the story by shifting from distanced appraisal to close implication in her response to the question asking about the film's approach to its themes: 'madness and identity were dealt with admirably – what kind of identity could Vincent develop?' Almodóvar's presumed talents at storytelling rather than his skills at challenging normative constructions of gender are the aspects that Jessica praises. Another respondent, Susan, a retired lecturer who did not give her age and ethnicity, diverges from Jessica in her opinion of the film, commenting that she did not like *La piel que habito* because it was 'very strange, [with an] unbelievable plot. [I] didn't like the cruelty, but [I] loved the soundtrack'. However, like Jessica, she conveys the affective impact the film had on her (even if she describes this in negative terms).

In contrast perhaps to some of the criticisms cited above in response to the portrayal of lesbian desire in *La Vie d'Adèle*, those non-professional viewers who engage with the film's sexual politics – namely its staging of transgender identities and rape – are few. Often omitted is reference to the fact that Robert Ledgard (Banderas) inflicts a vaginoplasty on Vicente (Jan Cornet), who then becomes Vera (Elena Anaya), because Robert suspects him of having raped his daughter Norma (Bianca Suárez). This issue is broached occasionally in reviews in the film and general press, but these tend towards generalisation by broadening it out to a universal quest for gender/sexual identity (Schwartz 2011; Gandillot 2011) or they read it through a more philosophical lens, as in *Télérama*'s reviewer whose choice of vocabulary makes a passing nod to Hegelian phenomenology: 'variation virtuose sur la dialectique du maître et de l'esclave, le film est hanté . . . par l'énigme de l'identité sexuelle' (L.G. 2011) ('admirable variation on the master–slave dialectic, the film is haunted . . . by sexual identity'). The *Cahiers* critic Isabelle Zribi interprets one of the rape scenes as a secondary incident, but she does not engage with the political implications of this perfunctory approach to such a grave and contentious theme (Zribi 2011: 46). The well-known critic Jean-Marc Lalanne, writing in *Les Inrockuptibles*, briefly considers the approach to the transgender subject by noting the divergence between *La piel que habito*, in which a sex change is imposed, and *Todo sobre mi madre*, in which it is chosen by one of the protagonists and utilised, according to Lalanne, to question biological essentialism (2011). Lalanne's allusion to the issue of self-determination and its absence in *La piel que habito* aligns with some of the academic reception of the film in English and of this theme in Almodóvar's cinema. Some have argued that Almodóvar may be criticised for trivialising trans existence and rape within an *exercice de style* (Waldron and Murray 2014: 1–14). Others counter this perspective and maintain that Almodóvar's portrayal of themes such as transgender and rape contributes to his overarching interest in destabilising normative categories of sexuality and gender (Allinson 2009: 151; Lev 2013: 203).

Resisting the compulsion to come down on one side or the other of this particular debate, one of our respondents to the questionnaire expresses a more balanced reading. Craig, a forty-three-year-old white British caseworker, admitted that he liked *La piel que habito*, but added that '[possibly some] scenes went too far, especially the rape scene'. For Craig, though, whether the film is problematic or not because of these representations is open to question. Commenting on its approach, he notes '[it] could be read as misogynistic or feminist, we lack empathy with Vicente as a man but feel it for him as Vera'. A moral position is implied – audience response is generalised as favourable to the 'victim' as opposed to the 'assailant' – but Craig leaves the question of whether the film can be categorised as politically regressive or progressive relatively open.

Like the online LGBTQ and audience responses to *La piel que habito*, the reception of *Los amantes pasajeros* by its digital viewers is similarly immediate and free of any critical and cinephile agendas, although here it works in an opposing way, as an expression of general apathy towards the film. While some in the gay press in France have proclaimed this as a 'comédie très gay' (Martet 2013) ('very gay comedy') and, in a more traditionally aesthetic reading, as 'un huit [*sic*] clos aérien très réussi' ('a very well executed aerial *Huis clos*' – a reference to Sartre's play of that name) with stylistic echoes of 'loufoque' ('crazy') comedies of the 1930s and 1940s (Maury 2013), its online viewers appear largely unmoved either to critique or praise *Los amantes pasajeros*, with one unnamed contributor to za-gay specifically rejecting it as lacking Almodóvar's habitual intelligence and subtlety. Two other contributors dismiss it as nothing extraordinary ('rien de transcendant') (Anonyme1 2013; and a month later, Rhythm 2013), which contrasts with some of the professional criticism of the film that attempts to redeem it as worthy of critical evaluation, probably because of their esteem for its auteur. Thomas Sotinel, for instance, identifies 'une précision, un esprit (certes dissimulé sous un humour presque adolescent), qui sont ceux d'un grand metteur en scène' (Sotinel 2007) ('a precision, a spirit (of course hidden underneath an almost adolescent humour) which are those of a great filmmaker'); his use of 'metteur en scène', which Truffaut distinguished from real film directors (1954), does not subtract from the fact that his reading echoes the former *nouvelle vague* 'luminary's' argument, drawing on Giraudoux, that there are no 'good and bad [films], just good and bad [filmmakers]' (Gramont 1969).

Such a reappraisal of *Los amantes pasajeros* is echoed and extended in the review for *Cahiers*, authored by Jean-Sébastien Chauvin. While other critics lament or praise (but most often lament) the accessible (or facile, depending on their viewpoint) humour and brash and bawdy dialogues, he lingers

Figure 5.2 Passengers and crew sky-high in in *Los amantes pasajeros* (Pedro Almodóvar, 2013). Image © EL DESEO, D.A., S.L.U. Photo by Paola Ardizzoni and Emilio Pereda.

pensively on what he interprets as Almodóvar's rediscovered joy at filming 'corps et visages inscrits dans le présent des choses' (Chauvin 2013) ('bodies and faces inscribed firmly in the present'). In an attempt at poetic reformulation, he ponders about the reappearance of 'cet épanchement de la parole, ces logorhées verbales tranquilement impudiques. Loin de tout narcissisme, elles constituent un véritable art partagé, un humus chaud et tendre sur lequel peut s'épanouir le vivre-ensemble' (Chauvin 2013) ('this effusion of speech, these calmly shameless verbal logorrhea. Far from all narcissism, they constitute a veritable shared art, a warm and tender topsoil on which cohabitation can flourish'). Elsewhere, the persistent compulsion to convey a director's auteur status via comparisons with other esteemed filmmakers makes an appearance; Pascal Mérigeau, in *Le Nouvel Observateur*, finds a link between Almodóvar as illustrated in *Los amantes pasajeros* and Alain Resnais, although he accepts that their inspiration and tone are very different (Mérigeau 2013).

If Sotinel tempers the impact of the film's sexual innuendo humour on his otherwise upbeat and respectful review by containing it within a bracketed remark, another contributor to the za-gay thread is more dismissive, casually writing that they found it 'un peu lourd au bout du 81ème "bite"' (Anonyme2 2013) ('a bit heavy after the eighty-first mention of cock'). On another thread on the same site, entitled 'cinéma gay: noms de films' ('gay cinema: film titles') and in which contributors rank gay films, one lists *Los amantes pasajeros* in the 'bof' (which denotes indifference and may be translated as 'meh' in English) section and adds '10 fois le mot b*** par minute c'est lourd, très lourd, même si c'est Almodóvar!' (Anonyme3 2014) ('the word c[ock] ten times a minute, it's heavy, very heavy, even if it's Almodóvar!'). In opinion, if not in tone, such comments approximate some of the criticism of the sexual innuendo in the general press; Thibaut Sardier, reviewer for *Libération*, dismisses the film as gratuitous and vulgar (2013) and rejects the three male stewards as 'gay caricatures' (Sardier 2013). Self-declared Almodóvar adept Sotinel, by contrast, reads the portrayal of these men through a queer lens, arguing, perhaps idealistically, that they recall a period in which marriage interested neither gays nor heterosexuals (Sotinel 2013). Thus, while *Los amantes pasajeros* triggers journalistic responses that invoke well-oiled debates about positive representations of LGBTQ characters (which might also be said to replicate opposing views in academic publications on Almodóvar's sexual politics – Epps and Kadoudaki 2009: 12), the contributors to za-gay as illustrated by these responses, simply shrug *Los amantes pasajeros* off as of no interest, where interest may well refer to its potential both as a 'gay film' and as a source of entertainment. They seem unconcerned with the strategies of recuperation of journalists writing for the LGBTQ, film and general press, steeped in the traditions of 'legitimate' appreciation, with their attention to film history, creativity and canonicity. Almodóvar's pre-existing reputation fails, in this case, to convince them to overlook what they characterise as an eminently forgettable film of no importance. Unlike Truffaut and those whose work has been influenced by his doctrine, then, they qualify films freely, without being constrained by received critical value systems or questions of taste, as either good or bad, irrespective of the director. Self-styled 'Pédéblogeur' ('queer blogger') Matoo, on another site, is less casual in his criticisms, rejecting *Los amantes pasajeros* for lacking direction and the conviction to pursue its crazy comedy to its craziest and campest extreme, although he notes that there were 'quelques répliques assez cultes et souvent bien "cul" des stewards en folie' ('some cult and often 'blue' one-liners by the insane stewards') (Matoo 2013). While one respondent to his blog reminds him that he had forgotten the 'excellent' choreography performed by the three stewards to the Pointer Sisters' 'I'm So Excited!' (Philoo 2013), another is more dismissive than the contributors to za-gay by qualifying *Los amantes pasajeros* as 'raté' ('failed') and 'baclé' (Cyrille 2013) (sloppy).

Concluding Remarks

Much of the discussion in this chapter has been set in the context of further developments of what Jenkins (2006b) had already in the mid-2000s explored as a culture of convergence that 'alters the relationship between existing technologies, industries, markets, genres, and audiences' (15) (as mentioned in Chapter 4). The blend of opinion and online comment with response from audience members physically on site (at festivals and in focus group discussions, as explored in previous chapters) reveals both convergence with and divergence from institutionalised critical comment in various forms. Divergence is the more expected of the two processes, of course, where LGBTQ filmmaking and audience preferences run counter to – even while in dialogic relation to – critical value systems inflected by heterosexist assumptions and more or less high cinephile tastes in France and Spain. In this way, it should be emphasised that, although not bound together as a community like the interpretive community of fandom as studied in the early 1990s by Fiske (1992), these more recent audiences constitute an intervention – a disruption – in the established critical view. There is convergence too, in the more general sense, between critics and the audiences being studied here: simply, they agree, as has been seen, on certain points of interpretation and taste; in a more theoretical sense, they share a habitus, which 'provides a way of seeing the world, a structure which organises and interprets experience, and a generative framework for actions (or, in Bourdieu's terms, practices)' (Thomas 2002 : 14 drawing on Bourdieu 1984). They also share a legitimising, normative tendency (Pujol Ozonas 2011: 126–7, 186–7), and both are 'agents of maintaining social and cultural systems of classification and . . . hierarchies', as again fans were thought of as doing in the second wave of fandom studies as reviewed by Gray et al. (2007: 6). Furthermore, in talking of convergence in the particular sense of his own study, Jenkins observes that 'entertainment content isn't the only thing that flows across multiple media platforms. Our lives, relationships, memories, fantasies, desires also flow across media channels' (Jenkins 2006b: 17), and so also do they flow into and across the separated but related discourses of response that have been the subject of this chapter.

CONCLUSION

In this book we have been tracing cinematically mediated, cross-cultural flows and exchange of tastes, opinions, experiences, desires and values between France and Spain and, as a space of reception, Britain. Through our encounters with events and audiences (including the responses of 440 individuals), we have been asking how LGBTQ experiences and communities are inflected by divergences and commonalities mobilised by certain films and their reception. The various encounters between audience and film, between comment and image, and, indeed, present and past, have revealed some specific ways in which tastes, values, desires and fantasies translate between LGBTQ communities in three wide geographical locations. They have shown how thematic preoccupations of a social or political nature connect across languages through films which either were programmed at festivals and in special screenings or that we separately identified as being perceived as key interventions in terms of their tone, their attack or their structuring of issues. By looking through an LGBTQ lens at what France means for Spain and vice versa, and how certain viewers from Britain themselves apprehend or embrace those meanings, we have tried to forge new articulations between film audience research and our knowledge of sexuality in transnational contexts. This has been facilitated by the emerging range of different films covering varied issues and subject positions. In particular, the major themes that run through the responses – love and relationships, ageing, what is or might be living as a lesbian, gay, bisexual, trans or queer Catalan, citizen of France or Spanish subject – have shaped the discussion. The responses we gathered, as well as being concerned, often in self-questioning ways, with individual identity – like Antonio responding to *Eastern Boys* on the basis of his own particular life or like the very many respondents who were careful to state that they identified with some but not all aspects of a given character or situation experience – have expanded and nuanced the idea of 'sense of community'. We have been able to explore how respondents in the particular circumstances of their viewing of the films (at festivals, at focus groups, at home, abroad, online) themselves configure such notions as belonging, connection, shared history, shared experience, shared values (and, of course, identification).

In some cases, the sense of recognition was used as a means of articulating a political allegiance to an idea of LGBTQ community that transcends national, cultural and linguistic barriers. For Sarah, in London, the subjects of *Les Invisibles* represent the community of which she claims membership. In Barcelona, Oriol extols *Bambi* for providing a record of trans history that they feel belongs to them and, in Manchester, Steve similarly acclaims *Les Invisibles*. The specific and local contexts and configurations of that history are not usually highlighted as impacting on the viewer's expressed ability to claim it as theirs (although for Kenneth the history depicted in *Bambi* is one in which he suggests he had participated). Others, such as the Lyon focus group, used solidarity as a means of engaging with and conveying understanding of the political and social issues facing the trans subjects in *Guerriller@s*. In other cases, the connection was described in more personal terms, as we saw in Andrew's recollections when watching *Les Invisibles* of caring for his older partner in his later years, and the unnamed respondent who claimed to see themselves clearly in that film's subjects' candid accounts of love and desire. In another, perhaps more guarded case, Pedro recognises aspects of Laure/Michäel's crossdressing in *Tomboy* as something he did when he was young, but nonetheless uses this to reaffirm his own gender normativity and to transmit a conventional account of gender development in children.

The two main chapters presenting the audience responses have shown a broad range of ways in which representations from other, but proximate, cultures inform processes of self-recognition in terms of sexuality, politics and needs among local audiences. For some, responding to *Les invisibles*, an enthusiastic investment in the subject matter of older lesbian, gay and queer lives transcended national and linguistic differences; the recurrence of this subject matter across festivals and films and the textured responses we received became a notable aspect of our project. Responses to *80 Egunean* showed a preoccupation not only with empathy but even more so with the issue of age and with contrasting views on whether British or Spanish social attitudes are the most retrograde. While for some the slow, intense style of *L'Inconnu du lac* is a nationally marked, French, disadvantage, for others it lets them talk variously about the emotional lives of the characters or raw social realism.

Responses to the films made by trans people or on trans issues in some cases showed close political allegiances and awareness, as in the case of those who talked about *Guerriller@s*, or empathy based on an appreciation of queer political history, as in *Bambi*. They also revealed some of the detail underlying misreadings of trans issues by those viewing them from positions strictly LGB or cisgender. The range of positions occupied by respondents was restricted by their being largely external to the communities portrayed and at least one remove from the individual protagonists in terms of direct identification. In this sense, our project was again restricted by its dependence on festivals (and their imperfect inclusion of the 'T' in their self-styling and remit) and mainstream films (and their representations of trans lives and issues to melodramatic or even comic ends); but it also revealed a surprisingly varied – indeed, sometimes conflicted – set of responses ranging across materiality, identity, and politics bridging the trans and the queer.

In Chapter 1 we used the perspectives of film history, sexual politics and LGBTQ cultural exchange to sketch a cross-cultural map of the interconnected histories of France and Spain, Frenchness and Spanishness. We found throughout that many respondents are alert to and have recourse to talking in terms of perceived typical qualities of French or Spanish film in relation to their own LGBTQ experience. Responses were also found to be non-specifically informed by historical connections such as the influence on Spanish gay film of the 1970s and 1980s of French New Wave and experimental and radical filmmaking, or the influence of the Almodóvar phenomenon on popular French film cultures and the role of Spanish characters and locations in the visibilisation and pluralisation of LGBTQ issues in mainstream and genre cinema in France.

As we saw, respondents in Spain – David and Lucas – convey a knowledge of French LGBTQ cinema and strong attachments to the films they mention (*Les Témoins*, *Drôle de Félix* and *Les Roseaux sauvages*) which both characterise as canonical in terms of LGBTQ representations. They acclaim the approaches to LGBTQ themes as typically French because of their proximity to lived experience (David) and because they are raw, realistic and sexually enticing (Lucas). This association of closeness to actual human experiences with French cinema counters some of the discourses circulated in France – as we saw in Chapter 1 – wherein it is Spain and the Spanish that are constructed as achieving a more embodied connection with human affect and emotion than France. And yet, some of the French respondents' constructions of Spanish culture align with this connection of a more visceral, felt and sensed experience of and engagement with the social world with Spain. In France, Maxime and Cyprien claim that Spain is more open and accepting of trans identities than France, Benjamin and Flora imply that Ocaña's freedom is partly related to his being from Spain, and Daphne describes *El Sexo de los ángeles* as typifying Spain's relaxed and open attitude towards non-normative sexualities and relationships. However, in some of these cases, Spain and Spanish LGBTQ cinema were appropriated as prompts for critiquing France rather than for expressing any real claims of informed awareness of the realities of Spanish life. Elsewhere, sense of shared history, experience and values is not confined to the LGBTQ-identifying viewers. Damla, as we saw in the Manchester focus group, conveyed a strong connection to Thérèse and Pierrot in *Les Invisibles*, projecting herself forwards into the future and claiming to want to have experienced pasts like theirs. Shared values do not always depend on exact same experience.

Throughout, our concern has been with audiences' engagements with 'foreign' films and the construction of self and community identity. In this way, from the London screening of the documentary *Born Naked* (Andrea Esteban, 2012) (briefly discussed in Chapter 3), nine respondents allude to other cultures and to similarities or differences in queer and lesbian lives across Europe, with FD, a thirty-seven-year-old black British student and consultant, writing that she 'love[d] the three country perspective' and encapsulating her motive for coming to the film as, simply, but comprehensively, its being 'international, lesbian, queer'.

It was striking to see that identification with feelings, ideals, emotional situations or with a point in LGBTQ history was both common and specific. The experience of love, in its more romantic manifestations, was often the feeling or range of feelings that our respondents highlight as having allowed them to connect with, in many cases, the extraordinary existences and situations portrayed in the films. John claimed to understand and relate to Franck's self-destructive attraction for the deadly Michel in *L'Inconnu du lac* by citing his need to find love and give his life meaning. A similar attraction for *amour fou* was found to be the explanation offered by some of the respondents to both *Notre paradis* (by Rubén and Jose María) and *Eastern Boys* (by Roberto and Manuel) for their feelings of recognition, understanding and proximity. For some (Saraiva and Aldo, in London) the non-normative, intentionally queer and destabilising queer characters are sources for declarations of self-recognition, for others (Marc in Barcelona, and Santiago in Madrid) they are points of contention and serve as illustrations of an outdated cliché. Elsewhere, as we saw, situations known and experienced, and feelings recognised, recur as narratives of engagement with regards to trans films among non-trans-identifying and cisgender respondents. Here, the coming-out narrative, with self-acceptance and acceptance by others, is the most common point of similarity for our respondents.

Situations known and experienced are also highlighted as causes of empathy by some of the respondents to *El sexo de los ángeles*, who write or convey that they have lived similar bisexual or tripartite relationships in their pasts. For others, though, the triadic, polyamorous relationships between Raï, Bruno and Carla correspond to situations that they claim to aspire to. For others still, a life beyond dyadic coupledom is something they may well desire, but that they know they may not be able to live in the physical, material sense. In such cases, films offer the potential to experience something vicariously, possibly as a means of escaping the drudgery and restraints of a particular individual's reality, but not always. The fantasy scenario depicted on screen is a core element of that reality, of that engagement with the world rather than a separate entity altogether.

On the other hand, divergences between respondents' experiences and interpretations of social reality and those portrayed on film are highlighted as barriers to empathy and identification. We saw in London that Zadie and Rupah, in their comments about *80 Egunean* and *Les Invisibles*, implied that either racist attitudes depicted or the absence of subjects from different racial or ethnic backgrounds tempered their expressed ability to relate to the films. Similarly, Pablo and Antonio (Barcelona) are alone in highlighting the story of migration portrayed in *Eastern Boys*. This confirms the importance of the salience of a viewer's lived reality for the subject positions they claim in response to films, but it simultaneously raises concerns about the range of images of LGBTQ lifestyles we encounter, at festivals and special screenings and online. Although the filmmakers – and, to a degree, the audience – claim *Les Invisibles* as giving voice to a broad range of different interviewees and allowing a broad range of personal stories to be told, other voices – from those LGBTQ people from different racial or ethnic backgrounds for instance – remain silenced, their stories are untold within that particular film (or at that particular event).

The focus on selected LGBTQ film festivals in France and Spain helped us to define not only our audiences but also specific effects within the formation of community and of identity through engagement with films and values both foreign and familiar. Across the range, the festivals' spokespeople and self-promotional materials invoke the raising of awareness, responsibility, audience as community, and film of all genres as intervention; when quality and creativity are also invoked it is with an eye on affiliation, on connecting with a target audience. For several respondents, going to these festivals is part of who they are; indeed, for Michel, an attender at FIRE!!, going to the festival is a question of necessity. We found that working with festivals, while restricting the range of responses in some ways, in others allowed us to reach audiences and to focus pointedly on certain films in ways that other methods might easily close off.

Lastly, in cross-mapping professional critical reception with audience and other user responses to queer films with a wide box office appeal we explored patterns of convergence and divergence in views of films and key filmmakers. Tastes which might have seemed specifically part of a formation of LGBTQ community and identity – for example, an appreciation of the interconnectedness for some of loneliness and sexuality, in relation to *L'Inconnu du lac*; or a strong attraction towards the affirmative power of open sexual expression between women, as in *La Vie d'Adèle* – are seen to overlap and inform one another. While professional criticism attempts to establish an Ozon who is the French Almodóvar, there is little popular LGBTQ-authored buzz around the French director in Spain to match that around Almodóvar; and the Spanish director's latest films are popularly received in France from slightly unexpected angles – the liveliness and entertainment value of *La piel que habito* are noted, where the film critics see problems and allusions; *Las amantes pasajeros* is taken flatly, whereas the film critics are, in one way or another, highly excitable around the film. The two constituencies alight as often on the same as on different details. In the construction and emergence of critical discourses on these films and filmmakers the lines between the different approaches blur and intertwine.

In as much as we are part of the very audiences we have been studying, when we started off by asking if and how queer desires, values and tastes are translatable in our contexts of study we were asking a productively rhetorical question. We already supposed that these LGBTQ audiences, and program-mers and distributors, would be responding to what benign effects there may be in the transnational flow of moving images, to a generally shared Western European politics of diversity and to recognisable sets of personal concerns specific to LGBTQ experience and imagination. The granularity of the responses, however, has shown unexpected connections with these foreign films and odd directions in the passage of ideas and identifications between individuals, audiences and loose communities of commentators foreign and domestic, expert or amateur. The book thus reveals material evidence of the fragile, contested, negotiated and contingent nature of self and community identity as it plays out in the cross-cultural exchange between audiences and French and Spanish queer cinema.

APPENDIX I
STANDARD QUESTIONS FOR RESPONDENTS

Documentary Films

1. Why did you choose this film?
2. Did you like it? What did you like or dislike about it?
3. Did you think it was true to life? Why, or why not?
4. Did anything about the documentary surprise you?
5. Were you able to identify with any of the characters or events in the film?
6. What do you think of the way the themes of the film were dealt with?
7. Did you like the style of the documentary?
8. Do you think the director did a good job? Why, or why not?
9. Did you know anything about the film before coming to the screening? Where did you get this information?
10. Do you usually watch documentaries? What do you like or dislike about them?
11. Do you regularly attend LGBTQ film events/festivals or is this your first visit?
12. Do you have any other comments to add?

Fictional/Feature Films

1. Why did you choose this film?
2. Did you like it? What did you like or dislike about it?
3. Who was your favourite character? Why?
4. What was your favourite scene? Why?
5. Did you think it was true to life? Why or why not?
6. Did anything about the film surprise you?
7. What did you think of the actors?

8. Were you able to identify with any of the characters or events in the film?
9. What do you think of the way the themes of the film were dealt with?
10. Did you like the style of the film?
11. Did you know anything about the film before coming to the screening? Where did you get this information?
12. Do you have any other comments to add?

Other language versions for 'were you able to identify?' in question 5 for documentary films and question 8 for fictional/feature films: Cat., 'T'has sentit identificat?'; Fr., 'Vous êtes-vous senti proche?'; Sp., '¿Te has identificado?'.

Other language versions for 'true to life' in question 5 for fictional/feature films: Cat., 'representativa de la realitat'; Fr., 'vraisembable'; Sp. 'realista'.

PERSONAL DATA SOUGHT FROM RESPONDENTS TO BOTH TYPES OF FILM

Name:
Email address:
How old are you?
What is your place of residence?
What is your nationality?
How would you describe your ethnicity?
How do you identify (e.g. female, male, trans FTM, trans MTF, genderqueer, other)?
What kind of education/ training have you had?
What do you do?

APPENDIX II
PROJECT WEB PAGE

School of Arts, Languages and Cultures

Subjects | How to apply | Fees and funding | Graduate School | **School research** | School people | About the School

* Home
* School research
* All projects

Transnational Desires

▸ Who we are
▸ News and events
▸ Links
▸ Films

Transnational Desires

About us

This project focuses on lesbian, gay, transgender and queer films from France and Spain from the 1990s to the present day. As part of it, we are visiting LGBTQ festivals in France, Spain and the UK and engaging with local communities, groups and audiences through interviews, online questionnaires and blogs. Our aim is to investigate audience responses to LGBTQ films, asking broadly "how to images of queer desire travel?"

We are working in and out of French, Spanish, Catalan and English, on a range of materials from radical documentary through popular short-format entertainments to feature-length dramas, on-line, off-disc and in film theatres and archives. Links to the trailers and clips from some of the films can be found in the films section of this blog.

If you would like to get involved, please email us at: transnationaldesires@gmail.com.

Find us on facebook.

Transnational Desires

Who We Are

Transnational Desires is an AHRC-funded research project based in the School of Arts, Languages and Cultures at The University of Manchester. Chris Perriam is Professor of Hispanic Studies and writes about Spanish LGBTQ cinema.
Darren Waldron is Senior Lecturer in French and Screen Studies, and writes about French LGBTQ cinema and its audiences.

Transnational Desires / Deseos Transnacionales es un proyecto de investigación financiado por el AHRC (Arts and Humanities Research Council) y tiene base en la School of Arts, Languages and Cultures de la Universidad de Manchester. **Chris Perriam** es catedrático de Estudios Hispánicos y escribe sobre cine LGBTQ español.
Darren Waldron es profesor de francés y cine y escribe sobre cine LGBTQ y su público.

Transnational Desires / Desitjos Transnacionals és un projecte de recerca finançat per l'AHRC (Consell de Recerca d'Arts i Humanitats) amb base a l'Escola d' Arts, Languages and Cultures de la Universitat de Manchester. En **Chris Perriam** es catedràtic d'Estudis Hispànics i escriu sobre cinema LGBTQ espanyol. En **Darren Waldron** és professor de francès i cinema i escriu sobre el cinema LGBTQ i el seu públic.

Transnational Desires/Désirs transnationaux est un projet de recherche financé par le AHRC (Arts and Humanities Research Council) basé à la School of Arts, Languages and Cultures de l'université de Manchester. Chris Perriam est professeur d'Université d'Etudes Hispaniques et publie sur le cinéma LGTBQ espagnol. Darren Waldron est maître de conférences de français et de cinéma et publie sur le cinéma LGTBQ et son public. Ros Murray est assistant de recherche et publie sur le cinéma LGTBQ et la littérature avant-garde.

Links

- Casal Lamda
- Des Images aux mots Toulouse Festival
- Écrans Mixtes Lyon Festival
- In and Out Nice
- London Lesbian and Gay Film Festival
- LesGaiCineMad
- Fire!! Festival
- Barcelona International Lesbian and Gay Film Festival
- La Mostra Internacional de Films de dones
- Global Queer Cinema
- Queer Film Festivals
- Fundación triángulo
- Centre Audiovisuel Simone de Beauvoir
- Bifi
- Observatoire des transidentités
- Media G
- Têtu
- Centre LGBT Paris
- Fédération LGBT
- Cogam
- Revista Una Buena Barba
- Cartografías transfeministas

FILMOGRAPHY

FEATURE-LENGTH FILMS

8 Femmes, film, directed by François Ozon. Paris: Fidélité Films, 2002.

80 Egunean, film, directed by Jon Garaño and Jose Mari Goenaga. San Sebastian: Irusoin, 2010.

Agustina de Aragón, film, directed by Juan de Orduña. Madrid: CIFESA, 1950.

Alice et Martin, film, directed by André Téchiné. Paris: Les Films Alain Sarde, 1998.

A toute vitesse, film, directed by Gaël Morel. Paris: Magouric Productions, 1996.

Ander, film, directed by Roberto Castón. Bilbao: Berdindu, 2009.

Baise-moi, film, directed by Virginie Despentes and Coralie Trinh Thi. Paris: Canal+, 2000.

Belle de jour, film, directed by Luis Buñuel. Paris: Paris Film, 1967.

Cachorro, film, directed by Miguel Abaladejo. Madrid: Canal+ España, 2004.

Carmen, film, directed by Vicente Aranda. Madrid: Star Line TV Productions, 2003.

Carne trémula, film, directed by Pedro Almodóvar. Madrid: El Deseo, 1997.

Cet obscur objet du désir, film, directed by Luis Buñuel. Paris: Greenwich Film Productions, 1977.

Chroniques sexuelles d'une famille d'aujourd'hui, film, directed by Pascal Arnold and Jean-Marc Barr. Paris: Toloda, 2012.

Dans la maison, film, directed by François Ozon. Paris: Mandarin Films, 2012.

Donne-moi la main, film, directed by Pascal Alex-Vincent. Paris: Local Films, 2008.

Drôle de Félix, film, directed by Olivier Ducastel and Jacques Martineau. Issy-Les-Moulineaux: Arte France Cinéma, 2000.

Eastern Boys, film, directed by Robin Campillo. Paris: Les Films de Pierre, 2013.

Edward II, film, directed by Derek Jarman. London: British Screen, 1991.

El lugar sin límites, film, directed by Arturo Ripstein. Mexico: Conacite Dos, 1978.

El mar, film, directed by Agustí Villaronga. Barcelona: Issona Passola, 2000.

El sexo de los ángeles, film, directed by Xavier Villaverde. Rio de Janeiro: ANCINE, 2012.

El tambor del Bruch, film, directed by Ignacio F. Iquino. Barcelona: Emisora Films, 1947

Eloge de l'amour, film, directed by Jean-Luc Godard. Paris: Avventura Films, 2001.

En la ciudad sin límites, film, directed by Antonio Hernández. Madrid: Icónica, 2002.

Españolas en París, film, directed by Roberto Bodegas. Madrid: Ágata Films, 1971.

Exils, film, directed by Tony Gatlif. Paris: Princes Films, 2004.

Fucking Åmål, film, directed by Lukas Moodysson. Stockholm: Memfis Film, 1998.

Gazon maudit, film, directed by Josiane Balasko. Paris: Canal+, 1994.

Gouttes d'eau sur pierres brûlantes, film, directed by François Ozon. Paris: Fidélité Productions, 2000.

Goya's Ghosts, film, directed by Miloš Forman. Berkeley: The Saul Zaentz Company, 2006.

Habitación en Roma, film, directed by Julio Medem. Madrid: Morena Films, 2010.

Hable con ella, film, directed by Pedro Almodóvar. Madrid: El Deseo, 2002.

Intouchables, film, directed by Olivier Nakache and Eric Toledano. Clichy: Quad Productions, 2011.

Jean de Florette, film, directed by Claude Berri. Paris: DD Productions, 1986.

Jeune et jolie, film, directed by François Ozon. Paris: Mandarin Films, 2013.

Jules et Jim, film, directed by François Truffaut. Paris: Les Films du Carosse/ SEDIF, 1962.

Krámpack, film, directed by Cesc Gay. Madrid: Canal+ España, 2000.

L'Age d'or, film, directed by Luis Buñuel. Paris: Vicomte de Noailles, 1930.

L'Amour fou, film, directed by Pierre Thoretton. Paris: Les Films du Lendemain, 2010.

L'arbre de les cireres, film, directed by Marc Recha. Barcelona: Oerón Cinematográfica, 1998.

L'Auberge espagnole, film, directed by Cédric Klapisch. Paris: Bac Films, 2002.

L'Inconnu du lac, film, directed by Alain Guiraudie. Paris: Les Films du Worso, 2013.

La Folie des grandeurs, film, directed by Gérard Oury. Neuilly-sur-Seine: Gaumont International, 1969.

La Guerre est finie, film, directed by Alain Resnais. Stockholm: Europa Film, 1966.

La ley del deseo, film, directed by Pedro Almodóvar. Madrid: El Deseo, 1987.

La mala educación, film, directed by Pedro Almodóvar. Madrid: El Deseo, 2004.

La piel que habito, film, directed by Pedro Almodóvar. Madrid: El Deseo, 2011.

La Vie d'Adèle, film, directed by Abdellatif Khechiche. Paris: Quat'sous Films, 2013.

Las cosas del querer 2a parte, film, directed by Jaime Chávarri. Buenos Aires: Argentina Sono Film S.A.C.I., 1995.

Laurence Anyways, film, directed by Xavier Dolan. Montreal: Lyla Films, 2012.

Le Charme discret de la bourgeoisie, film, directed by Luis Buñuel. Paris: Greenwich Film Productions, 1972.

Le Clan, film, directed by Gaël Morel. Montreuil: Sépia Productions, 2004.

Le Refuge, film, directed by François Ozon. Paris: Eurowide Film Production, 2009.

Le Temps qui reste, film, directed by François Ozon. Paris: Fidélité Films, 2004.

Le Testament d'Orphée, film, directed by Jean Cocteau. Paris: Cinédis, 1960.

Les Biches, film, directed by Claude Chabrol. Paris: Les Films de la Boétie, 1968.

Les Chansons d'amour, film, directed by Christophe Honoré. Paris: Alma Films, 2007.

Les Dames du Bois de Boulogne, film, directed by Robert Bresson. Paris: Raoul Ploquin Films, 1945.

Les Enfants du paradis, film, directed by Marcel Carné. Paris: Société Nouvelle Pathé Cinéma, 1943–5.

Les Femmes du 6e étage, film, directed by Philippe Le Guay. Paris: Vendôme Production, 2010.

Les Garçons et Guillaume à table!, film, directed by Guillaume Gallienne. Paris: LGM Productions, 2013.

Les mans buides, film, directed by Marc Recha. Issy-les-Moulineaux: Arte France Cinéma, 2003.

Les Roseaux sauvages, film, directed by André Téchiné. Paris: Ima Films, 1994.

Les Témoins, film, directed by André Téchiné. Neuilly-sur-Seine: UGC, 2007.

Les Voleurs, film, directed by André Téchiné. Paris: Canal+, 1996.

Locura de amor, film, directed by Juan de Orduña. Madrid: CIFESA, 1948.

Loin, film, directed by André Téchiné. Neuilly-sur-Seine: Union Générale Cinématographique, 2001.

Los abrazos rotos, film, directed by Pedro Almodóvar. Madrid: El Deseo, 2009.

Los amantes pasajeros, film, directed by Pedro Almodóvar. Madrid: El Deseo, 2013.

Manon des Sources, film, directed by Claude Berri. Paris: DD Productions 1987.

Monster, film, directed by Patty Jenkins. Sherman Oaks, CA: Media 8 Entertainment, 2003.

Mujeres al borde de un ataque de nervios, film, directed by Pedro Almodóvar. Madrid: El Deseo, 1988.

Notre paradis, film, directed by Gaël Morel. Paris: Alfama Films, 2011.

Orphée, film, directed by Jean Cocteau. Paris: Films du Palais Royal, 1950.

Pas si grave, film, directed by Bernard Rapp. Paris: Canal+, 2003.

Pau i el seu germà, film, directed by Marc Recha. Paris: Canal+, 2001.

Petit Indi, film, directed by Marc Recha. Issy-les-Moulineaux: Arte France Cinéma, 2009.

Piedras, film, directed by Ramón Salazar. Madrid: Alquimia Cinema, 2002.

Plein sud, film, directed by Sébastien Lifshitz. Paris: Ad Vitam Production, 2009.

Potiche, film, directed by François Ozon. Paris: Mandarin Films.

Pourquoi pas moi?, film, directed by Stéphane Giusti. Paris: Alhena Films, 1999.

Presque rien, film, directed by Sébastien Lifshitz. Issy-les-Moulineaux: Arte France Cinéma, 2000.

Reinas, film, directed by Manuel Gómez Pereira. Madrid: Warner Bros. Pictures de España, 2005.

Romeos, film, directed by Sabine Bernardi. Cologne: Boogiefilm, 2011.

Ruy Blas, film, directed by Pierre Billon. Paris: Productions André Paulvé, 1948.

Sagitario, film, directed by Vicente Molina Foix. Madrid: Fernando Colomo Producciones Cinematográficas, 2001.

Sitcom, film, directed by François Ozon. Paris: Fidélité Productions, 1998.

Tacones lejanos, film, directed by Pedro Almodóvar. Madrid: El Deseo/CIBY, 1991.

The Living End, film, directed by Gregg Araki. Toronto: Cineplex Odeon Films, 1992.

The Rocky Horror Picture Show, film, directed by Jim Sharman. Los Angeles: Twentieth Century Fox Film Corporation, 1975.

Todo sobre mi madre, film, directed by Pedro Almodóvar. Madrid: El Deseo, 1999.

Tomboy, film, directed by Céline Sciamma. Paris: Hold Up Films, 2011.

Une nouvelle amie, film, directed by François Ozon. Paris: Mandarin Films, 2014.

Volver, film, directed by Pedro Almodóvar. Madrid: El Deseo, 2006.

Wild Side, film, directed by Sébastien Lifshitz. Paris: Maïa Films, 2004.

XXY, film, directed by Lucía Puenzo. Buenos Aires: Historias Cinematograficas Cinemania, 2007.

SHORT AND MEDIUM-LENGTH FILMS

Fireworks, film, directed by Kenneth Anger. Self-produced, 1947.

Le Testament d'Orphée, film, directed by Jean Cocteau. Paris: Cinédis, 1960.

Mathi(eu), film, directed by Coralie Prosper. Paris: Ecole Supérieure de Réalisation Audiovisuelle, 2011.

Un chant d'amour, film, directed by Jean Genet. Paris: Nico Papatakis, 1950.

One Night Stand, video, directed by Emilie Jouvet. Paris: Emilie Jouvet Production, 2006.

Une Robe d'été, film, directed by François Ozon. Paris: Fidélité Productions, 1996.

DOCUMENTARIES

Bambi, film, directed by Sébastien Lifshitz. Montreuil: Un Monde Meilleur, 2013.

Born Naked, film, directed by Andrea Esteban. Madrid: Pilar Comesaña, 2012.

El camino de Moisés, film, directed by Cecilia Barriga. Barcelona: self-produced, 2003.

Etre et avoir, film, directed by Bertrand Philibert. Paris: Maïa Fims, 2002.

Fake Orgasm, film, directed by Jo Sol. Barcelona: Zip Films , 2010.

Fille ou garçon: mon sexe n'est pas mon genre, film, directed by Valérie Mitteaux. Strasbourg: Arte, 2011.

Guerriller@s, video, directed by Montse Pujantell. Barcelona: self-produced, 2012.

Ignasi M, film, directed by Ventura Pons. Barcelona: Els Films de la Rambla, 2013.

L'Ordre des mots, film, directed by Cynthia Arra and Mélissa Arra. Paris: self-produced, 2007.

Las ventanas abiertas, film, directed by Michèle Massé. [Paris]: self-produced, 2014.

Les Invisibles, film, directed by Sébastien Lifshitz. Paris: Zadig Films, 2012.

Mi sexualidad es una creación artística, film, Lucía Egaña Rojas. Barcelona: self-produced, 2011.

Ocaña, retrat intermitent, film, directed by Ventura Pons. Barcelona: Prozesa, 1978.

Queer Artivism, film, directed by Maša Zia Lenárdič and Anja Wutej. Ljubljana: White Balance, 2013.

Race d'Ep, film, directed by Lionel Soukaz. [Paris]: Little Sisters Production, 1979.

Test de la vida real, film, directed by Florencia P. Marano. Barcelona: SF Produccions, 2009.

Vides transsexuals, film, directed by Maria Popota. Barcelona: Ajuntament de Barcelona, 2011.

REFERENCES

Abrams, Lynn (2010), *Oral History Theory*, London and New York: Routledge.

Acadèmia del Cinema (2015), 'Ventura Pons, Gaudí d'Honor-Miquel Porter 2015' Acadèmia del Cinema Català website news item, 27 November, <http://www.academiadelcinema.cat/en/actualitat/actualitat-activitats-acad emia/2086-ventura-pons-gaudi-d-honor-miquel-porter-2015> (last accessed 6 February 2015).

Agencia EFE and Jordi Font Comas d'Argemir (2014), 'Valls, un primer ministro francés de Barcelona, culé y que habla catalán', *La Vanguardia Internacional*, 31 March, <http://www.lavanguardia.com/internacional/ 20140331/54405315438/valls-primer-ministro-frances-barcelona-cule-habla-catalan.html> (last accessed 8 April 2014).

Agora (2015), Agora Films website entry for *Tomboy*, <http://www.agora films.net/film/195/TOMBOY> (last accessed 17 February 2015).

Ahmed, Sara (2006), *Queer Phenomenology: Orientation, Objects, Others*, Durham, NC: Duke University Press.

Alessandrin, Arnaud, Karine Espineira and Thomas Maud-Yeuse (2012), *La Transcyclopédie*, Paris: Des ailes sur un tracteur.

Allinson, Mark (2009), 'Mimesis and Diegesis: Almodóvar and the Limits of Melodrama', in Brad Epps and Despina Kadoudaki (eds), *All About Almodóvar: A Passion for Cinema*, Minneapolis: University of Minnesota Press, pp. 141–65.

Amago, Samuel (2005), 'Why Spaniards Make Good Bad Guys: Sergi López and the Persistence of the Black Legend in Contemporary European Cinema', *Film Criticism*, 30.1, 41–63.

Ang, Ien (1989), 'Wanted. Audiences. On the Politics of Empirical Audience Studies', in Elle Seiter, Hans Borchers, Gabriele Kreutzner and Eva Maria Warth (eds), *Remote Control: Television Audiences and Cultural Power*, London: Routledge, pp. 96–115.

Angoustures, Aline (2004), *L'Espagne (Idées reçues)*, Paris: Editions Les Cavaliers Bleu.

Anonyme1 (2013), Comment on Pedro Almodovar: cinéaste espagnol on-line forum, za-gay.com, 1 June, 22:33, <http://www.za-gay.org/forum/viewtopic/40253/pedro-almodovar-cineaste-espagnol/0/> (last accessed 20 August 2015).

Anonyme2 (2013), Comment on Pedro Almodovar: cinéaste espagnol on-line forum, za-gay.com, 12 June, 20:39, <http://www.za-gay.org/forum/viewto pic/40253/pedro-almodovar-cineaste-espagnol/0/> (last accessed 20 August 2015).

Anonyme3 (2014), Comment on Cinéma gay: noms de film on-line forum, za-gay.com, 2 July, 22:58, <http://www.za-gay.org/forum/viewtopic/44896/cinema-gay-noms-de-films/2/> (last accessed 9 September 2015).

Argüelles, Manu (2011), '*Potiche: Mujeres al poder*', in El espectador imaginario blog site, April, <http://elespectadorimaginario.com/pages/abril-2011/criticas/potiche-mujeres-al-poder.php> (last accessed 17 April 2015).

Arranz, Fátima, Pilar Aguilar, Javier Callejo, Pilar Pardo, Inés París and Esperanza Roquero (2010), *Cine y género en España. Una investigación empírica*, Madrid: Cátedra.

Attali, Danielle (2013) 'Almodóvar nous envoie en l'air', *Le Journal du Dimanche*, Culture, 24 March, <http://www.lejdd.fr/Culture/Cinema/Actualite/Almodovar-nous-envoie-en-l-air-598129> (last accessed 14 October 2015).

Aubert, Jean-Paul (2002), 'Le cinéma de l'Espagne démocratique. Les images du consensus', *Vingtième Siècle. Revue d'histoire*, 2.74, 141–51, DOI: 10.3917/ving.074.0141.

Aubert, Jean-Paul (2009), *L'Ecole de Barcelona: un cinéma d'avant-garde en Espagne sour le franquisme*, Paris: Broché.

Austin, Guy (1996), *Contemporary French Cinema*, Manchester: Manchester University Press.

Austin, Guy (2003), *Stars in Modern French Film*, London: Arnold.

Austin, Thomas (2002), *Hollywood Hype and Audiences: Selling and Watching Popular Film in the 1990s,* Manchester: Manchester University Press.

Azo, Toni (1994), 'Michel Foucault, pensar de l'altra banda', *Lambda*, 14, 40–1.

Banens, Maks (2014), 'Doing Same-Sex Families in Europe', shared open access resource, <https://www.academia.edu/5756731/Doing_same-sex_families_in_Europe> (last accessed 4 June 2015).

Barbe, Yannick (2011), 'Festival Ecrans Mixtes', *Yagg* online magazine, <http://yagg.com/2011/03/02/festival-ecrans-mixtes-a-lyon-il-est-urgent-de-prendre-soin-de-notre-memoire-collective/> (last accessed 5 October 2015).

Bardou, Florian (2015), 'Espagne: dix ans après, le marriage pour tout.e.s ne suffit pas', <http://yagg.com/2015/07/12/espagne-dix-ans-apres-le-mariage-pour-tout-e-s-ne-suffit-pas (last accessed 1 October 2015)

Barker, Emma (2007), 'Mme Geoffrin, Painting and Galanterie: Carle Van

Loo's *Conversation espagnole* and *Lecture espagnole*', *Eighteenth-Century Studies*, 40.4, 587–614.

Barker, Martin (2006), 'On Being Ambitious for Audience Research', in Isabelle Charpentier (ed.), *Comment sont reçues les œuvres*, Versailles: Créaphis, pp. 27–42.

Barker, Martin (2014), 'Crossing Out the Audience', in Ian Christie (ed.), *Audiences*, Amsterdam: Amsterdam University Press, pp. 187–205.

Barker, Martin (2016), '"Legolas, he's cool . . . and he's hot!": The Meanings and Implications of Audiences' Favorite Characters', in CarrieLynn D. Reinhard and Christopher J. Olson (eds), *Making Sense of Cinema: Empirical Studies into Spectators and Spectatorship*, London and New York: Bloomsbury/Continuum, pp. 147–76.

Barker, Martin and Kate Brooks (1998), *Knowing Audiences: 'Judge Dredd', Its Friends, Fans and Foes*, Luton: University of Luton Press.

Barker, Martin and Ernest Mathijs (eds) (2008), *Watching The Lord of the Rings: Tolkien's World Audiences*, New York: Peter Lang.

Basford, Jake (2012), '*Girl or Boy, My Sex Is Not My Gender* (*Fille ou garçon, mon sexe n'est pas mon genre*)' [review], in BFI London Lesbian & Gay Film Festival: Round-Up 4, 30 March, <http://sosogay.co.uk/2012/bfi-london-lesbian-gay-film-festival-round-up-4> (last accessed 8 April 2015).

Baudrand, Michel-Antoine (1701), *Dictionnaire géographique universel*, Amsterdam: François Halma, Guillaume van der Water.

Baxter, John (1994), *Buñuel*, London: Fourth Estate.

beapbeap (2013), Comment on FAQ report on *La vida de Adèle*, in Hay una lesbiana en mi sopa blog, 27 October 10:30, <http://www.hayunalesbian aenmisopa.com/2013/10/25/20-curiosidades-que-siempre-quisiste-saber-de-la-vida-de-adele/> (last accessed 8 April 2015).

Behlil, Melis (2005), 'Ravenous Cinephiles: Cinephilia, Internet, and Online Film Communities', in Marijke de Valck and Malte Hagener (eds), *Cinephilia: Movies, Love and Memory*, Amsterdam: Amsterdam University Press, pp. 111–23.

Bertrand, Ina and Peter Hughes (2005), *Media Research Methods: Audiences, Institutions, Texts*, London and New York: Palgrave Macmillan.

Betz, Dorothy M. (2005), 'Orientalism as Freedom in Hugo's *Les Orientales*', *Romance Quarterly*, 52.1, 54–63.

BFI (2013), Programme for London Lesbian and Gay Film Festival, London, 14–24 March, London: British Film Institute.

BFIPlayer (2014), Synopsis to *Les Invisibles*, online rental access page, BFIPlayer website, <http://player.bfi.org.uk/film/watch-les-invisibles-2012/> (last accessed 15 September 2015).

Binnie, Jon and Christian Klesse (2012), 'The Politics of Age, Temporality and Intergenerationality in Transnational Lesbian, Gay, Bisexual, Transgender and Queer Activist Networks', *Sociology*, 47.3, 580–95.

Bobo, Jacqueline (2003), 'The Color Purple: Black Women as Cultural

Readers', in Will Brooker and Deborah Jermyn (eds), *The Audience Studies Reader*, London and New York: Routledge, pp. 305–14.

Bond Stockton, Kathryn (2009), *The Queer Child or Growing Sideways in the Twentieth Century*, Durham, NC, and London: Duke University Press.

Bourcier, Marie-Hélène (ed.) (1998), *Q comme Queer*, Paris: Gai, Kitsch, Camp.

Bourcier, Marie-Hélène (2001), *Queer Zones: Politiques des identités sexuelles, des représentations et des savoirs*, Paris: Balland.

Bourcier, Marie-Hélène (2005), *Sexpolitiques, Queer zones 2*, Paris: La Fabrique Editions.

Bourcier, Marie-Hélène (2011), *Queer zones 3*, Paris: Editions Amsterdam.

Bourdieu, Pierre (1979), *La Distinction: critique sociale du jugement*, Paris: Les Editions de Minuit.

Bourdieu, Pierre (1984), *Distinction: A Social Critique of the Judgement of Taste*, translated by Richard Nice, Cambridge, MA: Harvard University Press.

Bourgeois, Charlotte (2008), 'Premier festival de films sur la transidentité de Paris', *Têtu*, 10 January 2008, <https://www.tetu.com/2008/01/10/news/culture/premier-festival-de-films-sur-la-transidentite-de-paris/> (last accessed 1 July 2015).

British Film Institute (2012), Note on *Notre paradis*, in programme for 26th London Lesbian and Gay Film Festival catalogue, March 2012, n.p., reproduced at, <http://mubi.com/films/our-paradise> (last accessed 15 August 2014).

Brooker, Will and Deborah Jermyn (2003), 'Conclusion: Overflow and Audience', in Will Brooker and Deborah Jermyn (eds), *The Audience Studies Reader*, London and New York: Routledge, pp. 322–34.

Buckingham, David (1991), 'What Are Words Worth?: Interpreting Children's Talk about Television', *Cultural Studies*, 5.2, 228–45.

Buñuel, Luis (1994), *Mon dernier soupir*, Paris: Editions Laffont.

Buse, Peter, Núria Triana-Toribio and Andrew Willis (2007), *The Cinema of Álex de la Iglesia*, Manchester: Manchester University Press.

Butler, Judith (1990), *Gender Trouble: Feminism and the Subversion of Identity*, London and New York: Routledge.

Cairns, Lucille (2006), *Sapphism on Screen: Lesbian Desire in French and Francophone Cinema*, Edinburgh: Edinburgh University Press.

Calphi (2008), 'IndentiT, 1er festival de films trans de Paris: premier bilan du festival', 20 January, <http://caphi.over-blog.fr/article-15541154.html> (last accessed 1 July 2015).

Caparrós Lera, José María (1999), *El cine de nuestros días (1994–1998)*, Madrid: Ediciones RIALP.

Carbonell, Àngel (2006a), 'Gilles Deleuze: el desig rebel', *Lambda*, 58, 28–30.

Carbonell, Àngel (2006b), 'Simone de Beauvoir, la passió de les dones', *Lambda*, 60, 26–7.

Casas, Quim (2014), 'Cuerpos y reacciones', *Dirigido por*, 443, 20–1.

Cate-Arries, Francie (2010), *Spanish Culture Behind Barbed Wire: Memory and Representation of the French Concentration Camps 1939–1945*, Cranberry, NJ: Associated University Presses / Rosemont Publishing.

CCCB (2005), 'Àmbits', in exhibition catalogue Literatures d'exili, Centre de Cultura Contemporània de Barcelona, <http://www.cccb.org/ca/exposicio-literatures_of_exile-13166> (last accessed 6 October 2014).

Cerdán, Josetxo and Miguel Fernández Labayen (2013), 'Almodóvar and Spanish Patterns of Film Reception', in Marvin D'Lugo and Kathleen M. Vernon (eds), *A Companion to Pedro Almodóvar*, Oxford: Wiley-Blackwell, pp. 129–52.

Cervulle, Maxime and Nick Rees-Roberts (2010), *Homo Exoticus: Race, classe et critique queer*, Paris: Armand Colin.

Chault, Paul (2013), 'Manif anti-mariage gay: Manuel Valls agite le chiffon rouge', *L'Express*, 27 May, <http://www.lexpress.fr/actualite/politique/manif-anti-mariage-gay-manuel-valls-agite-le-chiffon-rouge_1252038.html#CFU8hJU6GxVXRpaS.99> (last accessed 8 April 2014).

Chauvin, Jean-Sébastien (2013), 'C'est la mousse finale', *Cahiers du Cinéma*, 688, 50.

Chéries-Chéris (2001), 'Présentation historique du festival', in Chéries-Chéris festival archive, December, <http://www.cheries-cheris.com/archives/festival2001/presentation_historique.htm> (last accessed 31 August 2015).

Chéries-Chéris (2002), 'Pourquoi ce festival', Presentation 8th Chéries-Chéris festival, Chéries-Chéris festival archive, <http://www.cheries-cheris.com/archives/festival2002/pourquoi_ce_festival.htm> (last accessed 31 August 2015).

Chéries-Chéris (2004), Presentation page 10th Chéries-Chéris festival, Chéries-Chéris festival archive, <http://www.cheries-cheris.com/archives/festival_2004/> (last accessed 31 August 2015).

Chéries-Chéris (2006), Presentation page 12th Chéries-Chéris festival, Chéries-Chéris festival archive, <http://www.cheries-cheris.com/archives/festival_2006/> (last accessed 31 August 2015).

Chéries-Chéris (2011), Presentation page 17th Chéries-Chéris festival, Chéries-Chéris festival archive, <http://www.cheries-cheris.com/2011/> (last accessed 31 August 2015).

Chéries-Chéris (2012), Note on *El sexo de los ángeles*, in programme for 18th Chéries-Chéris festival website, Paris, 5–14 October, <http://www.cheries-cheris.com/2012/Le_sexe_des_anges.html> (last accessed 15 September 2015).

chueca.com (2006), '*El tiempo que queda*', in chueca.com website, 3 January, <http://www.chueca.com/articulo/el-tiempo-que-queda> (last accessed 17 April 2015).

Cineffable (2011), Note on *Guerriller@s*, in programme for 23rd Cineffable Festival International du Film Lesbien et Féministe de Paris, Paris, 29 October–2 November, p. 33.

Cineffable (2014), Cineffable festival newsletter, April, <http://www.cine ffable.fr/docs/ClapInfo/ClapInfo-04-2014.pdf> (last accessed 31 August 2015).

CineLGBT (2014), Membership page of the Spanish Film Market/CineLGBT network, <http://www.cinelgbt.com/miembros> (last accessed 5 August 2014).

Cinemanía (2013), 'Lesbianismo en el cine', stills gallery with text by Rubén Lardín, *Cinemanía*, October, 91–5.

Cinémarges (2015), Archived programme note for *En 80 jours*, screened at 12th Cinémarges Festival, Bordeaux, 1 May 2011, <http://www.cinemas-utopia.org/bordeaux/index.php?id=1316&mode=film> (last accessed 12 June 2015).

Cinespagne (2007), 'Bilan 2006 du cinéma espagnol en France' , cinespagne. com website, 13 July, <http://www.cinespagne.com/actualites/2102-bilan-2006-du-cinema-espagnol-en-france> (last accessed 3 September 2015).

Clews, Colin (2013), '1981. London's First Festival of Gay Film and Video', post in Gay in the 80s blog, 10 June, <http://www.gayinthe80s.com/2013/06/1981-londons-first-festival-of-gay-film-and-video/> (last accessed 31 August 2015).

Contra La Vida de Adele (2014), Comment on review of *La vida de Adèle* in CGnauta blog, 16 February, <http://cgnauta.blogspot.co.uk/2014/01/la-vida-de-adele-2013-resena-y-critica-de-la-pelicula.html#sthash. DJs5HQbf.dpuf> (last accessed 30 March 2015).

Corner, John (2008), 'Documentary Studies: Dimensions of Transition and Continuity', in Thomas Austin and Wilma de Jong (eds), *Rethinking Documentary: New Perspectives, New Practices*, Maidenhead and New York: Open University Press; Oxford University Press, pp. 13–28.

Costa, Jordi (2007), 'La vida como práctica de riesgo', *El País*, digitally archived print edition, 21 September, <http://elpais.com/diario/2007/09/21/cine/1190325607_850215.html> (last accessed 15 September 2015).

Creton, Laurent and Anne Jäckel (2004), 'A Certain Idea of the Film Industry', in Michael Temple and Michael Witt (eds), *The French Cinema Book*, London: British Film Institute, pp. 209–20.

Cuadrado, Luis José (2014), 'La vida de Adèle', *Revista Atticus*, 24, 110–16, <http://revistaatticus.es/old/Revistas/Revista_Atticus_24.pdf> (last accessed 2 April 2015).

Cunningham, Stuart and Jon Silver (2012), 'On-Line Film Distribution: Its History and Global Complexion', in Dina Iordanova and Stuart Cunningham (eds), *Digital Disruption: Cinema Moves On-Line*, St Andrews: St Andrews Film Studies, pp. 33–66.

Cyrille (2013), Response to comment on 'Les Amants passagers' by Matoo, on Matoo's blog, Cinéphage section, 22 July, 12:45, <http://blog.matoo. net/index.php/archives/2013/07/22/les-amants-passagers/> (last accessed 22 July 2015).

Czach, Liz (2004), 'Film Festivals, Programming, and the Building of a National Cinema', *The Moving Image*, 4.1, 76–88.

D'Lugo, Marvin (1991), *The Films of Carlos Saura: The Practice of Seeing*, Princeton: Princeton University Press.

D'Lugo, Marvin and Paul Julian Smith (2012), 'Auteurism and the Construction of the Canon', in Jo Labanyi and Tatjana Pavlović (eds), *A Companion to Spanish Cinema*, Chichester: Wiley-Blackwell, pp. 113–51.

Dalton, Stephen (2013), '*Me, Myself and Mum* (*Les Garçons et Guillaume, à table!*): Cannes Review', *The Hollywood Reporter*, 20 May, 18:10, <http://www.hollywoodreporter.com/review/me-myself-mum-les-garcons-525727> (last accessed 3 September 2015).

Damiens, Antoine (2012), 'Publics et spectateurs hétérosexuels du Festival Ecrans Mixtes 2012', Mémoire de Séminaire, Lyon: Université Lumière Lyon 2.

Daniel, Xavier (1996). 'Untitled', Homocinefilies, *Lambda*, 22, 40–1.

Daniel, Xavier (1997), 'Carmen Miranda a Sodoma', *Lambda*, 27, 40–1.

Davies, Anne (2007), *Pedro Almodóvar*, London: Grant and Cutler.

de Taillac, Matthieu (2014), 'L'Espagne fière du choix de Manuel Valls pour Matignon', *Le Figaro*, 1 April, <http://www.lefigaro.fr/politique/2014/04/01/01002-20140401ARTFIG00093-l-espagne-fiere-du-choix-de-manuel-valls-pour-matignon.php> (last accessed 8 April 2014).

de Valck, Marijke (2007), *Film Festivals: From European Geopolitics to Global Cinephilia*, Amsterdam: Amsterdam University Press.

de Valck, Marijke (2010), 'Reflections on the Recent Cinephilia Debates', *Cinema Journal*, 49.2, 132–9.

de Valck, Marijke (2013), 'Film Festivals: Successful or Safe?', in Dina Iordanova (ed.), *The Film Festival Reader*, St Andrews: St Andrews Film Studies, pp. 97–108.

Delgado Gomez-Escalonilla, Lorenzo (2009), 'Inmigración, educación, integración: La última oleada de españoles en Francia', in *Un siglo de inmigración española en Francia*, Vigo: Grupo de Comunicación Galicia en el Mundo, pp. 159–80.

Díaz, Jordi (1996), 'Jean Genet i el Districte Cinquè (1932–34)', *Lambda*, 23, 38–9.

Donaghue, Courtney B. (2014), 'Death of the DVD Market and the Rise of Digital Piracy: Industrial Shifts in the Spanish Film Market Since the 2000s', *Quarterly Journal of Film and Video*, 31.4, 350–63. DOI 10.1080/10509208.2012.660443.

Doyle, J. D. (2015), Queer Music Heritage blog, <http://www.queermusicheritage.com/fem-madame.html> (last accessed 8 April 2015).

Eamon, William (2009), '"Nuestros males no son constitucionales, sino *circunstanciales*": The Black Legend and the History of Early Modern Spanish Science', *The Colorado Review of Hispanic Studies*, 7, 13–30.

Ecrans Mixtes (2013), synopsis of *Ocaña, retrat intermitent*, in programme for 3rd Ecrans Mixtes festival, Lyon, 6–12 March, p. 13.

Edelman, Lee (2004), *No Future: Queer Theory and the Death Drive*, Durham, NC: Duke University Press.

Edwards, Gwynne (2009), *The Discreet Art of Luis Buñuel: A Reading of His Films*, London and New York: Marion Boyers.

Ekman, Mary C (1992), 'Concealing Identities, Revealing Stories: Marie-Catherine d'Aulnoy's Relation du voyage d'Espagne', *Society for Interdisciplinary French Seventeenth Century Studies*, 6.2, 49–64.

Elsaesser, Thomas (2005) 'Cinephilia or the Uses of Disenchantment', in Marijke de Valck and Malte Hagener (eds), *Cinephilia: Movies, Love and Memory*, Amsterdam: Amsterdam University Press, pp. 27–44.

Elsaesser, Thomas (2013), 'Film Festival Networks: The New Topographies of Cinema in Europe', in Dina Iordanova (ed.), *The Film Festival Reader*, St Andrews: St Andrews Film Studies, pp. 69–96.

elputojacktwist (2007), '*Los testigos*', review posted in dosmanzanas.com blog, 28 September, <http://archivo.dosmanzanas.com/index.php/archives/3623> (last accessed 18 August 2015).

Emma (2014), Comment on review of *La vida de Adèle* in CGnauta blog, 8 February, <http://cgnauta.blogspot.co.uk/2014/01/la-vida-de-adele-2013-resena-y-critica-de-la-pelicula.html#sthash.DJs5HQbf.dpuf> (last accessed 30 March 2015).

Epps, Brad (2013), 'Echoes and Traces: Catalan Cinema, or Cinema in Catalonia', in Jo Labanyi and Tatiana Pavlović (eds), *Companion to Spanish Cinema*, Chichester: Wiley-Blackwell, pp. 50–79.

Epps, Brad and Despina Kakoudaki (2009), 'Introduction: Approaching Almodóvar: Thirty Years of Reinvention', in Brad Epps and Despina Kakoudaki (eds), *All About Almodóvar*, Minneapolis and London: University of Minnesota Press, pp. 1–34.

Eribon, Didier (1999), *Réflexions sur la question gay*, Paris: Fayard.

Espineira, Karine (2008), *La Transidentité: de l'espace médiatique à l'espace publique*, Paris: L'Harmattan.

Espineira, Karine (2015), *Transidentités: Ordre et panique de genre, le réel et ses interprétations*, Paris: L'Harmattan.

Espineira, Karine, Maud-Yeuse Thomas and Arnaud Alessandrin (eds) (2012), *Trans-yclopédie: Tout savoir sur les transidentités*, Paris: Editions des Ailes sur un Tracteur.

Espineira, Karine, Maud-Yeuse Thomas and Arnaud Alessandrin (2013), 'Queer, trans et féminisme: je t'aime . . . moi non plus', in Karine Espineira, Maud-Yeuse Thomas and Arnaud Alessandrin (eds), *Corps Trans, Corps Queer*, Paris: L'Harmattan, pp. 13–20.

Ezpeleta, Joako (2009), 'Manifesto FIRE!! 2009', in Casal Lambda (eds), *FIRE!! 14ª Mostra Internacional de Cinema Gai i Lesbià*, press pack, p. 1,

<http://www.lambdaweb.org/cinema/ediciones_anteriores/2009/pdf/fire 2009dossierpremsa.pdf> (last accessed 22 August 2014).

Ezpeleta, Joako (2014), 'Entrevista a Antoine Leonetti', *Lambda*, 80, 13.

Fabre, Clarisse (2013), 'Une pétition s'oppose à la projection de *Tomboy* dans les écoles', *Le Monde*, Culture, 21 December, <http://www.lemonde. fr/culture/article/2013/12/21/une-petition-s-oppose-a-la-projection-de-tom-boy-dans-les-ecoles_4338625_3246.html#1YbhM7U4ky8uTvIe.99> (last accessed 15 September 2015).

Fancinegay (2012), 'Vídeo Promocional FanCineGay 2012'. YouTube post, 25 October, <https://www.youtube.com/watch?v=Nr4oYU8x0G8> (last accessed 22 August 2014).

Faulkner, Sally (2013), *A History of Spanish Film: Cinema and Society 1910– 2010*, London: Bloomsbury Academic.

Feenstra, Pietsie and Vicente Sánchez-Biosca (eds) (2014), *Le Cinéma Espagnol: Histoire et Culture*, Paris: Armand Colin.

Fernàndez, Josep-Anton (2000), *Another Country: Sexuality and National Identity in Catalan Gay Gay Fiction*, Leeds: Maney/MHRA.

Fernàndez, Josep-Anton (2007), 'The Authentic Queen and the Invisible Man: Catalan Camp and Its Conditions of Possibility in Ventura Pons's *Ocaña, retrat intermitent*', *Journal of Spanish Cultural Studies*, 5.1, 83–99.

Fernández-Santos, Ángel (2002), 'Ahí, muy cerca', *El País*, digitally archived print edition, 17 May, <http://elpais.com/diario/2002/05/17/cine/ 1021586405_850215.html> (last accessed 18 August 2015).

FICGLB (2014), Festival website landing page for Barcelona International Gay and Lesbian Film Festival, <http://www.barcelonafilmfestival.org> (last accessed 14 August 2014).

Filmin (2015), 'Biofilmografía de François Ozon', in Filmin website data-base, <https://www.filmin.es/director/francois-ozon> (last accessed 9 April 2015).

FIRE!! (2012), Synopsis for *Les Témoins*, in programme for FIRE!!, 17th Casal Lambda Film Festival, 5–15 July, <http://www.lambda.cat/cinema/ 2012/10_cat.html> (last accessed 8 September 2015).

FIRE!! (2013a), Programme (English version) for FIRE!!, 18th Casal Lambda Film Festival, 4–14 July, <http://www.lambda.cat/cinema/2013/01_eng. html> (last accessed 15 February 2015).

FIRE!! (2013b), Synopsis for *Bambi*, in programme for FIRE!! 18th Casal Lambda Film Festival, 4–14 July, <http://www.lambda.cat/cinema/2013/ 13_cat.html> (last accessed 5 June 2105).

FIRE!! (2013c), Synopsis for *Les Invisibles*, in programme for FIRE!!, 18th Casal Lambda Film Festival, Barcelona, 4–14 July, <http://www.lambda.cat/ cinema/2013/13_eng.html> (last accessed 5 June 2105).

FIRE!! (2014), Synopsis for *Eastern Boys*, in programme for FIRE!!, 19th Casal Lambda Film Festival, Barcelona, 2–13 July, <http://www.lambda.cat/ cinema/2014/07_eng.html> (last accessed 1 July 2015).

Fish, Stanley (1980), *Is There a Text in This Class? The Authority of Interpretive Communities*, Cambridge, MA and London: Harvard University Press.

Fiske, John (1992), 'The Cultural Economy of Fandom', in Lisa A. Lewis (ed.), *The Adoring Audience: Fan Culture and Popular Media*, London and New York: Routledge, pp. 30–49.

Fluvià, Armand de (1989), '200 anys de Revolució Francesa: 20 anys de Revolució Gai', *Casal Lambda*, 2, 6–7.

Foerster, Maxime (2012), *Elle ou lui? Une histoire des transsexuels en France*, Paris: La Musardine.

Fouz-Hernández, Santiago (2013), *Cuerpos de cine: Masculinidades carnales en el cine y la cultura popular contemporáneos*, Barcelona: Edicions Belleterra.

Fouz-Hernández, Santiago and Alfredo Martínez-Expósito (2007), *Live Flesh: The Male Body in Contemporary Spanish Cinema*, London and New York: I. B. Tauris.

Fouz-Hernández, Santiago and Chris Perriam (2007), 'El deseo sin ley: la representación de "la homosexualidad" en el cine español de los años noventa', in Félix Rodríguez and Angie Simonis (eds), *Cultura, homosexualidad, homofobia*, Barcelona: Laertes, pp. 61–79.

Frith, Hannah (2000), 'Focusing on Sex: Using Focus Groups in Sex Research', *Sexualities*, 3.3, 275–97.

Fundación Triángulo (2010), 'Quienes somos – Presentación', landing page of the website of the Fundación Triángulo, <http://www.fundaciontriangulo.org/quienes-somos> (last accessed 22 August 2014).

Galt, Rosalind (2010), 'Impossible Narratives: The Barcelona School and the European Avant-Gardes', *Hispanic Review*, 78.4, 491–511.

Galt, Rosalind and Karl Schoonover (2014), 'Minds, Bodies, and Hearts: Flare London LGBT Film Festival 2014', 21 November, in *Necsus. European Journal for Media Studies*, <http://www.necsus-ejms.org/minds-bodies-hearts-flare-london-lgbt-film-festival-2014/> (last accessed 1 July 2015).

Gamson, Joshua (1996), 'The Organisational Shaping of Collective Identity: The Case of Lesbian and Gay Film Festivals in New York', *Sociological Forum*, 11.2, 231–61.

Gandillot, Thierry (2011), 'Dans la peau d'Almodóvar', *Les Echos*, 17 August, <http://www.lesechos.fr/17/08/2011/LesEchos/20996-042-ECH_dans-la-peau-d-almodovar.htm> (last accessed 15 September 2015).

Gara (2014), 'Quiero acercar el festival aún más a la gente; vamos a exprimir a los invitados', interview with Pau Guillén, 4 February, <http://gara.naiz.eus/paperezkoa/20120204/320021/es/Quiero-acercar-festival-aun-mas-gente-vamos-exprimir-invitados> (last accessed 22 August 2014).

García, Javi (2006), 'Les primeres pel.lícules cent per cent gais', *Lambda*, 57, 26.

Gaut, Beryl (1999), 'Identification and Emotion in Narrative Film', in Carl

Plantinga and Greg M. Smith (eds), *Passionate Views: Film, Cognition and Emotion*, Baltimore: Johns Hopkins Press, pp. 200–16.

gayles.tv (2013), 'Festival Internacional de Cine Gay y Lésbico de Barcelona 2013', interview with Xavier Daniel, <https://www.youtube.com/watch?v=a61X1CLM4qo&feature=youtu.be> (last accessed 22 August 2014).

Gever, Martha (1990), 'The Names We Give Ourselves', in Russell Ferguson, Martha Gever, Trinh T. Minh-ha and Cornel West (eds), *Out There: Marginalisation and Contemporary Cultures*, New York: New Museum of Contemporary Art; Cambridge, MA: MIT Press, pp.191–202.

Gies, David (2008), "Staging the Revolution(s)', Institute of European Studies, University of California EScholarship working paper, 22 February, <http://escholarship.org/uc/item/6rg3b4bw> (last accessed 15 August 2014).

Gil, Jaume (2002), '*Primer verano*', *Lambda*, 43, 26.

Gil, Jaume (2003), '*8 mujeres*', *Lambda*, 48, 24.

Goscinny, René and Albert Uderzo (1969), *Astérix en Hispanie*. Paris, Lausanne and Montreal: Dargaud.

Goytisolo, Juan (2009), *Genet en el Raval*, Barcelona: Galaxia Gutenberg.

Gramont, Sanche de (1969), 'Life Style of Homo Cinematicus', *New York Times*, Books, 15 June, <https://www.nytimes.com/books/99/04/18/specials/truffaut-style.html> (last accessed 22 July 2015).

Gray, Jonathan Cornel Sandvoss and C. Lee Harrington (2007), 'Introduction: Why Study Fans?', in Jonathan Gray, Cornel Sandvoss and C. Lee Harrington (eds), *Fandom: Identities and Communities in a Mediated World*, New York: New York University Press, pp. 1–23.

Griffiths, Robin (ed.) (2008), *Queer Cinema in Europe*, Bristol: Intellect.

Gubbins, Michael (2012), 'Digital Revolution: Active Audiences and Fragmented Consumption', in Dina Iordanova and Stuart Cunningham (eds), *Digital Disruption: Cinema Moves On-Line*, St Andrews: St Andrews Film Studies, pp. 67–100.

Guerrilla Travolaka (2009), Identity statement, Guerrilla Travolaka blog, <http://guerrilla-travolaka.blogspot.co.uk> (last accessed 10 February 2015).

Guilhem, Florence (2005), 'Les Réfugiés espagnols en Haute-Garonne', in José Jornet (ed.), *Républicains espagnols en Midi-Pyrénées: Exil, histoire et mémoire*, revised edn, Toulouse: Presses Universitaires du Mirail, pp. 293–8.

Gusfield, Joseph R. (1975), *The Community: A Critical Response*, New York: Harper Colophon.

Gutiérrez-Albilla, Julián (2008), *Queering Buñuel: Sexual Dissidence and Psychoanalysis in His Mexican and Spanish Cinema*, London and New York: I. B. Tauris.

Harbord, Janet (2002), *Film Cultures: Production, Distribution and Consumption*, London: Sage.

Harbord, Janet (2009), "Film Festivals-Time-Event', in Dina Iordanova and Ragan Rhyne (eds), *The Film Festivals Reader*, St Andrews: St Andrews Film Studies, pp. 40–6.

Hayward, Susan (2000), *Key Concepts in Cinema Studies*, London and New York: Routledge.

Heredero, Carlos F. (2013), 'La misteriosa verdad del arte', *Caimán Cuadernos de Cine*, 20, 8.

Higbee, Will and Song Hwee Lim (2010), 'Concepts of Transnational Cinema: Towards a Critical Transnationalism in Film Studies', *Transnational Cinemas*, 1.1, 7–21.

Hilton, Ronald (2002). *La Légende noire au 18e siècle. Le Monde hispanique vu du dehors*, Historical Text Archive, <http://www.historicaltextarchive. com/books.php?action=toc&bid=8> (last accessed 3 June 2015).

Hirsch, Marianne (2012), *The Generation of Postmemory: Writing and Visual Culture after the Holocaust*, New York: Columbia University Press.

Hollway, Wendy (1989), *Subjectivity and Method in Psychology: Gender, Meaning, Science*, London: Sage.

HOME (2015), Archived programme note for *The Invisibles*, screened at Poutfest, Cornerhouse, Manchester, 22 August 2013, < http://homemcr.org/ film/the-invisibles/> (last accessed 12 June 2015).

Huard, Geoffroy (2014), *Los antisociales. Historia de la homosexualidad en Barcelona y en París, 1945–1975*, Madrid: Marcial Pons.

Iglesias, Eulália (2014), 'Extraños en el paraíso: *El desconocido del lago* de Alain Guiraudie', *Caimán Cuadernos de Cine*, 26, 32–3.

Ilie, Paul (1976), 'Exomorphism: Cultural Bias and the French Image of Spain from the War of Succession to the Age of Voltaire', *Eighteenth-Century Studies*, 9.3, 375–89.

Institut Francès (2013), 'Missió', landing page of the Institut Francès de Barcelona, <http://www.institutfrancais.es/barcelona/los-institutos-en-espa na/mision> (last accessed 7 August 2013).

Iordanova, Dina (2012), 'Digital Disruption, Technological Innovation', in Dina Iordanova and Stuart Cunningham (eds), *Digital Disruption: Cinema Moves On-Line*, St Andrews: St Andrews Film Studies, pp. 1–31.

Iordanova, Dina and Stuart Cunningham (eds) (2012), *Digital Disruption: Cinema Moves On-Line*, St Andrews: St Andrews Film Studies.

Jackson, Julian (2009), *Living in Arcadia: Homosexuality, Politics, and Morality in France from the Liberation to AIDS*, Chicago and London: University of Chicago Press.

Jean-Yves (2005), '30 ans de culture gay au cinéma', in the blog Contribution subjective à une mémoire gaie: littérature, cinéma, arts, histoire, <http:// culture-et-debats.over-blog.com/> (last accessed 22 July 2015).

Jenkins, Henry (2006a), *Fans, Bloggers and Gamers: Exploring Participatory Culture*, New York and London: New York University Press.

Jenkins, Henry (2006b), *Convergence Culture: Where Old and New Media Collide*, New York: New York University Press.

Jenkins, Henry (2007), 'Afterword: The Future of Fandom', in Jonathan Gray, Cornel Sandvoss and C. Lee Harrington (eds), *Fandom: Identities and*

Communities in a Mediated World, New York: New York University Press, pp. 357–64.

Jhally, Sut and Justin Lewis (1992), *Enlightened Racism: The Cosby Show, Audiences, and the Myth of the American Dream*, Chicago: University of Chicago Press.

Jones, Angela (ed.) (2013), *A Critical Inquiry into Queer Utopias*, New York: Palgrave Mcmillan.

Jornet, José (ed.) (2004), *Républicains espagnols en Midi-Pyrénées: Exil, histoire et mémoire*, revised edn, Toulouse: Presses Universitaires du Mirail.

Jullier, Laurent and Jean-Marc Leveratto (2014), 'Cinephilia in the Digital Age', in Ian Christie (ed.), *Audiences*, Amsterdam: Amsterdam University Press, pp. 143–54.

Junta Directiva AET-Transexualia (2007), '"Crónica de acuerdo político insuficiente": Transexualia detalla carencias sanitarias a transexuales', website of Izquierda Unida, <http://www.izquierda-unida.es/node/2423> (last accessed 11 February 2015).

Kaganski, Serge (2013), '"Les Garçons et Guillaume, à table!", magistrale comédie de genres', online review, in *Les Inrocks* (online version of *Les Inrockuptibles*), 19 November, 18:30, <http://www.lesinrocks.com/cinema/films-a-l-affiche/les-garcons-guillaume-table/> (last accessed 3 September 2015).

Katz, Elihu and Tamar Liebes (1990), 'Interacting with "Dallas": Cross Cultural Readings of American TV', *Canadian Journal of Communication*, 15.1, 45–66.

Képénékian, Georges (2013), Presentation, in programme for 3rd Ecrans Mixtes festival, Lyon, 6–12 March, p. 3.

Képénékian, Georges (2015), Presentation, in programme for 5th Ecrans Mixtes festival, Lyon, 4–10 March, p. 3.

Killer Queen (2014), '*El desconocido del lago*', review, *Críticas en 8 mm*, 26 March, <http://www.criticasen8mm.com/2014/03/el-desconocido-del-lago-killer-queen.html> (last accessed 15 September 2015).

Kinder, Marsha (1993), *Blood Cinema: The Reconstruction of National Identity in Spain*, Berkeley: University of California Press.

Kirschen, Marie (2008), 'Quand le cinéma se met en trans', *L'Humanité*, 17 January, <http://www.humanite.fr/node/490> (last accessed 1 July 2015).

Kirschen, Marie (2009), 'Deuxième édition du festival IdentiT, le festival international de films trans de Paris', interview with Jihan Ferjani, *Têtu*, digital edition, 10 June, 11:20, <https://www.tetu.com/2009/06/10/news/culture/deuxieme-edition-du-festival-identit-le- festival-international-de-films-trans-de-paris/> (last accessed 2 September 2015)

L.G. (2011), 'Plus Almodóvar que jamais. *La piel que habito*, de Pedro Almodóvar', *Télérama*, Cinéma, 28 May, <http://www.telerama.fr/cinema/ils-ont-fait-cannes,69229.php> (last accessed 9 September 2015).

Labory, Marie (2013), Presentation, 19th Chéries-Chéris festival, Chéries-Chéris festival archive, October, <http://www.cheries-cheris.com/2013/editoriaux/> (last accessed 31 August 2015).

Lacroix, Thomas and Isabelle Bouhet (2004), *La Population espagnole en France* (Tome 2), HAL open access, <http://hal.archives-ouvertes.fr/docs/00/82/06/60/PDF/LAcroix_2004_POPULATION_ESPAGNOLE_EN_FRANCE_4.pdf> (last accessed 27 March 2014).

Lalanne, Jean-Marc (2011), '*La piel que habito* de Pedro Almodóvar', *Les Inrocks*, 16 August 2011, <http://www.lesinrocks.com/cinema/films-a-l-affiche/la-piel-que-habito-un-parcours-palpitant-entre-les-genes-et-les-genres/> (last accessed 15 September 2015).

Lambda (1995), 'Cent anys de cinema', editorial, *Lambda*, 20, 5.

Larraz, Emmanuel (1984), 'La Guerre d'Indépendance dans le cinéma franquiste', in *Les Espagnols et Napoléon. Actes du colloque international d'Aix-en-Provence 13–15 octobre 1983*, Aix-en-Provence: Université de Provence / J. Lafitte, pp. 241–53.

Larraz, Emmanuel (1986), *Le Cinéma Espagnol, des origines à nos jours*, Paris: Editions du Serf.

Le Corre, Maëlle (2015), 'Un nouveau départ pour Chéries-Chéris?', *Yagg Ciné Plus*, 4 August, 16:02, <http://yagg.com/2015/08/04/un-nouveau-depart-pour-cheries-cheris/> (last accessed 3 September 2015).

Le Parisien (2013), 'Mariage gay à Paris: Anne Hidalgo unit le maire du IVe et son compagnon', *Le Parisien*, 8 June, <http://www.leparisien.fr/societe/paris-anne-hidalgo-a-marie-le-maire-ps-du-ive-a-son-compagnon-08-06-2013-2878515.php> (last accessed 8 April 2014).

Le Parisien (2014), 'Valls à Matignon: la presse catalane salue le "Français de Barcelone"', *Le Parisien*, 1 April, <http://www.leparisien.fr/municipales-2014/valls-a-matignon-la-presse-catalane-salue-le-francais-de-barcelone-01-04-2014-3730929.php> (last accessed 8 April 2014).

Leberg, Dan (2011), 'Fanboys in the Ivory Tower: An Attempted Reconciliation of Science Fiction Film Academic and Fan Culture', *Gnovis*, 8 August, <http://www.gnovisjournal.org/2011/08/08/fanboys-in-the-ivory-tower-an-attempted-reconciliation-of-science-fiction-film-academia-and-fan-culture/> (last accessed 30 March 2015).

Lebrun, Hervé Joseph (2012), Presentation, 18th Chéries-Chéris festival, Chéries-Chéris festival archive, October, <http://www.cheries-cheris.com/2012/editoriaux/> (last accessed 31 August 2015).

Legann, Cyril (2013), Presentation, 19th Chéries-Chéris festival, Chéries-Chéris festival archive, October, <http://www.cheries-cheris.com/2013/editoriaux/> (last accessed 31 August 2015).

Leonetti, Antoine (2010), 'Agridulce Francia', presentation text, web brochure for FIRE!!, 15th Casal Lambda Film Festival, 2010 (July), <http://www.lambdaweb.org/cinema/ediciones_anteriores/2010/es/largometrajes.php> (last accessed 22 August 2014).

LesGaiCineMad (2012), Programme for 17th LesGaiCineMad festival, Madrid, 1–11 November, Madrid: Fundación Triángulo.

LesGaiCineMad (2014a), '9,000 fans del cine LGBT', Facebook post, 2 July, <https://www.facebook.com/photo.php?fbid=720225774701435> (last accessed 31 August 2015).

LesGaiCineMad (2014b), Synopsis of *Las ventanas abiertas*, in programme for 19th LesGaiCineMad festival, Madrid, 30 October – 13 November, <http://lesgaicinemad.com/peliculas/documentales/p/2> (last accessed 8 April 2015).

Lev, Leora (2013), 'On Rapists Ourselves', in Marvin D'Lugo and Kathleen M. Vernon (eds), *A Companion to Pedro Almodóvar*, Malden, MA and Oxford: Wiley-Blackwell, pp. 524–50.

Lillo, Natacha (2009), 'La emigración española a Francia a lo largo del siglo XX: Entre la "perfecta integración" y el retorno', in *Un siglo de inmigración española en Francia*, Vigo: Grupo de Comunicación Galicia en el Mundo, pp. 11–28.

Lillo, Natacha (2013), 'L'Immigration espagnole en France au XXe siècle', Musée de l'Histoire de l'immigration website, <http://www.histoire-immi gration.fr/des-dossiers-thematiques-sur-l-histoire-de-l-immigration/l-immi gration-espagnole-en-france-au-xxe-siecle> (last accessed 27 March 2014).

Loist, Skadi (2012), 'A Complicated Queerness: LGBT Film Festivals and Queer Programming Strategies', in Jeffrey Rouff (ed.), *Coming Soon to a Festival Near You: Programming Film Festivals*, St Andrews: St Andrews Film Studies, pp. 157–72.

Loist, Skadi (2013), 'The Queer Film Festival Phenomenon in a Global Historical Perspective (the 1970s–2000s)', in Anaïs Fléchet, Pascale Gœtschel, Patricia Hidiroglou, Sophie Jacotot, Caroline Moine and Julie Verlaine (eds), *Une histoire des festivals: XXe–XXIe siècle*, Paris: Publications de la Sorbonne, pp. 109–21.

Loist, Skadi and Ger Zielinski (2012), 'On the Development of Queer Film Festivals and Their Media Activism', in Dina Iordanova and Leshu Torchin (eds), *Film Festival Yearbook 4: Film Festivals and Activism*, St Andrews: St Andrews Film Studies, pp. 49–62.

L'Ordre des Mots (2015), English-language presentation of *L'Ordre des mots*, official website, <http://www.lordredesmots-lefilm.com/en/> (last accessed 15 September 2015).

Losilla, Carlos (2014), 'Los límites del deseo, el deseo sin límites: La representación del sexo gay en *La vida de Adèle* y *El desconocido del lago*', *Caimán Cuadernos de Cine*, 24, 18–19.

Lourdes L (2015), Comment on SensaCine review of *Une Nouvelle Amie*, 17 May, <http://www.sensacine.com/peliculas/pelicula-223933/criticas-espec tadores/> (last accessed 11 June 2015).

Loureda, Carlos (2012), 'Los actores españoles dopados por el cine francés', post on Cine Invisible blog, *Fotogramas*, 12 March, <http://cine-invisi

ble.blogs.fotogramas.es/tag/natalia-verbeke/> (last accessed 15 September 2015).

Manea, Ioana (2009), 'L'Espagne chez La Mothe Le Vayer ou comment utiliser les stéréotypes de la littérature politique pour exprimer des opinions libertines', *Loxias*, 26, <http://revel.unice.fr/loxias/index.html?id=2993> (last accessed 4 June 2015).

Martel, Frédéric [1996] (1999), *The Pink and the Black: Homosexuals in France since 1968*, translated by Jane Marie Todd, Stanford: Stanford University Press.

Martet, Christophe (2013), 'Les Amants Passagers: Almodóvar au 7ème ciel', post on *Yagg* website, 27 March, 18:03, <http://yagg.com/2013/03/27/les-amants-passagers-almodovar-au-7e-ciel/> (last accessed 22 July 2015).

Martet, Christophe (2014), 'Découvrez la bande annonce sexy de Rémi Lange pour les festival Ecrans Mixtes', post on *Yagg* website, 11 January 09:30, <http://yagg.com/2014/01/11/decouvrez-la-bande-annonce-sexy-de-remi-lange-pour-le-festival-ecrans-mixtes/> (last accessed 1 July 2015).

Martínez, Beatriz (2013), '*La vida de Adèle*. La pasión es de un color cálido', *Dirigido por*, 437, archived at <http://www.dirigidopor.com/dirigidopor/Dirigido_Archivo_La_vida_de_Adele.html> (last accessed 8 September 2015).

Martínez, Moisès (2005), 'Mi cuerpo no es mío. Transexualidad masculina y presiones sociales de sexo', in Grupo de Trabajo Queer (ed.), *El Eje de mal es heterosexual: figuraciones, movimientos y prácticas feministas queer*, Madrid: Traficantes de Sueños, pp. 113–20.

Martin-Márquez, Susan (1999), *Feminist Discourse and Spanish Cinema: Sight Unseen*, Oxford: Oxford University Press.

Matoo (2013), '*Les Amants passagers*', comment on Matoo's blog, Cinéphage section, 22 July, <http://blog.matoo.net/index.php/archives/2013/07/22/les-amants-passagers/> (last accessed 22 July 2015).

Maury, Louis (2013), 'Au ciné: la nouvelle comédie de Almodóvar, le conte de Bryan Singer', 27 March, <http://www.tetu.com/2013/03/27/news/culture/au-cine-la-nouvelle-comedie-de-almodovar-le-conte-de-bryan-singer/> (last accessed 22 July 2015).

McCaffrey, Enda (2006), 'From Universalism to Post-universalism; the PaCS and Beyond', *Modern and Contemporary France*, 14.3, 291–304.

McMillan, David W. and David M. Chavis (1986), 'Sense of Community: a Definition and Theory', *Journal of Community Psychology*, 14, 6–23.

Méjean, Jean-Max (2011), *Almodóvar, les femmes et les chansons*, Paris: L'Harmattan.

Melero, Alejandro (2010), *Placeres ocultos: Gays y lesbianas en el cine español de la transición*, Madrid: Notorious Ediciones.

Melero, Alejandro (2011), 'Hacia la construcción de una teoría queer española. Foucault y la homofobia del tardofranquismo', *La torre del Virrey*, 10,

49–54, <http://www.latorredelvirrey.org/viejaltv/pdf/10/alejandromelero. pdf> (last accessed 8 April 2014).

Méndez, Marcos (2007), 'Los testigos', in Kane3, online cultural magazine, no date, <http://www.kane3.es/dvd/los-testigos.php> (last accessed 18 August 2015).

Mérigeau, Pascal (2013), 'Une lucidité délirante', *Le Nouvel Observateur*, Culture, 28 August.

Merino, Imma (2013), 'El sexo entre mujeres existe', *Caimán Cuadernos de Cine*, 20, 10–12.

Merton, Robert K. and Patricia L. Kendall (1946), 'The Focused Interview', *American Journal of Sociology*, 51, 541–57.

Mira, Alberto (2004), *De Sodoma a Chueca: Una historia cultural de la homosexualidad en España en el siglo XX*, Barcelona and Madrid: Egales.

Mira, Alberto (2005), 'Introduction', in Alberto Mira (ed.), *The Cinema of Spain and Portugal*, London: Wallflower Press, pp. 1–11.

Mira, Alberto (2013), '*Ocaña, retrat intermitent / Ocaña. An Intermittent Portrait* (Ventura Pons, 1977): the Mediterranean Movida and the Passing Away of Francoist Barcelona', in María M. Delgado and Robin Fiddian (eds), *Spanish Cinema 1972–2010: Auteurism, Politics, Landscape and Memory*, Manchester: Manchester University Press, pp. 49–63.

Missé, Miquel (2012), *Transsexualitats: altres mirades possibles*, Barcelona: Col.lecció textos del cuerpo.

Missé, Miquel and Gerard Coll-Planas (eds) (2010), *El género desordenado: críticas en torno a la patologización de la transexualidad*, Barcelona and Madrid: Egales.

mm (2013), 'Cuatro pelis maricas (que deberías ver)', post in Planetamurciano blog, 17 December, <http://www.planetamurciano.com/?p=10176> (last accessed 8 September 2015).

Molina Foix, Vicente (2001), 'Ozon', *El País* digitally archived print edition, 25 September, <http://elpais.com/diario/2001/09/25/cultura/1001368803_ 850215.html> (last accessed 22 April 2015).

Monnot, Olivier (2001), Interview with Florence Radelizi and David Dibilio, in Chéries-Chéris festival archive, December, <http://www.cheries-cheris. com/archives/festival2001/presentation_interview.htm> (last accessed 31 August 2015).

Montpelliergay (2015), Montpelliergay.com Lesbian and Gay Pride website landing page, <http://www.montpelliergay.com/collectif-martine/> (last accessed 31 August 2015).

Moonray (2007), Comment under LGBT tag, Wikepédia discussion list, 24 April, <https://fr.wikipedia.org/wiki/Discussion:Pedro_Almodóvar> (last accessed 20 August 2015)

Morley, David (1980), *The Nationwide Audience*, London: British Film Institute.

Morley, David (2006), 'Unanswered Questions in Audience Research', *The Communication Review*, 9.2, 101–21.

Morrison, David (1998), *The Search for a Method: Focus Groups and the Development of Mass Communication Research*, Luton: University of Luton Press.

MosTra'ns (2009), 'Presentació', MosTra'ns festival website, <http://mostrans. wordpress.com/presentacio/> (last accessed 22 August 2014).

Muñoz, Abelardo (1999), *El baile de los malditos. Cine independiente valenciano, 1967–1975*, Valencia: Filmoteca de la Generalitat Valenciana.

Muñoz, Jose Esteban (2009), *Cruising Utopia: The Then and There of Queer Futurity*, New York: New York University Press.

Musée de l'histoire de l'immigration (2013), 'Les Français émigrent-ils à l'étranger?', in Musée de l'histoire de l'immigration website, <http:// www.histoire-immigration.fr/histoire-de-l-immigration/questions-contem poraines/les-migrations/les-francais-emigrent-ils-a-l-etranger> (last accessed 31 August 2015).

nemo (2007), Comment on entry on '*Los testigos*' by elputojacktwist, dosman-zanas blog, 30 September, 12:46, <http://archivo.dosmanzanas.com/index. php/archives/3623> (last accessed 18 August 2015).

Neuhoff, Eric (2011), 'Le docteur Almodóvar abuse', *Le Figaro*, digital edition, Culture, 16 August, < http://www.lefigaro.fr/cinema/2011/08/16/ 03002-20110816ARTFIG00525-le-docteur-almodovar-abuse.php> (last accessed 15 September 2015).

Nichols, Bill (1991), *Representing Reality: Issues and Concepts in Documentary*, Bloomington: Indiana University Press.

Nichols, Bill (1994), 'Discovering Form, Inferring Meaning: New Cinemas and the Film Festival Circuit', *Film Quarterly*, 47.3, 16–30.

Nichols, Bill (2008), 'The Question of Evidence, the Power of Rhetoric and Documentary Film', in Thomas Austin and Wilma de Jong (eds), *Rethinking Documentary: New Perspectives, New Practices*, Maidenhead: Open University Press and New York: Oxford University Press, pp. 29–38.

Obadia, Paul (2002), *Pedro Almodóvar, l'iconoclaste*, Paris: Editions du Cerf; Editions Corlet.

Observatoire des transidentités (2012), 'Entretien avec Miquel Missé – STP 2012', Observatoire des transidentités blog site, 20 October, <http://www. observatoire-des-transidentites.com/article-entretien-avec-miguel-misse-stp-2012-111459905.html> (last accessed 18 July 2014).

Odicino, Guillemette (2013), 'Entretien avec Sébastien Lifshitz', from *Les Invisibles*, DVD extras, Paris: Ad Vitam.

Oso Casas, Laura (2009), '"Chambras", porterías, "pubelas" y "burones": estrategias de movilidad social de las españolas en París', in *Un siglo de inmigración española en Francia*, Vigo: Grupo de Comunicación Galicia en el Mundo, pp. 79–98.

Ourbih, Pascale (2013), Presentation, 19th Chéries-Chéris festival,

Chéries-Chéris festival archive, October, <http://www.cheries-cheris.com/2013/editoriaux/> (last accessed 31 August 2015).

Pageaux, Daniel-Henri (2007), 'Un aspect des relations culturelles entre la France et la Péninsule Ibérique: l'exotisme', Alicante: Biblioteca Virtual Miguel de Cervantes, <http://www.cervantesvirtual.com/obra/un-aspect-des-relations-culturelles-entre-la-france-et-la-pninsule-ibrique-l-exotisme-0/> (last accessed 8 April 2014).

Paschalidis, Gregory (2009), 'Exporting National Culture: Histories of Cultural Institutes Abroad', *International Journal of Cultural Policy*, 15.3, 275–89.

Pautent (2013), Comment on FAQ report on *La vida de Adèle*, in Hay una lesbiana en mi sopa blog, 26 October, 15:07, <http://www.hayunalesbianaenmisopa.com/2013/10/25/20-curiosidades-que-siempre-quisiste-saber-de-la-vida-de-adele/> (last accessed 8 April 2015).

Peccadillo Pictures (2015), About Us, in Peccadillo Pictures website, <https://www.peccapics.com/about-us-2/> (last accessed 31 August 2015).

Pérez-Sanchez, Gema (2007), *Queer Transition in Contemporary Spanish Culture: From Franco to La Movida*, New York: SUNY Press.

Perks, Robert and Alistair Thomson (2006), 'Introduction to Second Edition', in Robert Perks and Alistair Thomson (eds), *The Oral History Reader*, 2nd edn, London and New York: Routledge.

Perriam, Chris (2013a), *Spanish Queer Cinema*, Edinburgh: Edinburgh University Press.

Perriam, Chris (2013b), '*En la ciudad sin límites* (Antonio Hernández, 2002); dos o tres pasos hacia el pasado, y un paso hacia delante', in Manuel Palacio Arranz and Antonia Cuvalo (eds), *Las imágenes del cambio: Medios audiovisuales en las transiciones a la democracia*, Madrid: Biblioteca Nueva, pp. 165–78.

Petit, Jordi (2004), 'De la Llei sobre perillositat social a la revolució del preservatiu i el matrimoni. Aproximació al moviment de lesbianes i gais a Catalunya (1970–2000)', in Enric Prat (ed.), *Els moviments socials a la Catalunya contemporània*, Barcelona: Universitat de Barcelona/Biblioteca Els Juliols, pp. 111–32.

Philoo (2013), Response to comment on '*Les Amants passagers*' by Matoo, on Matoo's blog, Cinéphage section, 22 July, 11:15, <http://blog.matoo.net/index.php/archives/2013/07/22/les-amants-passagers/> (last accessed 22 July 2015).

Pidduck, Juliane (2002), 'After 1980: Margins and Mainstream', in Richard Dyer (ed.), *Now You See It*, 2nd edn, New York and London: Routledge, pp. 265–94.

Pidduck, Julianne (2011), 'The Visible and the Sayable: The Moment and Conditions of Hypervisibility', in Florian Grandena and Cristina Johnston (eds), *Cinematic Queerness: Gay and Lesbian Hypervisibility in Contemporary Francophone Feature Films*, Oxford and New York: Peter Lang, pp. 9–40.

Plantinga, Carl (1999), 'The Scene of Empathy: The Human Face on Film', in Carl Plantinga and Greg M. Smith (eds), *Passionate Views: Film, Cognition and Emotion*, Baltimore, MD: Johns Hopkins University Press, pp. 239–55.

Plantinga, Carl and Greg M. Smith (1999), 'Introduction', in Carl Plantinga and Greg M. Smith (eds), *Passionate Views: Film, Cognition and Emotion*, Baltimore, MD: Johns Hopkins Press, pp. 1–17.

Plummer, Ken (2010), 'Generational Sexualities, Subterranean Traditions, and the Haunting of the Sexual World: Some Preliminary Remarks', *Symbolic Interaction*, 33.2, 163–90.

Potter, Jonathan and Margaret Wetherell (1987), *Discourse and Social Psychology: Beyond Attitudes and Behaviour*, London and Beverly Hills: Sage Publications.

Powell, Philip Wayne [1971] (2008), *La leyenda negra: un invento contra España*, translated by Carlos Sáinz de Tejada, Barcelona: Áltera.

Powrie, Phil (2006) (ed.), *The Cinema of France*, London: Wallflower.

Powrie, Phil, Bruce Babington, Anne Davies and Christopher Perriam (2007), *Carmen on Film: A Cultural History*, Bloomington: Indiana University Press.

Preciado, Beatriz [2000] (2002), *Manifiesto contra-sexual*, Madrid: Opera Prima.

Prosser, Jay (1998), *Second Skins: The Body Narratives of Transsexuality*, New York: Columbia University Press.

Provencher, Denis M. (2007), *Queer French: Globalisation, Language and Sexual Citizenship in France*, Aldershot and Burlington: Ashgate.

Pujol Ozonas, Cristina (2011), *Fans, cinéfilos y cinéfagos: Una aproximación a las culturas y los gustos cinematográficos*, Barcelona: Universitat Oberta de Catalunya.

Quet, Antoine (2013), Presentation, 19th Chéries-Chéris festival, Chéries-Chéris festival archive, October, <http://www.cheries-cheris.com/2013/edi toriaux/> (last accessed 31 August 2015).

Quintana Morraja, Ángel (2013), '*La vida de Adèle*: porque ella es una mujer', *Caimán Cuadernos de Cine*, 21, 6–13.

Rajchman, Olivier (2013), 'Pedro Almodóvar: L'ibère barock', in *L'Express* magazine online, 19 March, <http://www.lexpress.fr/culture/cinema/pedro-almodovar-l-ibere-barock_1232159.html> (last accessed 22 July 2015).

Ramón Solans, Francisco Javier (2008), 'El legado historiográfico de Miguel Artola', *Rolde*, 1 January, <http://www.rolde.org/content/files/magazine_ 32_03_solans.pdf> (last accessed 8 April 2014).

Ramos Cantó, Juana (2007), 'Cronología Trans en España', ILGA website, Zona Trans, <http://trans_esp.ilga.org/trans/bienvenidos_a_la_secretaria_tra ns_de_ilga/zona_trans/historia/cronologia_trans_en_espana> (last accessed 11 February 2015).

Rees-Roberts, Nick (2008), *French Queer Cinema*, Edinburgh: Edinburgh University Press.

Rees-Roberts, Nick (2015), '"*Hors milieu*": Queer and Beyond', in Raphaelle

Moine, Hilary Radner, Alastair Fox and Michel Marie (eds), *A Companion to Contemporary French Cinema*, Chichester: Wiley-Blackwell, pp. 439–60.

Regnier, Isabelle (2005), 'En France, le concept de film gay n'est pas clair', interview with Jacques Martineau and Olivier Ducastel, *Le Monde*, Cinéma, 29 March, <http://www.lemonde.fr/cinema/article/2005/03/29/olivier-duca stel-et-jacques-martineau-cineastes-en-france-le-concept-de-film-gay-n-est-pas-clair_632783_3476.html> (last accessed 31 August 2015).

Reilhac, Philippe, David Dibilio and Florence Fradelizi (2004), Presentation 10th Chéries-Chéris festival, Chéries-Chéris festival archive, <http://www.cheries-cheris.com/archives/festival_2004/> (last accessed 6 October 2015).

Reinhard, CarrieLynn D. and Christopher J. Olson (eds) (2016), 'Introduction: Empirical Approaches to Film Spectators and Spectatorship', in CarrieLynn D. Reinhard and Christopher J. Olson (eds), *Making Sense of Cinema: Empirical Studies into Spectators and Spectatorship*, London and New York: Bloomsbury/Continuum, pp. 1–18.

Rhyne, Ragan (2007), 'Pink Dollars: Gay and Lesbian Film Festivals and the Economy of Visibility', Dissertation, New York: New York University Department of Cinema Studies.

Rhythm (2013), Comment on Pedro Almodovar: cinéaste espagnol on-line forum, za-gay.com, 2 July, 07:31, <http://www.za-gay.org/forum/viewtopic/40253/pedro-almodovar-cineaste-espagnol/0/> (last accessed 20 August 2015).

Riambau, Esteve and Casimiro Torreiro (1999), *La Escuela de Barcelona: el cine de la 'gauche divine'*, Barcelona: Anagrama.

Ribert, Evelyne (2009), 'Francia por costumbre, España como posibilidad: Miradas de hijos de emigrantes españoles', in *Un siglo de inmigración española en Francia*, Vigo: Grupo de Comunicación Galicia en el Mundo, pp. 181–96.

Rich, B. Ruby (2013a), *New Queer Cinema: The Director's Cut*, Durham, NC: Duke University Press.

Rich, B. Ruby (2013b), 'Why Do Film Festivals Matter?', in Dina Iordanova and Ragan Rhyne (eds), *The Film Festival Reader*, St Andrews: St Andrews Film Studies), pp. 157–65.

Ríos Pérez, Sergio (2010), 'Les publics du monde entier confirment leur goût pour le cinéma ibérique', Cineuropa website, 24 June, <http://www.cineuropa.org/cf.aspx?t=cfocusnewsdetail&l=fr&tid=1632&did=147676#cl> (last accessed 3 September 2015).

Rodríguez, Rafael (2009), '*Los juncos salvajes*', post, dosmanzanas blog site, 11 January, <http://archivo.dosmanzanas.com/index.php/archives/6225> (last accessed 18 December 2013).

Rodríguez Marchante, Oti (2014), '*La isla mínima* abre la competición y echa el primer órdago', Festival report in *ABC.es*, Hoy Cinema, 22 October, <http://hoycinema.abc.es/noticias/20140921/abci-isla-minima-festival-sebastian-201409201920.html> (last accessed 17 April 2015).

Rodríguez Ortega, Vicente (2013), 'Almodóvar, Cyberfandom, and Participatory Culture', in Marvin D'Lugo and Kathleen M. Vernon (eds), *A Companion to Pedro Almodóvar*, Oxford: Wiley-Blackwell, pp. 524–50.

Roquentin, Antoine (2015), Entry on *Une Nouvelle Amie*, in ¿Qué tal Francia? blog, 26 March (last accessed 11 June 2015).

rosagua (2015), Comment on SensaCine review of *Une Nouvelle Amie / Una nueva amiga*, 21 May, <http://www.sensacine.com/peliculas/pelicula-223933/criticas-espectadores/> (last accessed 11 June 2015).

Roth-Bettoni, Didier (2007), *L'Homosexualité au cinéma*, Paris: La Musardine.

Roth-Bettoni, Didier and Chéries-Chéris festival organising team (2009), Presentation, 15th Chéries-Chéris festival, Chéries-Chéris festival archive, November, <http://cheries-cheris.com//archives/index.html> (last accessed 31 August 2015).

Roth-Bettoni, Didier, Bruno Thévenon, Sylvie Tomolillo and Ivan Mitifiot (2013), 'Ecrans-mixtes: Sweet Transvestite', in programme for 3rd Ecrans Mixtes festival, Lyon, 6–12 March, p. 13.

Roth-Bettoni, Didier, Bruno Thévenon, Sylvie Tomolillo, Ivan Mitifiot, Nadia Benzaaza and Antonin de Saint Martin (2015), Programme for 5th Ecrans Mixtes festival, Lyon, 4–10 March, <http://festival-em.org/festival-2015/> (last accessed 22 July 2015).

Rouff, Jeffrey (2012), 'Programming Film Festivals', in Jeffrey Rouff (ed.), *Coming Soon to a Festival Near You: Programming Film Festivals*, St Andrews: St Andrews Film Studies, pp. 1–21.

Rowbotham, Sheila (1973), *Hidden from History: 300 Years of Women's Oppression and the Fight Against It*, London: Pluto Press.

Ruiz, Ainara (2013), Review in Zinegoak Facebook pages, <https://www.facebook.com/pages/ZINEGOAK/92153947621?sk=reviews> (last accessed 5 September 2015).

Sáez, Javier (2003), 'Excesos de la masculinidad: La cultura leather y la cultura de los osos', in Queeremos saber: El fanzine transmaribollo de internet, <http://www.hartza.com/osos4.htm> (last accessed 18 June 2015).

Sáez, Javier (2013), 'Miss Bear', in Las Disidentes colectivo artístico's blog site, 26 June, <http://lasdisidentes.com/2013/06/26/miss-bear-por-javier-saez/> (last accessed 18 June 2015).

Saïd, Edward [1978] (1998), 'Orientalism', in Julie Rivkin and Michael Ryan (eds), *Literary Theory: An Anthology*, Oxford: Wiley-Blackwell, pp. 873–6.

Salamon, Gayle (2010), *Assuming a Body: Transgender and Rhetorics of Materiality*, New York: Columbia University Press.

Salom, Ricard (2003), 'Lambda, cinematogràfic', *Lambda*, 45, 37.

Salom, Ricard and Alfonso Herranz (2003), 'Crònica de FIRE!!', *Lambda*, 47, 28.

Samsó, Jordi (2014), 'El voluntariat a la Mostra de Cinema del Casal Lambda', *Lambda*, 80, 17, <http://lambda.cat/Revista/80.pdf> (last accessed 22 August 2014).

Sardier, Thibaut (2013), 'Almodóvar, crash sexe', *Libération*, Cinéma, 27 March, http://next.liberation.fr/cinema/2013/03/26/almodovarcrash-sexe_891450> (last accessed 15 Septmebr 2015).

Sarita (2013), '1977: Els homosexuals al poble català', *l'aBORDatge* 2: 19–21, <http://issuu.com/brotbord/docs/num2/18?e=6492576/3112464> (last accessed 8 August 2013).

Schoonover, Karl (2015), 'Queer or Human? LGBT Film Festivals, Human Rights and Global Film Culture', *Screen*, 56.1, 121–32.

Schrøder, Kim, Kirsten Drotner, Stephen Kline and Catherine Murray (2003), *Researching Audiences*, London and New York: Hodder Arnold.

Schwartz, Arnaud (2011), 'Vertiges de l'apparence', *La Croix*, 17 August.

Sedgwick, Eve Kosofsky (1991), 'How to Bring Your Kids up Gay', *Social Text*, 29, 18–27.

Segal, Lynne (2014), *Out of Time: The Pleasures and Pitfalls of Ageing*, London: Verso.

Seguin, Jean-Claude (1994), *Histoire du cinéma espagnol*, Paris: Broché.

Seguin, Jean-Claude (2009), *Pedro Almodóvar: Filmer pour vivre*, Paris: Editions Ophrys.

Seguin, Jean-Claude (2013), 'Is There a French Almodóvar?', in Marvin D'Lugo and Kathleen M. Vernon (eds), *A Companion to Pedro Almodóvar*, Oxford: Wiley-Blackwell, pp. 432–52.

Seiter, Ellen (1999), *Television and New Media Audiences*, Oxford: Oxford University Press.

Sellier, Geneviève (2005), *La Nouvelle Vague: Un cinéma au masculin singulier*, Paris: CNRS Editions.

Silanoc (2007), Comment under LGBT tag, Wikepédia discussion list, 24 April, <https://fr.wikipedia.org/wiki/Discussion:Pedro_Almodóvar> (last accessed 20 August 2015).

Silberfeld, Judith (2015), 'Changement d'état civil: L'Association Nationale Transgenre demande "une vraie loi sur l'identité de genre"', *Yagg*, 29 September, <http://yagg.com/2015/09/29/changement-detat-civil-lassoci ation-nationale-transgenre-demande-une-vraie-loi-sur-lidentite-de-genre> (last accessed 1 October 2015).

skyzos (2009), Comment on Rodríguez (2009), dosmanzanas blog site, 13 January, 14:07, <http://archivo.dosmanzanas.com/index.php/archives/ 6225> (last accessed 18 August 2015).

Smith, Paul Julian (1992), *Laws of Desire: Questions of Homosexuality in Spanish Writing and Film, 1960–1990*, Oxford: Clarendon Press.

Smith, Paul Julian (2000), '*Pourquoi pas moi?*' [review], *Sight and Sound*, December, 53.

Solla, Fernando, '*El desconocido del lago* ¿No te dan miedo los siluros?', festival review in Cinedivergente website, <http://cinedivergente.com/festi vales/festivales-2014/atlantida-film-fest-2014/el-desconocido-del-lago> (last accessed 8 September 2015).

Sotinel, Thomas (2007), *Pedro Almodóvar*, Paris: Le Monde/Cahiers du Cinéma.

Sotinel, Thomas (2013), '*Les Amants passagers*: Retour aux fondamentaux de la Movida', *Le Monde*, Culture, 26 March, <http://www.lemonde.fr/culture/article/2013/03/26/retour-aux-fondamentaux-de-la-movida_3148053_3246.html> (last accessed 15 September 2015).

Staff RadioGay (2014), Review of *Tomboy*, in RadioGay web pages, Píldoras/Cine, 8 December, <http://radiogay.es/tomboy-celine-sciamma-2011/> (last accessed 18 May 2015).

Staiger, Janet (2005), *Media Reception Studies*, New York and London: New York University Press.

Stockton, Kathryn B. (2009), *The Queer Child, or Growing Sideways in the Twentieth Century*, Durham, NC: Duke University Press.

Strauss, Frédéric (1986), *Pedro Almodóvar: conversations avec Frédéric Strauss*, Paris: Broché.

Stringer, Julian (2001), 'Global Cities and the International Film Festival Economy', in Mark Shiel and Tony Fitzmaurice (eds), *Cinema and the City: Film and Urban Societies in a Global Context*, Oxford: Blackwell, pp. 134–44.

Stryker, Susan (2004), 'Transgender Studies: Queer Theory's Evil Twin', *GLQ: A Journal of Lesbian and Gay Studies*, 10.2, 212–15.

Suárez, Juan A. (2006), 'Surprise Me', in Queer Film and Video Festival Forum, Take Two: Critics Speak Out, special issue of *GLQ: A Journal of Lesbian and Gay Studies*, 12.4, 600–2.

Tarr, Carrie and Brigitte Rollet (2001), *Cinema and the Second Sex: Women's Filmmaking in France in the 1980s and 1990s*, London: Continuum.

Televisió de Catalunya 3/24 (2010), 'França, el principal consumidor de cinema català', news item, 18 November, <http://www.324.cat/video/3220390/altres/Franca-el-principal-consumidor-de-cinema-catala#> (last accessed 8 August 2013).

Tertois, Tomas (2008), 'Bilan 2007 du cinéma espagnol en France', Cineuropa website, 24 August, <http://www.cinespagne.com/actualites/2111-bilan-2007-du-cinema-espagnol-en-france> (last accessed 3 September 2015).

Tertois, Thomas (2009), 'Bilan 2008 du cinéma espagnol en France', Cineuropa website, 15 July, <http://www.cinespagne.com/actualites/2131-bilan-2008-du-cinema-espagnol-en-france> (last accessed 3 September 2015).

Tesson, Charles (1995), *Luis Buñuel*, Paris: Editions de l'Etoile / Cahiers du Cinéma.

Thomas, Lyn (2002), *Fans, Feminisms and 'Quality Media'*, London and New York: Routledge.

Thompson, Christopher W. (2012), *French Romantic Travel Writing: Chateaubriand to Nerval*, Oxford and New York: Oxford University Press.

Thornton, Sarah (1995), *Club Cultures: Music, Media and Subcultural Capital*. Cambridge: Polity Press.

Triana Toribio, Núria (2003), *Spanish National Cinema*, London: Routledge.

Triana Toribio, Núria (2014), 'Residual Film Cultures: Real and Imagined Futures of Spanish Cinema', *Bulletin of Hispanic Studies*, 91, 65–81.

Truffaut, François (1954), 'Une certaine tendance du cinéma français', *Cahiers du Cinéma*, 6.31, 15–29.

Tur, Bruno (2009), 'Estereotipos y representaciones sobre la inmigración española en Francia', in *Un siglo de inmigración española en Francia*, Vigo: Grupo de Comunicación Galicia en el Mundo, pp. 123–40.

Turnbull, Sue (2008), 'Beyond Words? The Return of the King and the Pleasures of the Text', in Martin Barker and Ernest Mathijs (eds), *Watching the Lord of the Rings: Tolkien's World Audiences*, New York: Peter Lang, pp. 181–90.

undesmots (2013), Comment on Pedro Almodovar: cinéaste espagnol online forum, za-gay.com, 11 July, 08:36, <http://www.za-gay.org/forum/viewtopic/40253/pedro-almodovar-cineaste-espagnol/0/> (last accessed 20 August 2015).

uniFrance Films (2009), *Le Cinéma français à l'étranger: resultats de l'année 2009 et de la décennie* [report], <http://medias.unifrance.org/medias/52/167/42804/piece_jointe/french-cinema-abroad-results-for-2009-and-the-past-decade.pdf> (last accessed 8 April 2014).

uniFrance Films (2011), 'French Films Attracted 57 Million Spectators Abroad in 2010', 13 January, <http://en.unifrance.org/news/5920/french-films-attracted-57-million-spectators-abroad-in-2010> (last accessed 5 June 2015).

uniFrance Films (2013), 'Update on Spanish Market Prior to the San Sebastian Film Festival', 16 September, <http://en.unifrance.org/news/10024/update-on-the-spanish-market-prior-to-the-san-sebastian-film-festival> (last accessed 5 June 2015).

UNWTO (2012), *Global Report on LGBT Tourism*, compiled by World Tourism Organisation in association with the International Gay and Lesbian Travel Association, <http://www.e-unwto.org/doi/pdf/10.18111/9789284414581> (last accessed 5 August 2015).

Uría, Lluís (2014), 'La española Anne Hidalgo deviene la primera mujer alcaldesa de París', *La Vanguardia*, 31 March, <http://www.lavanguardia.com/20140331/54405279836/la-espanola-anne-hidalgo-deviene-la-primera-mujer-alcaldesa-de-paris-lluis-uria.html> (last accessed 2 June 2015).

Vela, Carlos G. (2014), 'La crisis de la FNAC', *La Marea*, 1 May, <http://www.lamarea.com/2014/05/01/la-crisis-de-la-fnac/> (last accessed 22 August 2014).

Vélez-Pellegrini, Laurentino (2011), *Sujetos de un contra-discurso: una historia intelectual de la producción teórica gay, lesbiana y queer en España*, Barcelona: Ediciones Bellaterra.

Vidal, Xavier (2013), 'Crítica de *Los testigos*', post in Cinoscar & Rarities blog, 23 May, <http://cachecine.blogspot.co.uk/2013/05/especial-andre-techine-critica-de-los.html> (last accessed 15 September 2015).

Vidal Sanz, Rafael (2013), 'La homosexualidad en el cine de François Ozon', 400 News in 400 Films website, <http://www.400films.com/blog/2013/12/la-homosexualidad-en-el-cine-de-francois-ozon/> (last accessed 7 April 2015).

Viera, Àlex (2013), 'Cinema europeu, asiàtic i llatinoamericà', in FICGLB 2013 webpages, <http://www.barcelonafilmfestival.org/2013/ct/presentacio.htm> (last accessed 22 August 2014).

Vilaseca, David (2010), *Queer Events: Post-Deconstructive Subjectivities in Spanish Writing and Film, 1960s to 1990s*, Liverpool: Liverpool University Press.

Ville de Paris (2015), 'L'Education à l'image', in Les actions de Paris pour le cinéma, Ville de Paris public information website, <http://www.paris.fr/services-et-infos-pratiques/culture-et-patrimoine/cinema/les-actions-de-paris-pour-le-cinema-2313#l-education-a-l-image_7> (last accessed 31 August 2015).

Vives, Mélanie (2013), Presentation, 19th Chéries-Chéris festival, Chéries-Chéris festival archive, October, <http://www.cheries-cheris.com/2013/editoriaux/> (last accessed 31 August 2015).

Waldron, Darren (2009), *Queering Contemporary French Popular Cinema: Images and Their Reception*, New York: Peter Lang.

Waldron, Darren (2013), 'Embodying Gender Nonconformity in Girls: Céline Sciamma's *Tomboy*', *L'Esprit créateur*, 53.1, 60–73.

Waldron, Darren (2016), 'Transnational Investments: Aging in *Les Invisibles* (Sébastien Lifshitz, 2013), and Its Reception', in CarrieLynn D. Reinhard and Christopher J. Olson (eds), *Making Sense of Cinema: Empirical Studies into Film Spectators and Spectatorship*, London and New York: Bloomsbury/Continuum, pp. 87–116.

Waldron, Darren and Ros Murray (2014), 'Troubling Transformations: Pedro Almodóvar's *La piel que habito / The Skin I Live In* (2011)', *Transnational Cinemas*, 5.1, 57–71.

White, Patricia (1999), 'Introduction: On Exhibitionism', in Queer Publicity: a Dossier on Lesbian and Gay Film Festivals, *GLQ: A Journal of Lesbian and Gay Studies*, 5.1, 73–8.

Yaggvideo (2009), 'Le festival trans' IdentiT sur le site gay et lesbien Yagg', documentary interview with Jihan Ferjani and Catherine Oh, 6 December, <http://www.dailymotion.com/video/x9ked3_le-festival-trans-identit-sur-le-si_shortfilms> (last accessed 31 August 2015).

Yekani, Elahe, Eveline Kilian and Beatrice Michaelis (eds) (2013), *Queer Futures: Reconsidering Ethics, Activism, and the Political*, Burlington: Ashgate.

Yuki (2013), Comment on FAQ report on *La vida de Adèle*, in Hay una lesbiana en mi sopa blog, 26 October, 22:10, <http://www.hayunalesbianaenmisopa.

com/2013/10/25/20-curiosidades-que-siempre-quisiste-saber-de-la-vida-de-adele/> (last accessed 8 April 2015).

za-gay (2013), Pedro Almodovar: cinéaste espagnol on-line forum, <http://www.za-gay.org/forum/viewtopic/40253/pedro-almodovar-cineaste-espagnol/0/> (last accessed 20 August 2015).

Zinegoak 10 (2013), 'Premio honorífico / Ohoretzko Saria / Honour Award', in brochure for 10th Zinegoak festival, Bilbao, 31 January – 10 February, pp. 6–7, <http://www.zinegoak.com/CatalogoZG2013_BR.pdf> (last accessed 8 April 2014).

Zinegoak (2014), Programme for 11th Zinegoak festival, Bilbao, 20–7 January.

Zinentiendo (2014), Festival landing page for 9th Zinentiendo festival, Zaragoza, 30 May – 7 June, <http://zinentiendo.org/2014/05/07/ya-esta-en-marcha-la-9a-edicion-de-zinentiendo/> (last accessed 3 August 2015).

Zribi, Isabelle (2011), 'Nouvelle Eve', *Cahiers du Cinéma*, July–August, 46–8.

INDEX

EU Authorised Representative:

Easy Access System Europe Mustamäe tee 50, 10621 Tallinn, Estonia

gpsr.requests@easproject.com

Printed and bound by CPI Group (UK) Ltd, Croydon, CR0 4YY

24/02/2026

02059257-0005